UP YOUR SCORE

THE UNDERGROUND GUIDE TO THE SAT

by Larry Berger, Michael Colton,
Lisa Exler, Manek Mistry, and Paul Rossi

Illustrations by Chris Kalb

WORKMAN PUBLISHING • NEW YORK

Library of Congress Cataloging-in-Publication Data
Up your score : the underground guide to the SAT/ by Larry Berger ... [et al.]:
    Illustrations by Chris Kalb.---Rev. ed.
    p.cm.
    ISBN 0-7611-0483-6
    1. Scholastic Aptitude Test—Study guides.   I. Berger, Larry.
LB2353.57.U7   1996
378′.16′62—dc20   96-17390
                                                         CIP

Interior Illustrations: Chris Kalb
Cover Art: Jay Thompson

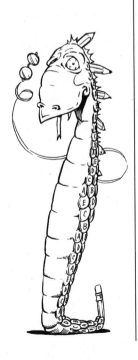

SAT questions selected from the following publications of the College Entrance Examination Board: 5 SATs (1981); 6 SATs (1982); 10 SATs (1983, 1986, 1990). Reprinted by permission of the Educational Testing Service, the copyright owner of the test questions.

Permission to reprint the SAT material does not constitute review or endorsement by the Educational Testing Service or the College Board of this publication as a whole or of any other testing information it may contain.

SAT is the registered trademark of the College Entrance Examination Board, which has not endorsed this publication.

Workman books are available at special discount when purchased in bulk for special premiums and sales promotions as well as for fundraising or educational use. Special editions or book excerpts also can be created to specification. For details, contact the Special Sales Director at the address below.

Workman Publishing Company, Inc.
708 Broadway
New York, NY 10003-9555

Manufactured in the United States of America

First Printing July 1996
10 9 8 7 6 5 4 3 2 1

Grateful acknowledgment is made for permission to reprint the following:
You Can Call Me Al by Paul Simon © 1986 Paul Simon

TO OUR PARENTS

FLORENCE AND TOBY BERGER
ELLEN AND CLARK COLTON
EMMA AND JACOB EXLER
VIRGINIA AND NARIMAN MISTRY
CHARLINE AND FAUST ROSSI

ACKNOWLEDGMENTS

There are many people who have helped us with *Up Your Score*. Listed in alphabetical order, the following people deserve our deep gratitude:

Doris Berger, for her devoted promotional work;

Florence Berger, professor of management at the Cornell University School of Hotel Administration, for helping with the memory and concentration chapters, and for revealing her secret recipe for Sweet and Tasty 800 Bars;

Toby Berger, electrical engineering professor at Cornell University, for calculating the statistics that prove our methods work, advising us on the math section, and correcting our mistayckes;

David Bock, Ithaca High School, for being a terrific math teacher, for the valuable ideas he gave us for the guessing section, and for his editing assistance;

Belle Cohen, for her good counsel, the use of her home and telephone, and for being the best public relations/marketing grandmother in the business;

Brian Colton, for being himself;

Clark Colton, for superb editing and negotiating;

Ellen and Jill Colton, for support, encouragement, and TLC;

Jason Colton, for his business savvy;

Emma Exler for her countless suggestions, help with the vocabulary list, editing, and support;

Jacob Exler for his encouragement and good advice;

Steven Exler for his suggestions and good humor;

Randy A. Faigin, for her suggestions and her terrific support-iveness;

Dennis Ferguson, for his excellent proofreading of our initial manuscript;

The Ferndale, California, Focus Group: Ryan Dixon, Dawn Eastin, Casey Laris, Michael Laris, and Jenny Russell, for their early enthusiasm for the book;

Nous remercions bien cordialement les Fougerays d'avoir si aimablement hébergé Paul, et les Warchol d'avoir hébergé Michael;

Florence Harris, for her generous editing assistance and advice;

Lynn C. Harris, for her extraordinary support, outstanding advice, and hilarious contributions;

Sharon Herbstman for helping with astuteness and zeal and everything in between;

All our friends in the Ithaca High School Class of '86, the Newton North High School Class of '93, and the Beth Tfiloh School Class of '96 for their all around greatness, encouragement, and suggestions;

Milton Kagan, one of the few SAT coaches who really knows his stuff, for sharing some of his excellent ideas with us;

Andrea Kochie, Ithaca High School, for being an amazing college admissions advisor, and for helping us acquire so much of the information that we needed;

Dr. Elizabeth Mandell, for her medical consultation for the "Little Circles" section;

Kevin McMahon, Ithaca High School math teacher, for his suggestions about the math section;

The people at New Chapter Press—Wendy Crisp, Kathryn Arnold, Mary Tooley, and Kate Walker—for deciding to publish the original book, for putting up with three neophyte co-authors, and for being a joy to work with;

James Pullman, amazing English teacher at IHS, for helping us plan the TSWE section;

Faust and Charline Rossi, for the many kind efforts they have made on our behalf;

Rita Rosenkranz, the agent John Grisham wishes he had, for scoring a perfect 1600 on the Super Agent Test;

Bob Schaeffer and FairTest, for advice and information;

David Schwarz, for his insightful editorial guidance;

Linda Shapiro, for recommending Michael and launching his literary career;

Helen Smith, for teaching Michael how to write good;

Steve Wendelboe, director of athletics, New Palestine High School, New Palestine, Indiana, for his support;

The folks at Workman Publishing for their astuteness, audacity, alacrity, and ardor—Margot Herrera for her brilliant editing, Suzanne Rafer for her important insights, Peter Workman for taking us on, Lori S. Malkin and Billy Kelly for the great layouts, Gwen Petruska for the cool cover; David Schiller for his promotional genius, and Lindsay MacGregor for publicizing the book with panache.

The Yale Class of '90: Deborah Bloom, Jeff Dolven, Amelia Eisch, David Franklin, James Hanaham, Chris Kincade, Julian Kleindorfer, Andrew Michaelson, Jim Rosenfeld, Zachary Silverstein, SM 1845J, Mike Warren, and Jay Withgott, for their contributions, humor, and support.

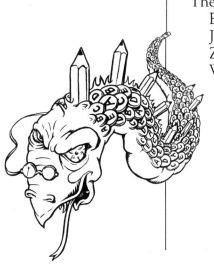

CONTENTS

Introduction:
A Brief History of This Book 1
    One Afternoon in the Ithaca High School
      Cafeteria Way Back in the Late '80s 2
    Nine Years Later 3
    Four Months Later 3

CHAPTER 1

About the SAT 5
    Before We Begin, Any Questions? 6
    The Story of the Evil Testing Serpent 17
    How to Practice 19
    Getting in Gear 21

CHAPTER 2

The Verbal Section 23
    Mastering the Question Types 24
    Sentence Completions 26
    Analogies 31
    Critical Reading Passages 37
    About SAT Words 50
    Memorizing SAT Words 52
    The Word List 55
    Useful Synonyms 145
    Similar-Looking Words 146

CHAPTER 3

The Math Section 147
    Theory of Study 148
    Calculators 149
    Fractions/Units 152
    Word Problems 161
    Equations 170

Geometry Problems 172
Coordinate Geometry 185
Quantitative Comparisons 188
The Funny Symbol Question 190
Grid-in Problems 193

CHAPTER 4

Guessing, or The ETS Strikes Back: Impostors From Hell 197
Impostors From Hell 198
Guessing, the SAT, and the Specter
of World Destruction 201
The Six Rules of Guessing 203
A Final Word on Guessing 207

CHAPTER 5

SAT II Writing Test 209
The Story of Little-Read Writing Serpent . . .210
The Three Question Types 211
The 13 Rules of the Writing Test 216
Practice Questions 229
The Essay 232

CHAPTER 6

But Wait! You Also Get 243
Concentration 244
Proctors: Mindless Slaves of the ETS 249
Relaxation 251
Yoga and the SAT 253
Cheating 256

Little Circles 258
Is the SAT Biased? 263
SATing for Dollars 265
SATitis 266
Canceling Counseling 267
The SSS and the SDQ 267
The SAT and the Internet 268
Food Smuggling 270
Fashion and Beauty Tips 272
Stick It in Your Ear 273
Some Other Thoughts on Getting Into
    College 274
Parting Words of Advice 275

Who Are These People, Anyway? 277

A BRIEF HISTORY OF THIS BOOK

ONE AFTERNOON IN THE ITHACA HIGH SCHOOL CAFETERIA WAY BACK IN THE LATE '80s

"This book really sucks," Paul yawned as he pulled the crust off his sandwich, scattering Miracle Whip all over page 12 of Barron's SAT guide.

"Yeah, what's the point of the SAT anyway?"

"To cause us pain and suffering," Manek mumbled.

"You know what's wrong with all these SAT review books?"

"No, what?" asked Larry.

"They're all written by embalmed educators who were born before the invention of the number 2 pencil, before the SAT itself, and before *The Brady Bunch* went on the air."

"If I could write an SAT review book, it wouldn't be so boring."

"I know what you mean. If I wrote an SAT review book, it would be one that was erudite, yet not bombastic, one that would comprehensively elucidate the turbid depths of this baneful examination, one that would carry students to new heights of academic self-actualization, one that would . . ."

"Yeah, and one with lots of skin."

"You know, Larry's right. If we could write a kick-ass manual telling confused, bored, and sexually frustrated students like us across this great land how to rock on the SAT we would—"

"Yes indeed, we would be providing a contribution to society that . . ."

". . . that could bring us enough funds to pay for college."

". . . and a chance to get on Letterman."

"Letterman? Do you really think so?"

"Sure, why not?"

A few months later, after Larry, Manek, and Paul had each earned SAT scores over 1500, they began work on an SAT review book that would share their secrets of SAT success with their fellow students. Their book was called *Up Your Score*, and it helped many students get into prestigious colleges that cost more than they could afford.

Over the next nine years, as Larry, Manek, and Paul grew old and joined bingo and shuffleboard leagues, the SAT also changed. Because too many students had read *Up Your Score* and outsmarted the test, the SAT was revised. In order to meet this new challenge, Larry, Manek, and Paul searched long and hard for the perfect student to update the book. Eventually, they decided upon Michael Colton, a brilliant young rebel from Massachusetts who had achieved a perfect 1600 by reading *Up Your Score* and who also baked award-winning chocolate chip cookies.

Michael's revision of the book enabled a generation of youngsters to follow in his footsteps at Harvard, but age eventually took its toll on him. His hair grew gray, his face grew wrinkled, and he forgot who Sandra Bullock was. Students reading *Up Your Score* were confused by his references to the Cosby Show and Michael J. Fox. The book was losing its edge. Something had to be done.

Immediately Michael embarked upon a nationwide quest to find the next SAT genius, visiting 83 cities in only 6 days. No one met the stringent requirements until he reached the charming city of Baltimore, where he met Lisa Exler, an *Up Your Score* disciple who had also used the book and earned a 1600 (further proof that the book really works). In addition to her formidable vocabulary skills, she could run a three-minute mile, knew all the lyrics to Pearl Jam's *Vitalogy*, and had flawless skin. After consulting with the grumpy old men at the bingo tournament, Michael welcomed Lisa to the *Up Your Score* crew.

Four Months Later . . .

Hey, what's up? I'm Lisa Exler and I've spent the last several months dusting off *Up Your Score*. I've updated the information, clarified the examples and explanations, and added my own hints and strategies. In addition, I've replaced antiquated references in the book for those of us who relate better to *Friends*

than to *The Golden Girls*. I mean, the guys may have been cool in their day, but now they're over the hill. In the year 2000, Larry Berger will be 31. Thirty-one! He could be my grandfather! I, however, am in touch with today's teens. Heck, I *am* a teen; I've got the navel ring to prove it. My favorite toy is the telephone and the only thing I remember about Ronald Reagan's presidency is *We Are the World*.

Now sit back, relax, and prepare to rock the SAT.

ABOUT THE SAT

BEFORE WE BEGIN, ANY QUESTIONS?

Why do I have to read this book if I want to go to college?

Good question. The answer is, you don't. You can choose not to read this book, and halfway through the SAT have a nervous breakdown from which you never quite recover despite decades of psychiatric care, which will lead to all of your several marriages ending in bitter divorces that cost you every penny you make as a mediocre professional bowler, until your life is cut short by an agonizing disease for which they find a cure a week after no one comes to your funeral. Next question?

What is the SAT?

The SAT was developed in 1927 because colleges wanted an objective way of comparing students. It used to be that they had no way of knowing that Eggbert's D average at Impossible High School was actually much more impressive than Buffy's B average at Easy Academy. Supposedly, the SAT gives an accurate measure of a student's ability to do college work. Certain teenage review-book authors think that it fails miserably in its attempt to do this, but the fact remains that it is a very important part of the college application process. Your SAT score can make the difference between acceptance to and rejection from a college.

What exactly is on the SAT?

The SAT is made up of the SAT I and the SAT II. The SAT I, to which most of this book is devoted, is three hours long. It consists of 75 minutes of verbal testing (two sections of 30 minutes and one of 15 minutes), 75 minutes of math testing (same breakdown as verbal), and 30 minutes of an experimental section, either verbal or math, which will not count toward your score, but which you'll have to do anyway because they don't tell you which is experimental and which is real.

The SAT II tests cover individual subjects such as writing, literature, foreign languages, history, math, and science. The Educational Testing Service (the company that writes the tests) is pushing the SAT II Writing test as the most impor-

Before the SAT, colleges had no way of knowing that Eggbert's D average at Impossible High School was actually much more impressive than Buffy's B average at Easy Academy.

tant SAT II because it requires an essay, so we have included a chapter on it. Colleges usually ask for three SAT II scores, including Writing.

Note: In this book, we usually refer to the SAT I simply as "the SAT." However, references to the SAT II remain as "SAT II."

What is a "good score" on the SAT?

Each of the two sections of the test, math and verbal, is scored on a scale of 200 to 800. A perfect combined score (math plus verbal) is 1600; a bad combined score is 400.

No, seriously, what score should I shoot for?

Well, that depends. First, you have to consider what your goals are. Some of you are reading this book because the NCAA rules require that you get a composite score of at least 820 in order to be eligible to play on an intercollegiate team as a freshman. Some of you want to score in the 1500s to ensure your place at Harvard. The table on the next page gives the average SAT scores at a wide variety of schools.

What's all this about raising my score?

In 1995 the ETS "recentered" its scoring system. Because more and more students were taking the SAT every year, the average score on each section had dropped below 500, the middle score on a scale from 200 to 800. The scores became harder to interpret because a verbal score of 470, although below the middle score of 500, was actually above the national average of 428. As of April 1995, the scale was recentered so that a student's score on the test would more closely reflect his or her performance on the test and 500 would once again become the average. What this means for you is that your score will appear higher than it would have before 1995, while your percentile (how you did compared to how everyone else did) will stay the same. It also means that for the next year or two, you should ask colleges if the scores they report as averages are recentered or not.

Average Recentered Scores

School	Verbal SAT	Math SAT	Combined Scores
Boston University	619	610	1229
Brown	680	670	1350
Cal Tech	700	770	1470
UCLA	589	622	1211
Colorado State	553	560	1113
Dartmouth	700	700	1400
Johns Hopkins	670	685	1355
Morehouse	564	555	1119
U Penn	668	670	1338
Pomona	705	690	1395
Texas A&M	570	594	1164
Texas Tech	536	549	1085
U Vermont	563	568	1131
Wellesley	670	638	1308
Wesleyan	680	650	1330
Yale	720	690	1410

Source: *Insider's Guide to the Colleges 1996* (St. Martin's Press)

These scores are the average recentered scores. They are typical of the scores of the students entering these schools. They are not minimum requirements, nor do they guarantee your admission.

There are many other factors considered by admissions officers. High school grades and courses, work experience, application essays, leadership qualities, the admissions interview, ethnic background, legacy (having relatives who went to the school you are applying to), and many other things all have an impact on whether or not you get in. Although these other factors are all important, your SAT score may be the most crucial. If you are president of every club in your school, the admissions officers may be so impressed with your extracurricular activities that they'll accept you even if you scored noticeably below the school's average SAT score. But if you don't have legacy, your grades are ho-hum, and you have a boring list of extracurriculars, then you will need SAT scores well

We asked Jim Wroth, a sophomore at Yale, what he got on the SAT, and he said 1760. When we responded that it's impossible to score above 1600, he explained that he has Yale relatives who date back to the year 1760, so it didn't really matter what his scores were.

above the average. (For more on college admissions, see page 274.) Many admissions officers would try to deny this claim, but the admissions records show that if you have an SAT score above the average for the school to which you are applying, and there's nothing flagrantly wrong with the rest of your application, then you will almost certainly get in. While the other factors on your application are subjective, your SAT score is a big, fat, hairy, "objective" *number.* Even an admissions officer who claims that the SAT score is not particularly important is going to be subconsciously influenced by this number. It categorizes your application in the admissions officer's mind as "smart kid" or "dumb kid." It has an impact on the way an admissions officer interprets virtually everything else on your application.

What about the PSAT?

If you've already taken the PSAT and you didn't study for it, don't read this. It will only depress you.

A PSAT is the same as an SAT except that there are only two 30-minute math and two 30-minute verbal sections. That means about 108 questions instead of 138. Supposedly, the PSAT contains fewer of the most difficult questions. Another difference is that, while SAT does not have a *P* as its first letter, PSAT does. Here's why . . .

The *P* in PSAT stands for three things. The first is easy— Preliminary. The PSAT is a preliminary look at the real SAT. It's a sneak preview of what the real thing is going to be like and a good chance to practice. In fact, your PSAT score report will come with your test book and a computer printout telling you, for each question, the correct answer, your answer, and the level of difficulty of the question. You can use this information to help prepare for the SAT.

But the PSAT is more than just a chance to practice. The second thing the *P* stands for is Scholarships and Special Programs. A good score on the PSAT makes you eligible for all sorts of scholarship programs, the most famous of which is the National Merit Scholarship Program. The National Merit

A good score on the PSAT makes you eligible for all sorts of scholarship programs, the most famous of which is the National Merit Scholarship Program.

If you don't put your PSAT scores on your college application, admissions people may suspect your scores were poor.

Scholarship is based on your *selection index*, which is your math score plus twice your verbal score. Recognition by the National Merit Program is a big plus on your college applications and it can even win you some money. The top 50,000 scorers are recognized by the Merit Program. The top 15,000 scorers become semifinalists. Out of the top 15,000 they pick 14,000 to become finalists. And about 6,900 of the finalists get big bucks toward college. This program is described in-depth in the "PSAT/NMSQT Student Bulletin," which also lists the corporate and college sponsors of the program. You can pick up a copy in any guidance counselor's office.

The third thing the *P* stands for is *A*pplications. The ETS publishes a pamphlet on taking the PSAT that says the PSAT is not used as a college admission test. But some schools have a space for PSAT scores on their applications. Other times there will just be a space where you can put "other test scores." Of course, it's optional whether or not you tell them your PSAT scores, but it's impressive if you have good ones.

What about Sunday test dates?

The ETS offers the SAT seven times a year between October and June; most students take the test on a Saturday morning. However, those students who cannot take the SAT on a Saturday for religious reasons have the option of taking it on Sunday, usually the day after the scheduled Saturday test. The Sunday test doesn't cost any extra, but on your registration form you need to fill in the special 01000 test center code, and with your registration form you must send a signed letter on official letterhead from your clergyman explaining that religious convictions prevent you from taking the SAT on a Saturday.

Because the test given on Sunday is exactly the same as the Saturday test, you cannot register for both. The test is scored on the same scale, and percentages are calculated the same way for Sunday test-takers as for Saturday test-takers. In the end, therefore, there is no advantage or disadvantage to registering for a Sunday test. Only do it if you have to.

What special skills will I need to take the SAT?

A variety of abilities are necessary. First, you must be able to stay awake, which can be difficult even though you will be sitting for three hours in the most uncomfortable chair imaginable. (This is why we have included sections on yoga and concentration.) Second, you have to be able to sign a statement alleging that it is you and not some cyborg clone that is taking the test. Third, you must be able to read. (And if you're reading this, you've probably already cleared that hurdle, unless you're just looking at the pretty design of the pages.) Fourth, you must know a lot of math and verbal stuff so that you can answer the questions correctly. (That's what most of this book is about.) Fifth, you need to understand the proper strategies for taking the SAT and the many ways that you can outsmart the test. (We explain all of the tricks.) Sixth, after you find the right answer, you need to be able to fill in all the little circles on the computerized answer sheet, without going out of the lines. (We've provided several columns of little circles for practice and have done extensive experimentation on what is the most efficient way to fill them in.)

For more on the critical skills of food smuggling and secretive eating, see Chapter 6.

Other useful skills are food smuggling and secretive eating. These skills are covered in this book's final chapter.

How do I get psyched to study for the SAT?

You cannot study for the SAT unless you are mentally and physically prepared. Listed below are several ways of psyching yourself up.

1. Try to convince yourself that it is fun and challenging to learn new words and mathematical facts. (Good luck.)
2. Next, try to convince yourself that the things you learn in today's study session will enable you to think critically and to sound articulate and intelligent for the rest of your life. (This technique does not work either.)
3. Realize that the opposite sex is often attracted to equations and big words. (Nope.)

4. Note that the average teenager will burn approximately 115 calories during an hour of intense studying. (Maybe so, but walking up and down stairs for an hour is much more interesting and burns 350 calories.)

The above techniques do not work because they use positive thinking. The SAT does not inspire positive thinking. You must learn to think negatively. For example:

1. Recognize that if you do not do well on the SAT you will not get into a good college. You will have to go to school in the Yukon Territory and your college years will be disrupted by glacial migrations.
2. Go to the kitchen. Press your tongue against the metal freezer tray and hold it there for 10 minutes. Then rapidly yank it away. By comparison, studying for the SAT may actually be pleasurable.
3. Realize that the ETS is a wicked organization. By reading our book you are beating the system because you will score higher than you would otherwise.
4. Most of the dweebs who deserve to get into the colleges of their choice are probably too busy programming their computers and electronic pocket organizers to have time to read this book. It's fun to watch dweebs get mad when they don't get into a college that you get into.
5. The SAT is expensive:

$21.50	test fee
8.95	this book
14.00	*Real SATs*
1.00	gas to and from test
.40	four #2 pencils
4.00	food smuggled into test
$49.85	Total

You don't want to waste that kind of money.

You must learn to dwell on these negative thoughts. Let them gnaw at your insides. Begin to feel a hatred of this test and all that it stands for. Hate is a powerful emotion: It will give you the drive and determination you need for intense study.

An Authors' Note Intended to Build Your Confidence

Before we begin we must make one important point. In the extremely unlikely event that you read this book and still do miserably on the SAT, do not whine. Just make the best of going to college in the Yukon Territory. In addition, there are a number of small details that could go wrong during the test regardless of what you learn (or do not learn) from this book. A few examples:

1. You lose your admission ticket so they never even let you into the testing center.
2. You fall asleep during the critical reading passage about the history of celery.
3. You fall asleep while the proctor is reading the directions.
4. You fall asleep the night before the test and do not wake up until it is over.
5. You don't know the answer to question number 6 on the test, so you skip it. However, you forget to leave number 6 blank on your answer sheet. Then, you put the answer to number 7 in the space for number 6, the answer to number 8 in the space for number 7, etc. You don't realize that you have done this until you wake up from the passage about the history of celery and try to find your place. (Seriously, if you mess up your answer sheet like that, the proctor will probably give you some time to rearrange your answers after the test is over. Raise your hand and ask.)
6. All ten of your number 2 pencils break, and you end up having to use chalk.

Some distractions can be remedied. For example, if your desk squeaks, it's too hot, there's a fan that's blowing your papers away, or you're left-handed and the desks are made for right-handed people—tell the proctor! Although some proctors bite, most don't carry any dangerous diseases, and an occasional proctor will even try to help you. (See "Proctors: Mindless Slaves of the ETS" in Chapter 6.)

How should I prepare the day before the SAT?

There is much disagreement about the ideal way to prepare for the SAT. Each of the authors of this book has his or her own favorite method. Choose the one that is best suited to your personality.

1. Larry's Method: Be Prepared. Preparedness is the key. Have a healthy breakfast of juice, toast, milk, and organic cereal. Walk briskly to school so that you have time to giggle with your friends and clean your teacher's blackboard. Pay attention in all your classes. Go to the Honor Society meetings. While you are at varsity track practice, try your hardest to demonstrate your dedication to the coach and your pride in the school. Go home. Do your homework. Spend the night before the test relaxing—see a movie, practice your clarinet, play Scrabble. Don't bother with last-minute studying except to look at your list of the 10 words that have given you the most trouble. Put four number 2 pencils with unblemished erasers, your ID, your calculator, and your admission ticket by the door. Say your prayers, and go to bed early.

2. Manek's Method: Be Mellow. Tranquility is the key. Skip school the day before and relax—take the phone off the hook, lock the door, and put a cloth over your goldfish bowl so that you won't be distracted. Lie down on the floor with your favorite potato and breathe deeply. Starting with your toes and progressing to your earlobes, calm your entire body; feel yourself losing control of your muscles. When you're marvelously mellow, put your most prized possessions in the microwave and melt them. If you feel alarmed at this stage, then you're not totally tranquil—go back to the beginning and try biofeedback.

When you are entirely free of tension, center your thoughts on how wonderful it will feel to be done with the test, while pronouncing solemn and meditative syllables of wisdom. Close your eyes. Sleep.

3. Paul's Method: Get Pumped. Adrenaline is the key. Do not prepare for the SAT the day before. Instead, try to build up as much anxiety and fury as possible in your tortured, nerve-racked body. Do calisthenics. Mosh to hardcore ska. Invite a few friends over and engage in a primal-screaming session. Beat your body repeatedly with knotted cords and whips. Break lots of glass. When morning comes, make sure that your pulse is above 250 beats per minute, then break open the test center doors and destroy the test with your awesome animal energy.

Organizing materials such as your pencils, ID, admission ticket, and prayer manual the night before does not improve your score or general well-being. Disorganization forces you to think fast and deal rationally with unusual situations and problems like those tricky questions that will undoubtedly appear on the SAT. Finally, don't go to bed the night before the test. You can catch up on your sleep the first year you're dead.

4. Michael's Method: Be Superstitious. Superstition is the key. Find three live mice, a number 2 pencil, a proctor, and a college brochure. On the last full moon before the test, boil all of these together in a Teflon cauldron; simmer until golden brown. Chant the following:

> "O great *Up Your Score* lords, give me the strength to defeat the ETS! I am the Gatekeeper, and I will do as you command!"

If a black cat crosses your path, shoot a mirror with a silver bullet.

The clothes you wear on the test day are very important: If the test is on a rainy day, wear a raincoat. However, if the test is on a day when the Red Sox are playing at home, wear two

pairs of socks. If there has been an earthquake during the past week anywhere in Canada, make sure you wear a blindfold during the test (you can take it off during the breaks). Follow these rules, and you will be destined to score well.

5. Lisa's Method: Be Obsessive. Obsession is the key. The week before the test, begin to obsess over little things. Drink lots of fluids, take a variety of vitamins, and wear a surgical mask so you won't get sick. Reread your admissions ticket 50 times, each time checking that another piece of information is correct. Call ETS to make sure that your name is on the correct test center list. The night before the test, go into seclusion. Recharge and polish your calculator batteries and find five spare calculators to bring just in case. Sharpen 20 number 2 pencils and make sure that their points won't break. Dull the points of at least half of them to create a larger graphite area for filling in the little circles. Double check that your ID really belongs to you. Then triple check. Panic because your picture doesn't really look like you, and try to paste on a better one. Set four different alarms in order to ensure that you will wake up on time. By the time you arrive at the test center the next morning you'll be so relieved nothing went wrong that you won't mind taking the test.

Each of these methods has its merits. People using the first method tend to get higher scores, people using the second method get the most spiritual enrichment from the test, people using the third method tend to die young, people using the fourth method get locked up, and people using the fifth method usually get ulcers. No matter which method you use, be sure to read the wisdom on the last page of this book on the night before the test. Don't peek at it before then.

Who makes up the SAT?

The conventional answer to this question is that it is made up by the Educational Testing Service, a company based in New Jersey. However, we have discovered that this answer is a cover-up. The real truth about who makes up the SAT is revealed here for the first time in history . . .

THE STORY OF THE EVIL TESTING SERPENT

In the beginning, there was no SAT. Students frolicked in their high school paradise without knowledge of evil.

But then the Serpent silently slithered into the high school through the hot-lunch loading dock. He was the most nefarious, loathsome, malevolent, malicious, odious, insidious, cunning, beguiling, deceitful serpent who ever existed. It was because of this serpent that high school students have had to learn vocabulary words like the ones in the previous sentence. This was the Evil Testing Serpent (ETS). The ETS, an unfathomably long, mighty, mucus-encrusted beastie, was determined to bring evil and pain into the paradise. So he devised a plan that would put an end to the happiness of high school students.

This is how his plan worked. For three hours students would have to answer an incessant string of multiple-choice questions. The questions would be both boring and tricky. Students who gave too many wrong answers would have miserable futures and then die. He called this hideous ordeal the Slimy and Atrocious Torture (SAT).

The ETS inflicted his SAT upon the oppressed masses of students for many years, and the Serpent's power increased as he drained their meager life forces. Gradually, all resistance was crushed and the tormented youth became accustomed to taking the SAT. Parents and teachers began to view the SAT as a national institution. Long, bleak years of misery appeared to lie ahead for civilization.

Could no one defeat the ETS? Would this merciless serpent continue to strangle his victims into submission? Would *Saturday Night Live* ever be funny again? Was there no hope for humanity? Well, it turned out there was. . . . Five ordinary students, born under the tyranny of the ETS, suffered through the unholy SAT with the rest of their comrades. But afterwards, they made a secret blood-vow to avenge the misery they had suffered at the fangs of the Evil Testing Serpent. They delved into the mysteries of the SAT in the hope of uncovering its weaknesses and defeating it. They soon discovered many ways of psyching out the SAT and outsmarting the ETS. They transcribed their revelations in a stirring document wherein they demonstrated that although the Serpent was mean, their readers would be above the mean. The high school paradise was soon restored and students once again were able to pick freely from the Tree of College. *It is that document you now hold in your sweaty, trembling hands.*

Here, the cruel tricks of the ETS will be revealed and you will be shown how to use your understanding of the Serpent's methods to your own advantage. Throughout this book, the Serpent will make loathsome appearances and will secrete his foul venom all over the page to protest our revelations of his weaknesses and his trickeries. Soon you will be able to recognize the Serpent's infamous tricks and you will live forever free of the fear of his Slimy and Atrocious Torture.

HOW TO PRACTICE

We didn't put many practice problems in our book. This *does not* mean that you don't need to practice. It simply means that we didn't want to make up fake SAT questions when there are thousands of real SAT questions that have already been published by the ETS. Other review books contain tons of practice questions, but a lot of the questions are totally unlike the ones that are on the real SAT. Also, in many books, several of the given answers are *wrong*! The five of us got so frustrated with the questions in these books that we decided not to make the same mistake ourselves.

So, our advice is to practice on real SAT questions. However, there's a catch. Because the SAT was revised in 1994, few complete new SATs are available for you to practice on. Do not fear, however, for we at *Up Your Score* have been researching this problem and our experts have devised the following three-step practice plan.

1. Get the booklet *Taking the SAT I*, published by the College Board. It should be available from your guidance counselor for free. It contains one complete practice test along with sample verbal and math questions and explanations, as well as preparation and test-taking tips. You should also be able to pick up a copy of *Taking the PSAT* which will contain some practice questions and a full PSAT.

2. Get the book *Real SATs*, published by the College Board. This book contains three real, complete SATs and two PSATs (it's okay to practice on the PSATs; the questions are all similar). It also has more than 80 extra practice questions, many with clear explanations. The hints and strategies it provides are also worth reading. Of course, because it is published by the College Board, the official sponsor of the SAT, it doesn't tell you how foolish the SAT can be, nor does it show you any of the tricks on how to beat it, and it's not nearly as funny as we are.

3. Since many colleges consider only your highest SAT score, you can take the SAT more than once. For example, if you were planning to take the test in May or June, you could also register for the January test date and sign up for one of the new services that the College Board now offers to help you learn from your first test (and to make themselves more money). The Question-and-Answer Service will provide you with a copy of the test you took, your answers, the correct answers, scoring instructions, and information about the types and difficulty of each question. It costs $10.00, and you can order it either when you register for the test or up to five months after your test date. It takes three to seven weeks after your test is scored for you to receive the materials, but if you're willing to pay the $10.00 and wait a bit, you'll know exactly which areas of the SAT you need to concentrate on. Unfortunately, the College Board does not offer this valuable service for most of the test dates. So if you want to use it, be sure it's offered on your test date.

For the many test dates on which the Question-and-Answer Service is not available, the College Board offers the Student Answer Service. For $5.00 you will receive a computer-generated report which will tell you for each question, what type it was (analogy, geometry, etc.), if you answered correctly, incorrectly, or skipped it, and the level of difficulty on a scale of 1 to 5. You can order this service the same way you order the Question-and-Answer Service, and they'll mail it to you three to six weeks after they score your test. Although it doesn't provide you with as much information, you can still use it to gauge in which areas you need the most work.

Another thing to keep in mind is that you can always cancel your scores if you think you bombed the test; you can do this by informing the proctor before you leave the testing center or by contacting the ETS by the Wednesday after you take the test (see page 267). However, we don't really recommend doing this because most colleges look at your highest scores and you can always take the test again. Also, you'll never find out what your score was. Plus, it kills a Saturday morning.

GETTING IN GEAR

Of course you can think of thousands of things you'd rather do than prepare for the SAT, beginning with weeding and ending with sticking hypodermic needles in your eyes. But assuming that you recognize the necessity of preparing, how do you make yourself actually sit down and study?

1. Set a Score Goal

Establish a specific score as your goal. Pick a score that you think you can achieve but that will require some preparation. (A good score goal is one a bit above the average SAT score for students at the schools you're considering.) Once you've set this goal, don't stop studying and learning vocabulary words until you consistently achieve the score on practice tests.

2. Block Out Time in Your Schedule

Make an appointment with yourself to study and take practice tests. Don't compromise this time; treat it like a serious commitment that you can't break. Find a quiet, secluded place, and don't let yourself be disturbed—that means no food breaks, telephone calls, or pat-the-cat sessions. When you're finished, go outside and yell for a while to release your tension. Then reward your hard work and self-discipline by bathing in melted milk chocolate.

3. Study with Friends

Anything is more fun if you do it with friends (except maybe body piercing). Another advantage to studying with friends is that you can help each other with some of the harder math concepts and test each other on vocabulary words. Just make sure that you don't get carried away fooling around and forget to study. Also, don't have too good a time or the Serpent will hunt you down, hide under your bed, and stab a number 2 pencil into your little toe while you sleep. He doesn't like students to have any fun with his SAT.

Remember, if you don't prepare the first time, you'll just have to take the test again, and eventually you'll have to study. Unless, of course, you're aiming for college in the Yukon Territory.

THE VERBAL SECTION

MASTERING THE QUESTION TYPES

The verbal section of the SAT supposedly tests how skilled you are with words. It tests your vocabulary, your ability to understand the relationships between words, and your ability to read and comprehend. Basically, though, it's just a glorified vocabulary test. If you read the following strategies for answering analogy, sentence completion, and critical reading questions, and have fun with our vocabulary section, you'll be able to bury the serpent and maybe someday be a star contestant on *Wheel of Fortune*.

On every SAT there are 19 analogies, 19 sentence completions, and 40 critical reading questions, for a total of 78 questions. In this chapter we will go over each type of question individually in order to familiarize you with the different question types, and then show you some slick tricks.

Rule #1: Know Your Speed

You are given only 75 minutes for the three verbal subsections. So you figure, "Great, I have a minute per question." *Wrong.* You have to subtract about 20 minutes for the amount of time that you need to spend reading the reading passages. Then subtract another minute from the total test time for those moments you spend watching the kid in front of you pick his nose, and maybe another half second for the time that you spend picking your own nose. Now you have only about 40 seconds per problem. That's just about the amount of time most people need if they work efficiently. If you find yourself finishing ten minutes early, then you're probably working too fast and being careless, or you didn't spend enough time picking your nose. If you aren't finishing all the questions before the time runs out, you might have to be a little less careful (or skip the last reading passage of each section, as described in Strategy #5 of the reading passage section of this chapter, page 41). In any case, it's essential that you have practiced enough to know exactly how fast you should be moving. Good control of your speed and timing must be second nature to you when you take the real test.

Rule #2: Do the Sub-sections in the Best Order

All questions are worth the same number of points. Therefore, you want to have done as many problems as possible in the event that you run out of time. Sentence completions take the least amount of time, so do them first. Then do analogies. The critical reading passages take the longest; do them last. (This is usually the order given on the test.) The only exception to this rule would be if you consistently find that you score better on practice tests when you do things in a different order.

Rule #3: Realize That Questions Get Harder

The Serpent gets more and more cruel as each sub-section (a set of 10 sentence completions, a set of 10 analogies, etc.) progresses, except in the questions following each critical reading passage. The first question in a sub-section should be easy. The last question in a sub-section is usually hard. This is important to remember, because if you know that you're going to have to skip some questions, you might as well skip the hard ones.

On the last few questions in a sub-section, the most tempting answer is probably wrong.

This is also important because it can be used to outsmart the Serpent. You can use this principle to find correct answers to questions that you otherwise wouldn't be sure about. How? Since the first few questions in a sub-section are always easy, the obvious or most tempting guess is probably correct. The middle questions in a sub-section are a little harder; on these questions the obvious or most tempting guess is sometimes right and sometimes wrong. On the last few questions in a sub-section, the obvious, most tempting guess is probably wrong. This is a *crucial* concept. As we will explain in more depth later, a question is put at the beginning of a sub-section if, in the Serpent's experiments, most students get it right. It is put at the end if most students get it wrong. The trick is to learn to pick the answer that "most students" would pick on the questions at the beginning of the section, and, at the end of the section, avoid the answer that "most students" would pick. What we have explained here is just the basics of how to apply this concept. In Chapter 4 we provide a more advanced explanation, with additional useful strategies and tricks.

Remember, the questions only get harder within *sub*-sections, not from section to section. So, if you've finished with the analogies and you are moving on to sentence completion, you'll be starting afresh with relatively easy sentence completions.

If you want an in-depth explanation of this rule and its uses, read the book *Cracking the SAT and PSAT* by Adam Robinson and John Katzman. They call it the Joe Bloggs principle.

Rule #4: Know the Directions

The directions are the same every year. You should not waste any time reading them during the test. Memorize them from your copy of *Taking the SAT*, available from your high school guidance office.

A Quick Tip: If you skip a question because you don't know the answer, put a mark next to it. We suggest an X for the questions you don't think you'll be able to figure out, and a ? next to the ones you think you'd get with more time, but you don't want to spend the time on now.

SENTENCE COMPLETIONS

Definition:	Fill in the blank.
Number:	19 questions.
Priority:	Do them first.
Comment:	Not that bad once you get the hang of it.

For the sentence completion questions, the ETS presents you with a nice, logical sentence. The trouble is that one or two words are missing from it. Your job is to pick the correct missing word(s) from among five choices. All of the possible answers will make sense grammatically, but only one will make sense logically.

Some students consider sentence completions to be the hardest part of the verbal section because they test your sense of "sentence logic" in addition to testing your vocabulary. We think they are the easiest part because you have a context to help you figure out the answer. For example:

> The man was smelly so I plugged my _____.
> (A) ear
> (B) toe
> (C) eye
> (D) socket
> (E) nose

Each of these choices is okay grammatically, but why would you plug your eye, toe, ear, or socket if the man was smelly? You would plug your nose. Usually, the SAT questions are more sophisticated, but the basic idea is the same.

If you approach them properly, the sentence completion questions can be extremely gratifying. When you choose the right words to go in the blanks, the sentence will have a certain flow, a sort of magical aura that will suffuse your body with a warm, orgasmic glow.

The Basic Pattern

There is a basic thought pattern that you should follow whenever you attack a sentence completion question:

1. Read the sentence first, skipping over the blanks, just to get a feel for how the sentence is set up.
2. Read the sentence again, and this time, when you get to the blanks, think of *your own* initial guess as to what the missing words should be. You may not be able to come up with a specific word, but all you really need to determine is the answer's generic category—whether the word is a "negative" or a "positive" one.

In the blank write a "+" or "–" to remind yourself what type of word you're looking for. When there are two blanks, you should at least decide whether the two missing words are antonyms, synonyms, "good," or "bad."

3. Compare your guesses with the answer choices provided and see if any of them fit your general idea of what the answer should be.

4. Plug in the answer that looks best and see if it makes sense.

5. If it clearly makes sense, then go with it. Otherwise, try all of the other choices and pick the one that works best. As you're trying choices, cross out the ones that you're sure don't fit. Then, if you get stuck and decide to come back to the question, you won't have to waste time by reading all of the choices again.

Okay, enough rules. Here are some examples:

She insulted Irving's appearance by saying,
"Your face is _____."
(A) cheerful
(B) beautiful
(C) handsome
(D) charming
(E) a wart-ridden, misshapen mass of snotty
goo

So, that wasn't too tough. Anyway, did you notice that magical feeling when you chose (E)?

Let's try some from real SATs:

Until Florence Nightingale made nursing
_____, it was considered a _____
profession.
(A) scientific . . . painstaking
(B) essential . . . dangerous
(C) noble . . . lofty
(D) patriotic . . . worthy
(E) respectable . . . degrading

The way that you should read this question is, "Until Florence Nightingale made nursing *something good*, it was considered a *something bad that's the opposite of whatever's in the first blank* profession." You can eliminate (C) and (D) because *lofty* and *worthy* are both words that mean something good. You can eliminate (A) and (B) because they aren't opposites. Now you know the answer is (E).

> Although they are _____ by traps, poison, and shotguns, predators _____ to feast on flocks of sheep.
> (A) lured . . . refuse
> (B) destroyed . . . cease
> (C) impeded . . . continue
> (D) encouraged . . . attempt
> (E) harmed . . . hesitate

The correct answer here is (C). Any time that you see *although*, the sentence will have two parts. The first part will say "blah blah blah." The second part of the sentence will say something that you wouldn't expect considering that "blah blah blah" is true. In the above example, the first part of the sentence says, "Nasty things are trying to stop these predators from pigging out." Therefore, you would expect that they would decide not to pig out. However, the *although* indicates that the second part of the sentence will say the opposite of what you expected it to say. So you have to choose an answer that indicates that they are still pigging out. The only answer that would fit this idea is (C).

> As a scientist, Leonardo da Vinci was capable of _____, but his mistakes are remarkably few in light of his _____.
> (A) error . . . accomplishments
> (B) artistry . . . failures
> (C) genius . . . works
> (D) trivia . . . lapses
> (E) innovation . . . achievements

In the same way that *although* was the key word in the last example, *but* is the key word in this example. You should be able to figure out that the two missing words should be in the combination "bad thing" . . . "good thing." In other words, you should think to yourself, "As a scientist, Leo made some bad mistakes, *but* his screw-ups seem pretty minor when you look at the good things he did." Scanning down the list of possible answers, you may see that:

(A) is "bad" . . . "good"
(B) is "good" . . . "bad"
(C) is "good" . . . "irrelevant"
(D) is "irrelevant" . . . "bad"
(E) is "good" . . . "good"

Therefore, the correct answer must be (A).

Other key words that can change the logic of a sentence (like *although* and *but*) are:

- despite
- except
- far from (as in "*Far from* doing blah blah, the thing has done almost the opposite of blah blah.")
- in spite of
- instead of
- nevertheless
- unless
- while (*While* that is true, it is also true that this is true.)
- yet (That is true, *yet* we must also recognize that this is true.)

A Couple of Tricks

In the sentence completion section, as in the reading section, the ETS tries to be as nice as it can to women and minorities. So if you see a sentence that mentions women or minorities, it will usually be saying something good about them. For instance:

Although few in number, women in Congress have had _____ impact on a variety of issues.
(A) an arbitrary
(B) a negligible
(C) a substantial
(D) a minor
(E) an inadvertent

You could get this problem right without even reading more than the first few words in the sentence. All you have to realize is that "substantial" is the only positive word among the answer choices.

The ETS thinks that just knowing that congresswomen are influential on Capitol Hill will help every girl in SAT-Land do well on the test, get into her top-choice college, and then excel in her career.

Using the principle that the questions at the beginning of a section should be easy, you should avoid difficult vocabulary words at the beginning of a sentence completion section. For example, this question is the second one in its section:

> Just as congestion plagues every important highway, so it _____ the streets of every city.
> (A) delimits
> (B) delays
> (C) clogs
> (D) obviates
> (E) destroys

Delimits and *obviates* are difficult vocabulary words. If you had to know the meanings of these two words to answer this question correctly, then this question would be difficult and it would not be the second problem in the section. So eliminate (A) and (D). The correct answer is (C).

ANALOGIES

Definition: Comparisons.
Number: 19 questions.
Priority: Do them second.
Comment: Easy if you see the answer right away, confusing if you don't.

The word *analogy* begins with "anal" for a good reason. The format of this type of question is illustrated in the examples below. Your job is to find the pair of words that are related to each other in the same way that the two capitalized words are. Your mind will argue with itself about these questions forever if you let it. Think through each question thoroughly but not repetitiously. Most importantly, read *all* the answers— don't just grab the first one that looks good.

If you have trouble reading this type of question because of all those colons, use this simple rule:

Single colon (:) means "is related to"
Double colon (::) means "in the same way that"

So, for example

TUNA FISH : STARKIST ::
(A) peanut butter : Skippy

would be read: Tuna fish "is related to" Starkist "in the same way that" peanut butter "is related to" Skippy.

Words can be related in a whole bunch of ways. Although it would be impossible to list all of the possible relationships, here is a list of some common ones that the Serpent uses in the analogy section:

1. Synonyms (obscenity : profanity)
2. Antonyms (pain : pleasure)
3. A thing and what it's used for (the SAT : torturing students)
4. Cause and effect (*Up Your Score* : a 1600 score)
5. Things that go together (peanut butter : jelly)
6. Type of person and something that person would use (rapper : microphone)

7. Type of person and something that person would do (politician : lie)
8. Relative size (Curious George : King Kong)
9. Relative degrees of the same thing (happy : ecstatic :: interested : fascinated)
10. Description (school lunch : disgusting)
11. Part and whole (marshmallow surprises : Lucky Charms)

What to Do When You Don't See the Correct Answer

Situation #1: You Think You Know the Words, but You Don't See the Answer

There is a definite procedure that you should follow when you are in this situation. First, panic and scream. (This will distract the other test-takers and make your score look good in comparison.) Next, relax and apply the following two principles:

1. Make a sentence

When you're having trouble, the first thing you should do is make up a sentence that relates the two capitalized words. For example, here is a real SAT question:

LUNG : WHALE ::
(A) shell : clam
(B) claw : crab
(C) gill : fish
(D) fin : shark
(E) pearl : oyster

Make up a sentence like, "The lung is the organ that a whale breathes with." Then try that sentence out on all the other pairs of words.

"The *shell* is the organ that a *clam* breathes with." Nope.
"The *claw* is the organ that a *crab* breathes with." Nope.
"The *gill* is the organ that a *fish* breathes with." YEAH!
"The *fin* is the organ that a *shark* breathes with." Nope.
"The *pearl* is the organ that an *oyster* breathes with." Nope.

The answer is (C). Making a sentence forces you to clarify the relationship between the words. Make sure that your sentence is as specific as possible. If the sentence had been simply, "*Lungs* are part of a *whale*," then all of the answer choices except maybe (E) would have worked. You should keep changing your sentence, making it more specific until only one choice remains.

2. Look for other relationships

See if you can dream up another kind of relationship between the two capitalized terms. As the following example from a real SAT illustrates, two words can be related to each other in more than one way.

COMPLEX : BUILDING ::
(A) tapestry : fabric
(B) apple : tree
(C) classroom : campus
(D) federation : state
(E) highway : truck

If this problem seems *complex* to you, it is probably because you assumed that *complex* meant complicated. However, the definition of *complex* used here is the one that means, "a group of buildings," as in "apartment *complex*." Therefore, the sentence that connects them is: "A *complex* is a group of *buildings*." The best answer, therefore, is (D) because a *federation* is a group of *states*.

If you can't find a relationship between the two capitalized words other than the one you first thought of, try working backwards. Find the relationships between the words in each of the answer choices and then see if any of those relationships work for the capitalized words.

The parts of speech in the capitalized words will always be the same as the parts of speech in the answers. If the capitalized words are "VERB : NOUN," then all of the choices will be "verb : noun." So, in the example above you would have known that *complex* was a noun because *tapestry, apple, classroom, federation,* and *highway* are all nouns.

Situation #2: You Don't Know One or Both of the Capitalized Words

There is a definite procedure that you should follow in this situation. First, scream even louder than you did in situation #1, because you're in more trouble. Then look at the list of choices and eliminate any choice in which the two words are not related in a logical and definite manner. You should eliminate each choice for which you cannot answer "yes" to both questions of the DOPE. (The DOPE? Let us explain.)

The Dumb or Pointless Examination (DOPE)

Question 1

"Is there a logical and definite relationship between these words that I could make a sentence out of?"

Question 2

"Are they *almost always* related in that way or are they just related in that way in some rare contexts?"

If the answer to Question 1 is "no" or the answer to Question 2 is that the words are *not* "almost always related in that way," then the answer choice fails the DOPE and you should eliminate it.

For example, try this one from an old SAT:

PHOENIX : IMMORTALITY ::
(A) unicorn : cowardice
(B) sphinx : mystery
(C) salamander : speed
(D) ogre : wisdom
(E) chimera : stability

Suppose you don't know that a *phoenix* is a mythical, immortal being. You can still eliminate choice (A) because it fails Question 1 of the DOPE. There really isn't any relationship between *unicorn* and *cowardice*. Unicorns aren't known either for being cowards or for not being cowards. If there's no relationship between two words, they can't be part of an analogy. You can also eliminate (C) because there isn't much of a relationship between *salamander* and *speed*. Salamanders aren't particularly fast; if the Serpent wanted an example of something fast he would have used a cheetah. Salamanders also aren't particularly slow; if the Serpent had wanted an example of something slow he would have picked a snail. Choice (D) can be eliminated in the same way. *Ogres* aren't particularly wise or particularly unwise. If you know that a chimera is a female monster that breathes fire, you can also see that there's no relationship between *chimera* and *stability*. That leaves only choice (B), which is correct because a *phoenix* is a mythical being that represents *immortality* and a *sphinx* is a mythical being that is famous for posing *mysterious* riddles.

Let's do another.

> HPARGARAP : SECNETNES ::
> (A) cover : pages
> (B) book : chapters
> (C) grammar : errors
> (D) directory: graphs
> (E) summary : comments

You don't know what either of the capitalized words means. But that doesn't matter. You can still eliminate three of the answers because they are dumb or pointless.

Choice (C) does not pass the DOPE. There are such things as grammatical errors but grammar doesn't need to have errors and lots of things can have errors besides grammar. Therefore, choice (C) fails Question 2 of the DOPE. Moving on to choice (D) we see that it fails Question 1 of the DOPE. There is no logical and definite relationship between directories and graphs. Even if you say that some directories have graphs in them, choice (D) still fails Question 2 of the DOPE. Choice (E) fails the DOPE, too. Even if you say that some summaries have comments in them, or that people make comments in a summary, this relationship is not very logical and the two words are not usually related in this manner.

Choice (A) passes the DOPE. There are almost always

pages on the inside and a cover on the outside of a book. Choice (B) also passes the DOPE. A book is frequently composed of chapters. We've narrowed it down to (A) or (B). Now you have a 50-percent chance of getting it correct.

By the way, the capitalized words as they appeared on the SAT were actually PARAGRAPH : SENTENCES. We scrambled them. The correct answer is (B). A paragraph is made up of several sentences, just as a *koob* is made up of several *sretpahc*.

If you know one of the capitalized words, then you can narrow things down even further after you use the DOPE. For instance, in the above example, let's say the second word wasn't scrambled:

HPARGARAP : SENTENCES::

The DOPE has allowed you to narrow the choices down to (A) and (B). Now check to see if the relationships in those choices make sense with the word SENTENCES. In choice (A), the relationship is that a cover is wrapped around pages. Is there anything that wraps around sentences in the same way? Not really. However, in choice (B), the relationship is that a book is made up of many chapters; is there something that is made up of many sentences in the same way? Yes—a paragraph. So you know that (B) is the only answer that makes sense.

CRITICAL READING PASSAGES

Definition:	Passages followed by questions.
Number:	40.
Priority:	Do these last.
Comment:	Each consecutive passage is harder than the one before it. However, the questions following a particular passage are not arranged from easiest to hardest.

The reading passages make up 50 percent of the verbal section, so make sure you can do these well. However, it is difficult to study for this section in any direct way. Indirectly, you can study by improving your ability to read and comprehend.

We will start with the assumption that you know how to read. If, however, this is not a valid assumption, perhaps the first words that you should learn are *two hundred*, which is short for having to go to college in the Yukon Territory.

The ability to read fast can be a big advantage. So read only those words that start with *w*. "Hold it," you say, "but then I won't understand anything." To which we respond, "Oh yeah, you're right, sorry," and then suggest, "Try reading everything very carefully and make sure that you comprehend it all." To which you respond, "But then I won't have time to finish the test."

This is the heart-wrenching conflict that you must deal with on the critical reading section: to speed or not to speed. All we can say is, do as many practice tests as you possibly can so that you know how fast you can read and still understand as much as possible.

Fancy speed-reading tricks probably won't help much. Psychologists have found that speed-reading tricks really only teach you how to skim a text by skipping details. But for reading questions you have to know the details.

In order to improve your comprehension, we recommend that you expand your reading horizons. If your reading matter is presently limited to cereal boxes and the phone book, it's time to explore new possibilities. Caution: *Do not attempt to switch cold turkey!* Many a student has gone into intellectual shock after attempting to jump straight from *Teen Beat* to *The Plasma Physicist's Quarterly*. We suggest that you work up to quality reading material using this one-week plan:

Day 1: *Tattooed Bikers and Their Ladies* (this is a real mag!)
Day 2: *Teen Beat*

Day 3: *Pro-Wrestling Weekly*
Day 4: *The National Enquirer*
Day 5: *Soap Opera Digest*
Day 6: *Sassy*
Day 7: *People*

Now you should be ready to tackle the kind of reading that you are likely to find on the SAT. Read things like: *The New York Times, American Heritage, Time, Newsweek, The Atlantic Monthly, National Geographic, Sports Illustrated, The New Yorker, Harper's, Vogue,* and *Forbes.*

Attitude

The critical reading section is the one place where you should abandon negative thinking. As impossible as this may sound, it is important to assume a positive attitude toward the critical reading section. Why is this? Well, remember the chapter on oral hygiene in the health textbook you had in sixth grade? No, because it was boring and you didn't *want* to read it. But do you remember the chapter on sex? Yes, because you did want to read it. It's the same way with reading passages. You won't remember them if you have the attitude that they are boring and useless. (They are boring and useless, but that's not the point.) Instead, you must convince yourself that you are dying to read them because you are passionately interested in whatever they are about. Get psyched to read them. Treat them as you would a love letter. Treat them as you would a passage from a piece of great literature. Treat them as you would a section of *Up Your Score.*

There is sound psychological backing for this claim. Scientists have shown that comprehension and retention levels are much higher when people are interested in what they are reading than when people aren't. Your brain just doesn't bother remembering stuff that it finds totally dull.

Strategies for the Critical Reading Section

The following six strategies can be of help to you when taking the test. You probably shouldn't use all of them because that would take a lot of time. Which strategies you choose is a matter of personal preference. Try them all and see which ones you like.

Strategy #1

Skim the questions before reading the passage. This gives you an idea of what to look for while you read. Follow the four guidelines below if you use this method:

a. Only read the questions; don't read the answers, too. If the question is about a specific line in the passage, mark that line so that when you read the passage you will know to focus on the marked lines. (This is especially helpful for the vocabulary-in-context questions.)

b. When you see a question that asks for something general such as, "Which is the best title?" or "The main idea of the passage is . . . ," disregard it and go on to the next question. Why? Because you should always assume that there will be at least one question like that so you don't even have to bother reading it.

c. As you read the passage, circle anything that is an answer to one of the questions. Don't immediately go and answer the question because that will break your concentration and interfere with your comprehension.

d. Make sure that when you read the passage, you don't get so caught up in looking for the answers to the questions that you fail to understand the overall meaning.

Strategy #2

After you read a paragraph, ask yourself, "Self, what was that paragraph about?" Spend about two to six seconds summarizing the contents of the paragraph in your head. It helps to look at the paragraph while you are doing this because then you will remember where things are located in the passage.

This can save time later when you have to look for the answers. If you are a flake who, like Larry, can read an entire passage before realizing that you weren't paying attention and that you have no idea what it was about, then this strategy might be of help in forcing you to concentrate.

Strategy #3

Usually the passage will be composed of a few sentences that state the author's main idea and others that contain facts to support the main idea. As you read the passage, underline any sentence that is purely a statement of the author's main idea. It is guaranteed that there will be at least one question relating to these sentences and if you underline them, you won't have to waste time looking for them. We highly recommend that you use this strategy.

Strategy #4

While you are reading, underline the main sentence in each paragraph. The sound of your pencil will distract the other test-takers, making them lose concentration and improving your score in comparison. And when you are answering the questions, the underlining will automatically draw your attention to the main idea of each paragraph.

Strategy #5

The Princeton Review suggests that if you are having trouble finishing the verbal sections, you should skip the last reading passage. They argue that it takes several minutes to do the last section and, since it's the hardest passage, a lot of students get the questions wrong anyway. If you skip it, you will have much more time to devote to the rest of the questions that take less time, are easier, and are worth the same number of points.

Strategy #6

Read the passage, then translate the whole thing into Swedish. (This will only help if you are Swedish.)

The Passages

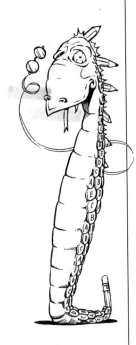

There are four reading passages on the SAT (actually five, because one is a double passage—more on that later). One passage runs between 450 and 600 words, one between 600 and 800 words, and two (one, plus the double passage) between 800 and 950 words. The number of questions relating to each passage is between five and 13. There is always a passage on something scientific and a passage that is an excerpt from a narrative, which could be fiction or nonfiction. The other passage topics include something historical, something about an art form, or something about a minority group. Each passage has a short introduction in italics. Read the introductions. They help you understand the passage, and often they define words or identify names that you need to know.

The Scientific Passage

Do not be intimidated by scientific jargon. The scientific passage will inevitably have some far-out scientific terms that you have never heard of. Don't worry. *You don't need to know scientific terms.* Either the terms will be totally irrelevant or they will be explained in the passage. Take for example the following excerpt from an actual SAT:

> ". . . Kinematic studies of such objects show them to be receding from us at a rate proportional to their distance. . ."

Some students might panic when reading this sentence because of the word *kinematic*. However, there is no need to panic. You don't have to know what *kinematic studies* are to answer the questions correctly.

The second reason why this sentence could be intimidating is that it refers to proportions. Proportions are math and math is intimidating. Once again, there is no need to worry. If you read the sentence that follows the above sentence in the passage you will see that it explains the math so that you don't have to do any thinking:

> "That is, those galaxies most distant from us have larger recessional velocities."

(You don't have to know what a *recessional velocity* is, either.) The expression, "that is, . . ." clues us in to the fact that this sentence is going to explain the previous sentence. You will frequently find this sort of thing in the scientific passages. If you don't understand a sentence, look at the sentences that precede and follow it. Chances are, one of them explains whatever you don't understand.

The Historical Passage

The historical passage will discuss a particular trend or period in history. The author will be making her own interpretation of that trend or period. She will support her interpretation with examples. When the author starts listing examples, read the first example, then skip the rest of the examples and put an "EX" (for "EX"ample) in the margin near the list of examples. In many cases, the author will also support her interpretation by referring to other historians who agree with her. In other cases, she will refer to other historians who disagree with her so that she can refute their interpretation. Circle the names of historians the author refers to—there will probably be a question about them.

The Art Passage

The author will never say, "Beethoven sucks."

The art passage will be about literature, painting, sculpture, crafts, music, etc., or a particular artist, musician, craftsman, writer, etc. In *all* of the examples that we looked at, the author had a positive attitude toward the artist or art form. The author might have some specific criticisms but the overall point of the passage will be complimentary. The author will never say, "Beethoven sucks." (This rule does not apply to the Double Passage.)

The Fiction Passage

The literature passage will be an excerpt from some piece of literary fiction. It is hard to predict what these passages will be like. Don't skim these too quickly. You have to read them carefully so that you pick up the subtleties. However, when you go to answer the questions, do not read too deeply. You might have to interpret the figurative meanings of parts of the passage, but don't try to be profound and read things into the passage that aren't there. Also, make sure that you pay attention to the author's style and tone. There will almost certainly be a question about that.

The Minority Passage

The ETS has been accused of being biased against minorities. In the 1970s, the ETS decided to respond to these accusations by putting a reading passage about minorities on each SAT. This is a pointless politically correct gesture on their part because it doesn't make the SAT any less culturally biased. (For more on the SAT and bias, see page 263.)

As far as we're concerned, the minority passage makes the SAT easier for everyone—minorities and majorities. This is because the ethnic passage is incredibly predictable. You *know* that the ETS is going to say good things about the minority group. That's the whole point of the passage. Therefore, many of the questions are giveaways, for example this one from a real SAT:

> The author's attitude toward the Chinese achievements mentioned in lines 1–45 is best described as one of
> (A) disbelief   (B) admiration
> (C) anxiety   (D) ambivalence
> (E) apathy

The only one of these choices that expresses a clearly positive attitude toward the Chinese is (B). Of course, (B) is the right answer.

The Double Passage

The Double Passage consists of two separate passages, which according to ETS, "oppose, support, or in some way complement" each other.

The selection is set up like this: an introduction, the first passage, the second passage, questions on the first passage, questions on the second passage, then questions on both passages.

Don't do it in this order. Here is our suggestion for the best order:

1. Read introduction
2. Read *first* passage
3. Do *first* passage questions
4. Read *second* passage
5. Do *second* passage questions
6. Do *both* passage questions

The reason is, the questions on the first passage will have nothing to do with the second passage. Therefore, it makes more sense to do the first passage questions immediately after reading the first passage. Likewise for the second passage. Then, after you have read and answered questions on both passages, you will have such a thorough knowledge that you will ace the questions on both passages.

You should be able to tell easily whether the two passages agree or disagree. Often, the introduction will help by saying that the two passages have "much in common" (in which case they'll probably agree) or "present two views" (in which case they'll probably disagree). If you're having trouble figuring out the relationship or you're running out of time, follow this general rule: If the context and subject matter of the two passages seem different, then what they say will almost certainly be similar, and vice versa. For instance, in some of the passages we've looked at, a speech from ancient Greece and a speech from the Civil War had the same view on war, and an essay on silent film and one on mime (two different art forms) showed the similarities between the two forms. However, another selection had two passages on architecture, both from the twentieth century, and they disagreed. So if the two passages were written in different times or places or if they concern different subjects, they probably agree. If they talk about the same subject and were written in the same time or place, they probably disagree. (Note: The passages will rarely strictly agree or disagree. One passage might concern only one point discussed in the other, or they may present two non-conflicting views on a subject.)

The ETS is not particularly creative in making up the questions for the reading section. He uses the same basic questions over and over. They fall into six main categories.

The Six Types of Questions

Type #1: General (main idea)

1. The author is primarily concerned with . . .
2. Which of the following titles best summarizes the passage?
3. The primary purpose of the passage is to . . .

Hint: Look at the topic paragraph and the concluding sentence.

Type #2: Explicit (facts)

1. According to the fourth paragraph, some economists feel that . . .
2. According to the passage, an atom of which of the following substances will split, releasing energy and more neutrons?
3. According to the passage, Margaret asked Mrs. Horn's opinion because she . . .

Type #3: Implicit (inferences, reading between the lines)

1. It can be inferred that the guilds were organized as they were because . . .
2. It can be inferred that each of the following applies to the *perfecti* except that they . . .
3. With which of the following statements about marketing would the author most likely agree?

Type #4: Author's Logic

1. What tone does the author take toward the chickens?
2. Which of the following best describes the development of the passage?
3. The author cites specific examples of the work of slave artisans primarily to . . .

Type #5: Vocabulary-in-Context

1. The word "obtrusive" is used in line 12 to mean . . .
2. The phrase "underlying themes" (line 7) refers to the . . .
3. Which of the following best captures the meaning of the word "alliance" in line 32?

Hint: Don't give up if you don't know the word; you should be able to figure it out from the context. Also, be careful—it may not be the most common definition of the word.

Type #6: Comparison (only on the Double Passage)

1. Which statement from Passage 1 does not have a parallel idea in Passage 2?
2. How would the author of Passage 1 respond to the idea of the "crazy spoons" in Passage 2?
3. Which statement is best supported by the two passages?

A note about outside knowledge:

Critical reading questions refer to what is "stated or implied *in the passage.*" You aren't supposed to use any outside information. So if the passage is about the history of celery and you happen to be an expert on that subject, you still have to read the passage. However, the passages almost never contradict accepted outside knowledge. You won't ever see a passage that claims that the Earth is flat. So never choose an answer that you know is making a false statement. On the other hand, never assume that you know the right answer just because you know that a statement is true. There might be other true statements among the choices that are more applicable to the passage.

Now it's time to attempt a sample passage. Following the passage are examples of the different types of questions and the answer choices that would accompany them.

A Serious Sample Passage

The following passage is an excerpt from a scientific journal about a recent scientific breakthrough.

Modern science has brought us many wonderful inventions—the television, the waterbed, "I Can't Believe It's Not Butter," and Michael Jackson. Many more marvelous technological breakthroughs loom on the horizon. The latest development in the field of applied science is no exception. Today, scientists have invented a process through which deceased family pets can be freeze-dried and saved for millennia.

Every pet owner knows that pets are integral parts of the household. When they have been around for so long, and have had such an influence on family members, it's hard to let them go when they pass on. Now, through freeze-drying, Fido or Fluffy can remain a household member forever.

When your pet dies, its lovable body will be kept intact. You can keep it on the mantel and take it down to pet it at your leisure—and a dehydrated pet does not require feeding, walking, or litter boxes. It emits much less of an odor than regular dead pets, and looks much better, also.

The projected uses for freeze-dried pets are numerous. If Spot happens to have died in a crouched pose, he can be placed on your lawn as a security device. Snookums can be used as a decorative centerpiece. Market analysts predict a boom in gerbil paperweights, goldfish refrigerator magnets, and poodle hood ornaments. They could even become collectors' items: You could trade them like baseball cards.

Detractors claim, however, that the dehydration wears off after several years, as moisture from the air enters the animal corpse and causes decomposition. This, it is feared, would attract bacteria into the home. Another flaw in the freeze-drying process is that the pet becomes brittle and breaks easily. For a young child, finding Ginger shattered on the living room floor could be extremely traumatic. Finally, it is feared that people who dislike their pets will have them freeze-dried before they actually die.

Although there are problems with the procedure, the concept of freeze-dried pets is a valuable one. If the method is

If Spot happens to have died in a crouched pose, he can be placed on the lawn and used as a security device.

perfected, it will allow a pet to remain an everyday part of the lives of its loved ones and, indeed, it will permit pets to be passed from generation to generation as family heirlooms.

1. This passage is primarily
   (A) a scientific description of the freeze-drying process
   (B) an essay on the religious and moral questions associated with the freeze-drying process
   (C) a general discussion intended to acquaint the reader with the subject of freeze-drying pets
   (D) an expression of someone's opinion
   (E) an advertisement pushing the freeze-drying process

2. The first paragraph is best described as
   (A) descriptive
   (B) introductory
   (C) irrelevant
   (D) sophomoric
   (E) existential

3. The word "detractors" in the fifth paragraph most nearly means
   (A) farm implements
   (B) critics
   (C) supporters
   (D) pet owners
   (E) scientific experts

4. According to the passage one of the most specific problems associated with the process is
   (A) a freeze-dried pet attracts viruses
   (B) cost is high
   (C) the lack of qualified individuals to perform the task
   (D) freeze-dried pets are not shatterproof
   (E) the fear the freeze-dried pets will stick to the wallpaper

5. The author seems to believe that
(A) freeze-drying is a worthless process when applied to animals
(B) the difficulties of freeze-drying outweigh the benefits
(C) it would be easier to freeze-dry an armadillo than a pine cone
(D) If you give a man a fish, he'll eat for a day; if you give a man two fishes, he'll eat for two days
(E) the goals of freeze-drying are worth striving for

Answers: 1. (C) 2. (B) 3. (B) 4. (D) 5. (E)

Now you have an idea of what the critical reading passages are all about. However, most passages won't be that interesting, that short, or that easy. (We couldn't help it; we're also interesting, short, and easy.) For practice, do the reading passages in *Real SATs*. The *Taking the SAT* booklet available at your high school guidance office will also have some reading passages.

Speak for yourselves, guys.
— Lisa

ABOUT SAT WORDS

Learning the Words You Need to Rock the Verbal Section

hypogyrrationalrhombocuboids
diffeomorphism
supermartingale
myelomeningocele
dacryocystorhinoscopy

You probably don't know what any of the above words mean. You probably don't care what any of the above words mean. Once you have finished this book, you still won't know what they mean.

The above words may be interesting and useful. But who cares? They were put here simply to intimidate you. They will not be on the SAT. This is because the SAT tests you on the type of words that a college student would be likely to run into. A college student who ran into any of the above words would suffer a concussion.

There is a certain type of word that just *is* an SAT word. It is impossible to define precisely what makes a word an SAT word, but by the time you have finished our word lists you will know what we mean. For the most part, they are words that you look at and say, "Fiddlesticks, I should know what that word means, but I don't. It's right here on the tip of my tongue but I can't quite . . ." Another characteristic of an SAT word is that it isn't particularly controversial. It won't have much to do with sex or violence or religion or anything that could offend someone.

The Two Types of Words

Type #1: Normal Words

Words that you would encounter in the course of doing your homework, listening to articulate people, or watching TV.

Example: If you saw the movie *The Wizard of Oz*, you heard the word *pusillanimous*. However, you probably didn't whip out your pocket dictionary and look it up. (If you did, consider a career with the ETS.) Now that you are in training for the SAT, you will have to start looking up any and all words that you encounter. Start now. Do you know what *amalgam* means?

Type #2: Decodable Words

Unusual words that they don't expect you to know off-hand but that you can figure out if you are clever.

Example: the word *decodable* is a decodable word. You could decode it like this:

"de" = take out; reverse
"code" = words or symbols with secret meanings
+ "able" = capable of being

decodable = capable of being taken out of its secret meaning

MEMORIZING SAT WORDS

Larry's Memoirs

Whan I started studying for the SAT, I had a feeble memory. I would spend a lot of time on the word lists, but nothing seemed to sink in. My feeble memory also affected other aspects of life. One day I met this gorgeous girl and she said, as girls are always saying to me, "I have an unquenchable desire for your body. My name is Jenny and my phone number is 867-5309." I went home and I was going to write her name down in my book of women who lust after me, but I couldn't remember her name or her phone number. I knew then it was time to do something about my memory problem.

So I read some stuff about how to improve my memory. Most of what I read sounded extremely dopey, but I gave it a try anyway. And, as they say in the world of laundry detergent, "It worked! It really worked!"

The moral of my story is that if you have a bad memory, it's not because there is something wrong with your brain, it's just that you haven't learned how to memorize. We will teach you how in this chapter. The techniques we present are more than cute little tricks. They will tremendously improve your ability to remember vocabulary words and may even change your life. You don't have to use them if you don't want to, but if you don't use them, it will take you much, much longer to learn the word lists.

The most important concept in memorizing things like vocabulary words is the *mnemonic* (nuh-mahn-eck) *device*. A mnemonic device is any technique, other than pure repetition, that helps you memorize something. So for each word in the list that you don't know, close your eyes for *12 seconds* and think of a mnemonic device.

Research has demonstrated that the most successful mnemonic devices are visual. If you can associate a word with a picture, you will be more likely to remember the word. For example, if you are trying to memorize the word *opulence* (luxury, great wealth), you could visualize a giant mansion surrounded by manicured lawns and lavish gardens. Above the gold-leaf foyer, the word *opulence* would be spelled out in precious gems. Within, you might imagine well-groomed fat gentlemen, the word *opulence* stitched in diamonds across their chests, eating huge amounts of caviar molded into the shape of the word *opulence*. If you make your mental pictures extreme in some way

they will be more memorable. So make your pictures extremely bizarre, extremely gross, extremely obscene, extremely comical, or extremely whatever you are likely to remember. (Detail is important in mental images like this one. The more details you are able to dream up, the more likely you are to remember the word.)

Move on to the other senses. *Hear* the chorus of castrati in the ballroom singing the word *opulence* over the gentle strains of Chopin played by a 50-piece symphony. *Feel* the silks the ladies and gentlemen wear sliding through your fingers as you trace the word *opulence* with champagne over your desktop. *Smell* the delicate and costly perfumes. And of course, *taste* the exquisitely fine wines enjoyed by *opulent* society.

After you have seen, heard, felt, smelled, and tasted the word you can open your eyes. You're still not done, though. Research has also shown that the more you do with a word, the more likely it will stay in your brain. So first read the word and its definition, then write the word and its definition, then sing the word and its definition, then make up a story about the word, then use the word in a conversation, then tattoo the word and its definition on your elbow, then staple the word and its definition to your goldfish.

Clinical tests have also proven that the pun is a very helpful memory technique. We have used puns to illustrate many of the words in the vocabulary list. (**Note:** Since we want to make sure that no one misses our subtlety, we have <u>pun</u>derlined each one.)

If none of these techniques works, there is one foolproof method. Neurologists say that if the word and its definition

Research has shown that the more you do with a word, the more likely it will stay in your brain. So read, write, sing, and say the word and its definition. Tattoo it onto your elbow and staple it onto your goldfish.

are repeated over and over during sexual activity, they will never be forgotten. There is no scientific explanation for this, but it is a widely accepted fact. Of course, we wouldn't know.

Another phenomenon you should be aware of is the *serial position effect*. Suppose you have a long list of words to memorize and you spend the same amount of time studying each word. According to the serial position effect, you will remember the words at the beginning of the list best, the words at the end of the list next best, and the middle words the worst. Therefore, spend the most time on the middle of the list.

Your chances of memorizing something improve if you study it right before you go to bed. While you sleep, your brain sorts out what occurred during the day. The last thought that goes into your brain right before you go to sleep gets special attention while your brain is doing its nightly sorting.

Finally, nobody studies better with music. Experiments have been done with people who swear that they study better with Pearl Jam in the background. But researchers have yet to find anyone who really does.

Two Essential Tools: Flash Cards and a Tape Recorder

You must keep flash cards and a tape recorder by your side while you study. When you come to a word you don't know, look it up and devote 12 seconds to thinking up a mnemonic device, be it a sentence, a quick drawing, or a bit of song lyric—whatever works for you. Then write the word on one side of a 3″ × 5″ card and its definition and your mnemonic device on the other.

Carry your flash cards with you everywhere. Study them during the ride to school, while you wait at the dentist's office, and during particularly boring classes. Every night before you go to sleep, test yourself on your words. Put the cards you know in one pile and the ones you don't know in another pile. Every night you should be able to add five cards to the pile of cards you know.

Do a similar thing with the tape recorder. When you come to a word that you want to remember, record the word, its definition, and either the example sentence that we give you or one that you make up. Then you can listen to the tape while you are in the shower or brushing your teeth. If you can rap or sing some of your words and definitions it's more fun to listen to. If you have a Walkman, you should listen to the tape wherever you go. If your friends ask you what you're listening to, respond casually, "It's 'Gretchen and the Vocab Lists'—they're new out of Seattle." If your friends ask to listen, say, "I would, but the record company asked me not to play it for anyone until it's been officially released."

Also, you may want to take a pocket notebook around with you to write down any unfamiliar words you come across. This will not only improve your vocabulary, but will also help your social life tremendously.

Then, after you've aced the SAT, you can sell your tape, flash cards, and notebook to your younger sibling.

THE WORD LIST

Don't be intimidated; there are only about 600 words here, and you probably know some of them already.

This is not a complete list of SAT words, but some of these *will* be on the test you take. Also, some of the words on this list could appear in another form. You therefore should learn to recognize various forms of a word like *refute* and *refutation*. The sentences and illustrations that follow the definitions are examples of the memorization techniques we described. Enjoy, and may you be blessed by the almighty vocabulary god until you get to "zyzzyva."

aardvark

Aardvark is the first real word in the dictionary, so we figured that we should start with it even though it has never been and probably never will be on the SAT.

abase — lower; humiliate
"I will not abase myself by going to a base with you on the first date," she said to Paul.

abash — embarrass
Arthur was abashed at a bash when he drank too much and fell in the trash.

abate — to lessen
Abigail's sister screamed, "Ab ate all the cookies!" Later, of course, her anger abated.

abominate — loathe; hate
The terrorist abominated his enemy Nate so much that he put a bomb in Nate's boxer shorts.

abstruse — profound; difficult to understand
If you could decipher them, you'd learn that the lyrics to Pearl Jam's "I Got ID" are abstruse.

accentuate — to stress; emphasize
An accent mark accentuates a syllable.
While in New York, it was rude of you to accentuate the fact that Brooklyn people speak with an accent you hate.

acclivity — sharp incline of a hill
A cliff is an example of an acclivity.

accolade — award; honor
When Mister Rogers received an accolade for being the most boring man alive he was not pleased.
Can you say accolade? Sure you can.

accost	to approach and speak to "That sn<u>ack cost</u> you $3.95!" the salesman said, <u>accosting</u> the customer who was about to leave without paying.
acne	zits
adroit	skillful R2D2 is an <u>adroit</u> <u>android.</u>
adulate	to flatter and praise so much it's sickening "B<u>rad, dual eight</u> hundreds on your SATs? You're a god!" she <u>adulated.</u>
adulterate	to make impure Never trust an <u>adult</u> with your bellybutton lint collection. He will definitely <u>adulterate</u> it.
adumbrate	to foreshadow by disclosing only partially The economic indicators <u>adumbrated</u> that the price of gas would rise to <u>a dumb rate.</u>
adverse	hostile; opposed; unfavorable (see AVERSE) "It's tough writing a national anthem during a British attack," complained Francis Scott Key. "The only light you have is the rockets' red glare. You have to <u>add verses</u> under <u>adverse</u> conditions."
advocate	urge; recommend <u>A</u>dvertisements <u>advocate</u> products.
aesthetic	artistic; pertaining to a sense of what is beautiful <u>As the tick</u> was sucking blood from my arm I squashed it. The dead insect smeared on my arm was not <u>aesthetic</u>ally pleasing.
affected	fake (think: a-FAKE-ted) His <u>affected</u> personality negatively <u>affected</u> our <u>affect</u>ion.
affinity	attraction There was a natural <u>affinity</u> between him and his new <u>Infiniti.</u>

affluent | rich
A flu went around the affluent passengers of the Concorde; their diamond tiaras and Rolexes sparkled when they sneezed.

affray | public brawl
The frog was afraid to enter the affray.

agape | open-mouthed
If you stand agape there is a gap in your mouth.

aghast | horrified
We were aghast when he "passed gas." (see EUPHEMISM. *Passed gas* is an example of a euphemism.)

agile | able to move in a quick and easy fashion
Age'll make you less agile.

alacrity | cheerful promptness
The empty auditorium was the result of a lack of alacrity amongst the sleep-deprived students.

alias | a false name
"Your real name was all I asked for; why did you give me an alias?" the reporter said to Ice Cube.

alimentary | supplying nourishment
When Watson asked, "What's a ten-letter word meaning 'supplying nourishment'?" Sherlock replied, "Alimentary, my dear Watson."

allay | to soothe; to make more bearable (see ALLEVIATE)
Note: This is one of a countless number of SAT words that means this.
He allayed his parents' fears by getting all As on his report card.

alleged | stated without proof
It was alleged that he died by falling off a ledge.

alleviate | **to make more bearable** (see APPEASE)
A leaf he ate failed to alleviate his hunger, even though it was a large leaf.

allude | **refer indirectly**
allusion | **a reference to something**
A lewd person alludes to salacious sexual endeavors (see SALACIOUS).

altercation | **a violent dispute**
An altercation broke out when, at the altar, Kate said, "I don't" to her groom.

amass | **collect; get a bunch of**
By publishing this book, we hope to amass a mass of 1600s for our readers.

ambulatory | **able to walk**
After he was run over by the ambulance, he was no longer ambulatory.

ameliorate | **improve a bad situation**
Amelia rated her love-life as having been ameliorated since last year.

amity | **peaceful relations; friendship**
The root "ami-" means friend, as in "amiable."
There was amity between the students at M.I.T. and their math professors.

amnesia | **loss of memory**
We forgot our sentence for this word because we have amnesia. (See, after this long wild night of vicious partying, combined with excessive exposure to the sun, and long, exotic massages with nameless, herbal oils, we became so fried that we lost our ability to recall things and to function normally in society, and . . . what word are we on?)

amorphous | shapeless
This word is decodable if you know all of the pieces:
      "a" = not (see ATYPICAL)
   "morph" = shape, form
  + "ous" = having the qualities of
amorphous = not having the qualities of shape
If you take too much morphine, you'll feel like an amorphous blob.

amuck | **freaked out and violently pissed off**
The schmuck in the muck got stuck, ran amuck, and guess what word he screamed? (answer: shucks)

anthropoid | **human-like**
The root "anthropo-" means human.
C3PO is an anthropoid droid.

antipathy | **hatred; aversion; dislike**
This word is also decodable:
    "anti" = against
 + "pathy" = feeling
  antipathy = feeling against
By this time you should be developing a strong antipathy to studying these words and their ridiculous definitions. Take a break. Put the book down, get a soda, or drink a bottle of Snapple. Then return to your work, refreshed and ready to continue.

apathetic | **indifferent; showing lack of interest**
apathy | **indifference; lack of interest**
    "a" = no
 "pathy" = feeling
  apathy = not feeling
It's a pathetic thing to be apathetic.
"They found the cure for apathy, but no one showed any interest in it."—George Carlin

apex | tip; peak; summit; way up there
This word is likely to be found in the analogy section. Its opposites are words such as *nadir* and *bottom*.
The <u>ape ex</u>ercised by jumping off the <u>apex</u> of the monkey house in the zoo.

appease | soothe; placate (think: a PEACE; see ASSUAGE)
He <u>appeased</u> his parents by eating <u>a piece</u> of slimy okra.

fishhead | the head of a fish
Just checking to see if you're still awake.

arbitrary | **chosen at random or without apparent reason**
If a college rejects you, its admissions process must be <u>arbitrary</u>.

ardor | heat; passion; zeal
With <u>ardor</u> she moaned, "You don't have to be so gentle—<u>ardor</u>, <u>ardor</u>."

askew | crooked; off to one side
Don't tell us our type is <u>a sk e w</u>. Did we <u>ask you</u>?

Who's that running away with *Ardor?*

Ardor

assuage | to ease; pacify (see APPEASE)
Buying <u>a suede</u> fringed jacket might <u>assuage</u> Donna's compulsive desire to shop.

astute | shrewd; wise; observing
<u>A student</u> must be <u>astute</u> to outwit the Evil Testing Serpent.

attribute | **a characteristic, usually a good one**
or **to explain by indicating a cause**
In her article on *Baywatch*'s Pamela Lee, the mean-spirited reporter <u>attributed</u> the actress's most prominent <u>attribute</u> to plastic surgery.

atypical	**not typical** (The prefix "a-" usually means not. For example, <u>amoral</u> means "not moral," <u>asexual</u> means "not sexual," <u>apolitical</u> means "not into politics," and, as we have seen, <u>amorphous</u> means "not shaped.") Michael Jackson's looks, voice, and clothing are <u>atypical</u> for an Earthling, so Lisa Marie left him.
audacity	**boldness** Their <u>audacity</u> was evident when they published their <u>odd SAT</u> book.
august	**majestic; awe-inspiring** When Cleopatra saw <u>Augustus</u> in all his finery, she said, "<u>Aw, Gus</u>, you look <u>august</u>."
austerity	**severity; strictness** His <u>austerity</u> is actually a rarity; sev<u>erity</u> is not his specialty.
averse	**opposed; unwilling** I was <u>averse</u> to writing <u>a verse</u> So at the teacher I did curse And put mounds of coleslaw in her purse. My verse started good but then got worse As I ran out of things that rhymed with -erse. <u>Averse</u> is a lot like <u>adverse</u>. It probably wouldn't matter if you got the two confused on the SAT, but for the record, you use <u>averse</u> when you want to say that a person or thing is opposed to something else. For example: Eggbert was <u>averse</u> to eating Frisbees. (**Note:** To or from always follows <u>averse</u>.) <u>Adverse</u>, on the other hand, is used when you want to say that something else is opposed to a person or thing. For example: Eggbert received <u>adverse</u> criticism for not eating Frisbees; or, Eggbert had to eat the Frisbee under <u>adverse</u> conditions. In the first example Eggbert is <u>averse</u> to eating, whereas in the second and third examples the criticism and the conditions are <u>adverse</u> to Eggbert.

avuncular	**a funky word meaning "like an uncle"** This word does not deserve a sentence because only your <u>avuncular</u> Uncle Herbert would ever use it.
awry	**twisted; crooked; out of whack; askew; wrong** "Waiter, there is something <u>awry</u> in my bread," she complained. "That thing?" he replied. "Why that's just <u>a rye</u> seed."

It is helpful to make up a story using as many of the vocabulary words as possible from the list you have just learned. We have written some sample stories, but you should write your own, too. Here is the first one.

An Adventurous Aardvark

The <u>audacious</u> <u>aardvark</u> was rooting around in the grass for some lunch with which to <u>assuage</u> his hunger when his <u>adroit</u> friend Bob the baboon waddled up with <u>alacrity</u> and <u>accosted</u> him. "Hey man," Bob said, beginning an <u>altercation</u>. "Why do you <u>abase</u> yourself in that <u>atypical</u> way? I <u>advocate</u> the <u>agile</u> use of a knife and fork."

"You are an ass," the <u>aardvark</u> replied politely. "It would be more <u>aesthetically</u> pleasing were I to eat that way, but the use of utensils would be too <u>affected</u> for a simple <u>aardvark</u> such as myself. I am <u>averse</u> to such an idea because it might <u>alleviate</u> my <u>acne</u>, which looks good on me."

"That has to be the <u>apex</u> of stupidity," Bob said, <u>aghast</u>. "Why are you so <u>apathetic</u> about your hygiene? At least you could <u>ameliorate</u> your looks and odor by taking a bath."

"Never <u>allude</u> to my <u>alleged</u> <u>antipathy</u> to cleanliness," the <u>aardvark</u> said with <u>austerity</u>. "Even with your nearly <u>anthropoid</u> form, you still pick lice out of strangers' hair."

Note: The characters in this story are entirely fictitious. Any resemblance to real people, alive or dead, is entirely coincidental.

B

bacchanalian

orgiastic; wild drunken revelry
Bacchus was the god of wine, and the Bacchanalia was the festival devoted to him.
He gave a <u>bacchanalian</u> party to welcome <u>back an alien</u>.

baleful
baneful

These words are similar in meaning but not entirely synonymous. <u>Baleful</u> refers to something that exerts an evil influence or foreshadows evil. <u>Baneful</u> refers to something that really is poisonous or deadly. (To remember this: <u>baneful</u> rhymes with painful—which deadly things tend to be.)
   We could see from the proctor's <u>baleful</u> look that he was going to do something <u>baneful</u> to us.

barrister

lawyer
What do <u>barristers</u> and sperm have in common?
Both have a one in a million chance of turning out human.
(Sorry, but we had to have a lawyer joke in here somewhere. Please don't sue us.)

bawdy

obscene; coarse; humorous (see LEWD)
Many <u>bawdy</u> jokes have to do with certain parts of the <u>body</u>.

beatific

displaying or imparting joy
"<u>Be terrific</u>," said the Hare Krishna with a <u>beatific</u> smile.

begrudge

to envy, to resent
To <u>be</u> holding a <u>grudge</u> for so long against me means that you must <u>begrudge</u> me my happy life.

beguile

trick
The [Evil Testing] Serpent <u>beguiled</u> me and I did eat the apple. (Genesis 3:13)

belated

delayed; <u>late</u>

We sent a <u>belated</u> birthday present and in return got a month-old piece of ice-cream cake.

bellicose

violent; warlike

You'll know you're sitting next to a <u>bellicose</u> person if during the test his sharpened number 2 pencil into your <u>belly goes</u>.

benevolent

kind

Superman may be the <u>benevolent</u> protector of the world, but have you ever noticed that he wears his underpants outside of his pants?

berate

scold severely

If you don't get into college, your parents will <u>berate</u> you. If you don't do A work, your teachers will <u>berate (B-rate)</u> you.

bereft

lacking something needed

When Norm learned that Sam had no <u>beer left</u>, he was <u>bereft</u>.

BEREFT

betroth

become engaged

She discovered that he wasn't wearing a tuxedo—she really was <u>betrothed</u> to a penguin.

biennial

every two years

This word is also decodable:

> "bi" = two
> + "ennial" = annual
>   biennial = 2 years

My social life has been reduced to <u>biennial</u> parties.

bland	not stimulating; dull
	(Remember, bland starts with bla.)
	I found the movie about the politics of cauliflower rather <u>bland</u>.
blandishment	flattery
	The sycophants obsequiously lavished me with <u>blandishments</u>. (Yes, you should look up each of these words.)
blighted	ruined; destroyed; withered
	After the Gulf War, when the Kuwaiti oil fields were <u>blighted</u> by fires, the Emir of Kuwait said, "No, I meant a <u>Bud Light</u>."
boisterous	rowdy
	We have male cheerleaders at our school. When they get in front of the crowd, those <u>boys stir us</u> up until we're <u>boisterous</u>.
bombastic	grandiloquent (wordy, pompous) in speech or writing
	At the end of his long, boring, <u>bombastic</u> speech, the self-satisfied tyrant received a <u>bomb basket</u> as a farewell gift.
braggadocio	cockiness; a braggart
	<u>Braggadocios</u> tend to do a lot of empty <u>bragging</u>.
brevity	briefness
	<u>Brave ET's</u> finger could heal a person with greater <u>brevity</u> than any earthling doctor could.
brusque	brief; curt; gruff; discourteous
	The Terminator is <u>brusque</u> with his enemies.
bucolic	pastoral; typical of farms and rural life
	The scene was <u>bucolic</u>
	So we started to fr<u>olic</u>
	In our feet so bare,
	Whoops! The cow chips were there!

bumptious | self-assertive
The <u>bumptious</u> people <u>bumped us</u> out of line, so we gave them all fierce head-butts.

burgeon | grow; sprout; flourish
Madonna's career <u>burgeoned</u> as soon as she changed the title of her unsuccessful song "Like a <u>Burgeon</u>."

burnish | polish
One of the housekeeper's jobs was <u>burnishing</u> the furnishings.

It's story time again, boys and girls:

A Bolivian Bacchanal | They threw us out of the helicopter <u>bereft</u> of any parachute, and the <u>brevity</u> of our flight and <u>brusqueness</u> of our landing were not described in the travel agent's <u>bland</u> brochure.

We found ourselves in a jungle with all sorts of <u>baneful</u> beasties crawling around our feet and <u>baleful</u> animal noises echoing in the <u>blighted</u> jungle.

"Yo," said my <u>bumptious</u> companion with <u>braggadocio</u> as he <u>burnished</u> his machete. "What say we bash our way out of this place?"

But before I could respond, we were captured by a <u>belli-cose</u> and <u>boisterous</u> tribe of natives about to perform its <u>be-lated</u> <u>biennial</u> human sacrifice to the fish goddess. In order to save our skins we both had to be <u>betrothed</u> to the chief's daughter Brunnehilde.

"Yo," said my companion. "This is a bit of a bummer. I should <u>berate</u> you for <u>bombastically</u> <u>beguiling</u> me into going on this vacation."

Then the axe fell and the <u>bacchanalian</u> rituals honoring the <u>benevolent</u> fish goddess began.

C

cache

hiding place (pronounced "cash")
The thieves <u>stashed</u> the <u>cash</u> in the <u>cache</u>.

cacophonous

sounding discordant; terrible and generally unpleasant to listen to; the opposite of euphonious
Just because the band's name is Human Sushi doesn't necessarily mean that they will sound <u>cacophonous</u>.
As Dracula arose from his <u>coffin</u>, the wolves let out a <u>cacophonous</u> wail.

cadaver

corpse
The medical students named their <u>cadaver</u> Ernie so that they could be "working in dead Ernest."

cajole

coax
"Yes, you <u>can, Joel</u>," they <u>cajoled</u> him. "You can become a professional dodgeball player if you set your mind to it."

callous

unfeeling; unsympathetic
Brian complained of the <u>callus</u> on his big toe, but Meg remained <u>callous</u>.

calumniate

to slander (This is one of a bunch of SAT words that mean this—see page 145.)

calumny

slander; defamation
It was <u>calumny</u> when I wrote the <u>column</u> in *The New York Times* that you enjoy poisoning Arctic wombats. I hated you, so I <u>calumniated</u> you.

candor

frankness; candidness
"Speaking with complete <u>candor</u>, Hansel," said the wicked witch, "I have chopped Gretel up and <u>canned her</u>."

cantankerous | ill-natured; quarrelsome
"Bloody screaming sea-dogs, I can't anchor us!" the cantankerous captain cried.

capacious | spacious
I wonder why they put such capacious boundaries around this word?

capitulate | **to surrender (see RECAPITULATE, which does not mean resurrender)**
Jean Claude Van Damme never capitulates.

capricious | **unpredictable; following whim**
The album charts were capricious; one week Alanis Morissette was on top, the next week Hootie and the Blowfish, and the next week, Mariah Carey.

captious | **fault-finding**
"What?! You're only in the Cs? And your room's still messy, and you haven't cooked me dinner," said the captious review book authors.

carrion | **rotting flesh**
The lion tore a hefty chunk of flesh out of the zebra's neck. Later the jackals came by and pulled more entrails out of the carrion. After the jackals left, the vultures remained to carry on with devouring it.

castigate | **punish**
Castration is a severe form of castigation.

cathartic	**cleansing; allowing a release of tension or emotion** Manek's method of preparing for the SAT is <u>cathartic</u> (see page 14).
caustic	**burning; characterized by a bitter wit** When she saw the ugly necklace that her boyfriend had bought her, she said to him <u>caustically</u>, "How much did that <u>cost? Ick!</u>" (Being sar<u>castic</u> and being <u>caustic</u> often go hand in hand, so relate them in your memory via the non-word sar<u>caustic</u>.)
cauterize	**to burn tissue (usually because a scar isn't healing)** When the bleeding <u>caught her eyes</u>, the doctor knew that she would have to <u>cauterize</u> the patient's skin.
cavil	**to raise unnecessary or trivial objections** When I told the vet that I feed my cow Diet Coke, he <u>cavilled</u> about how it would make my <u>calf ill</u>.
celerity	**swiftness, speed** When the light turned green, the chauffeur floored the gas pedal with <u>celerity</u> and we suddenly ac<u>celer</u>ated. I nearly spilled my <u>celery tea</u>.
celibacy **celibate**	**the condition of being <u>celibate</u>** **without sex; unmarried** If the prostitute does not <u>sell a bit</u>, she will have to be <u>celibate</u> tonight.
censor	**(v.) to remove inappropriate stuff** **(n.) someone who censors things** Fabio sensed her longing and with his rough hands caressed her voluptuous, heaving **CENSORED**
censure	**criticize; blame** When someone starts to criticize you, you can <u>sense you're</u> being <u>censured</u>.

cerebration	thought The guests at Einstein's birthday <u>celebration</u> were all deep in <u>cerebration</u>.
chagrin	embarrassment <u>She grinned</u> and blushed with <u>chagrin</u>.
chaos	state of utter confusion "We don't want to cause <u>chaos</u>," we told the customs official. "So just o<u>kay us</u> for passage!"

charlatan	quack; someone who pretends he's someone he's not <u>Charlotte in</u> *Charlotte's Web* was not a <u>charlatan</u>; she really could spell.
chaste	pure; unspoiled; virginal The virgin <u>chased</u> away the men so that she could remain <u>chaste</u>.
chicanery	trickery When I found the sneezing powder in my <u>Chicken</u> McNuggets, I knew you were up to some <u>chicanery</u>.
chimerical	far out; bizarre; really heady His dreams were so <u>chimerical</u> that it would ta<u>ke a miracle</u> for them to come true.

choleric | hot-tempered; easily made "hot under the <u>collar</u>"
The <u>choleric</u> pit bull did not enjoy it when his owner made him wear the electrified <u>collar</u>.

churlish | boorish; rude
Someone who is girlish
Is probably not <u>churlish</u>.

ciliated | having tiny hairs
"Oh Juliet, I love your deep blue eyes."
"Oh Romeo, I love the <u>ciliated</u> lining of your nostrils."

circumspect | prudent; cautious
This is one of those easily decodable words:
    "circum" = around (as in <u>circ</u>le)
    + "spect" = look (as in in<u>spect</u> and <u>spect</u>acles)
circumspect = look around (which suggests being cautious)
"<u>Search 'em</u>, in<u>spect</u>or," ordered the <u>circumspect</u> detective.

clemency | mildness of temper—especially leniency toward an enemy or in sentencing a criminal
The Mets kidnapped Roger <u>Clemens</u> from the Red Sox, but showed <u>clemency</u> by not forcing him to play on their team.

The following three "cog" words all have to do with thinking:

cogent | clear; logical; well-thought-out
The two men (<u>co-gents</u>) on the debate team gave a <u>cogent</u> argument.

cogitate | to think about deeply and carefully (see RUMINATE)
A good time to <u>cogitate</u> about dairy products is while eating <u>cottage</u> cheese.

cognizant	fully informed and aware; conscious When the factory repairman becomes <u>cognizant</u> that the <u>cog</u> <u>isn't</u> working, he will fix the gear.
comely	attractive; agreeable The more frequently you <u>comb</u> your hair, the more <u>comely</u> you become. Or maybe not.
comestible	food Banana flambé is a <u>combustible</u> <u>comestible</u>.
commensurate	equal; proportionate You don't think that the two piles of gold are <u>commensurate</u>? Well, <u>come measure it</u>.
commiserate	sympathize; be miserable together Decode: "co" = together + "miserate" = be miserable commiserate = be miserable together He <u>commiserated</u> with his friends, who also got 200s.
comport	to behave in a particular way The root "-port" means carry, as in the words im<u>port</u> (carry in), ex<u>port</u> (carry out), and trans<u>port</u> (carry across). In this context, <u>comport</u> has to do with how you carry yourself. <u>Comport</u> yourself in a <u>comfort</u>able way.
compunction	strong uneasiness caused by guilt (see REMORSE, CONTRITION) I felt <u>compunction</u> about puncturing your tires with Japanese throwing stars, but I went ahead and did it anyway.
concupiscence	sexual desire; lust; sensuality This word probably won't be on the test, but we like it.

concurrent	**at the same time** This is another decodable word: "con" = together (see CONVOKE) + "current" = at this time concurrent = at a time together John Adams's and Thomas Jefferson's deaths were almost <u>con-</u> <u>current</u>; they both died on Independence Day, 1826.
congenital	**existing at birth** This is decodable: "con" means together and "genital," well, you figure it out. Unless you've had a sex change, your <u>genitals</u> are <u>congenital</u>.
conjecture	**a statement made without adequate evidence** "<u>Can Jack sure</u>ly reach that conclusion?" I asked. "Or is it only a <u>conjecture</u>?"
conjugal	**pertaining to marriage** Unless you <u>can juggle</u> both your careers, you will not have <u>conjugal</u> happiness.
contort	**twist; bend** We recommend that you contact your local <u>contort</u>ionist in order to learn the skills necessary for sitting in an SAT chair.
contrition	**remorse; repentance; bitter regret felt owing to wrongdoing** When <u>Trish</u> broke his priceless gorilla sculpture she was over- come with <u>contrition</u>.
controversial	**of, relating to or causing dispute** Distributing <u>contra</u>ceptives in high school is a <u>controversial</u> issue.
convoke	**to call together; to cause to assemble** Decode: "con" = together + "voc" = call (<u>voice</u>) convoke = call together The mayor <u>convokes</u> a town meeting so that the citizens <u>can</u> <u>voc</u>alize their grievances.

corp-	a root meaning body example: <u>corp</u>se = dead body
corporal	of the body; bodily <u>Corporal</u> Thomas gave me <u>corporal</u> punishment because I saluted him with my foot instead of my hand.
corpulent	obese; having a fat body The <u>corpulent</u> corporal gave up eating for Lent.
corroborate	testify in agreement Do you have any witnesses who can <u>corroborate</u> that this is the restaurant where Bonnie and Clyde (<u>co-robbers) ate</u>?
countermand	cancel a command After Rachel spilled five cups of coffee, her boss <u>counter-manded</u> his order that she should always keep the <u>counter manned</u> at Central Perk.
covert	concealed; secret When the press finds out about the CIA's <u>covert</u> operations, the CIA tries to <u>cover it</u> up.
cower	quiver; shrink from fear The <u>coward</u> <u>cowered</u>.
crass	uncultured It is <u>crass</u> to scratch your <u>ass</u>.
credulity	gullibility His <u>credulity</u> led him to think that the pre-posterous alibi was <u>cred</u>ible. I found it too in<u>cred</u>ible to believe.
crestfallen	dejected "I'm sorry I dropped the toothpaste," he said, <u>crestfallen</u>.

I can't believe I dropped it!

Crestfallen

crux	main point; central issue; heart of the matter Crux is the Latin word for "cross," as you can tell from the word "crucifix," and a cross is always made when 2 lines meet in the center. "The crux of our work is to crucify crooks," explained the Roman policeman.
cull	select; weed out College admissions officers cull the best applications from the pile.
cupidity	greed; avarice (Although Cupid is usually associated with love, he's actually the god of desire, including desire for money.) Dan is possessed with stupidity as well as cupidity; he stole a lot of money, but then burned it to get rid of the evidence.
A Mystery	It was one of those steamy nights when the sky is lousy with stars. I was quietly cerebrating in the office of the Sure-Lock Homes Locksmith and Detective Agency. Suddenly, my cogitations were interrupted by a cacophonous sound and a cataclysmic vibration that reverberated through my capacious office. I stepped with circumspection into the hall because I was afraid someone might be up to some chicanery. I found a corpulent man lying contorted at the bottom of the stairs. Blood was gushing through a wound in his side, and I could see the ciliated lining of his small intestine. I decided to take charge. I asked with compunction, "Golly, are you okay?" He replied caustically, "Sure, I'm just swell. And how was your day?" "Peachy," I said. At that he bellowed cholerically, "Can't you see I've been shot? Did you think this hole in my chest was a congenital condition? Get me to a hospital with celerity!" "You don't have to be so captious and so churlish." "If I don't have this wound cauterized, I'll be a cadaver." At that moment a comely broad walked into the office. She was voluptuous and yet seemed chaste. I was overcome

with <u>concupiscent</u> thoughts. She pointed at the wounded man and said, "We were in my apartment; he got up to answer the door, and suddenly I heard a <u>cacophonous</u> sound and a cataclysmic vibration that must have reverberated in your <u>capacious</u> office."

Just then my assistant, Watt, entered. He said, handing me the phone, "My kid wants to know what sort of tree he should plant in our garden. What do you think, Sure-Lock?"

"A lemon tree, my dear Watt's son," I said.

Then Watt <u>cowered</u> and said, "What is that?"

"It's a plant with little yellow fruit and . . ."

He interrupted me, "No, that body on the floor."

"Oh golly, I forgot. We should get him to a hospital."

We all lifted the body <u>concurrently</u> and put him in my car. We stopped to buy some <u>comestibles</u> on the way.

When we arrived at the hospital, the doctor informed us that the <u>corpulent</u> man was dead.

"Golly, that's too bad," I said with <u>contrition</u> on the way.

Well, it was time for me to get to the bottom of this heinous crime. I asked the dame, "Who was that man?"

"My husband," she replied.

"Were your <u>conjugal</u> relations good?"

"Well, no, in fact we had been <u>celibate</u> for a long time."

"Why?"

"Speaking with <u>candor</u>, I chose to be <u>chaste</u>."

"Is it <u>crass</u> to ask why you chose to be <u>chaste</u>?"

"Because it starts with the letter C."

"Aha! Well, did you kill your husband?"

"How dare you <u>censure</u> me like that. What <u>calumny</u>!"

I repeated, "Did you kill him?"

With <u>chagrin</u>, she broke down. "Well, only a little, but Watt will <u>corroborate</u> that. He <u>cajoled</u> me into it."

"Watt! All the time I thought you were on the side of the law and you were really <u>covertly</u> planning this crime. You <u>charlatan</u>! I will bring you both to justice, and I'm sure you will be <u>castigated</u> with a prison sentence <u>commensurate</u> with the seriousness of the crime."

D

dais
a raised platform
The nervous speaker whispered, "Da is no way I am going up on the dais!"

daunt
to intimidate; frighten

dauntless
bold, unable to be daunted
The dauntless mouse daunted the lion with his .357 Magnum.

dearth
This word has nothing to do with the word death. It means scarcity (see PAUCITY).
When there is nothing but d'earth there is a dearth.
Because of Darth Vader, there was a dearth of laughter in the Death Star.

debase
lower in quality or value; adulterate (note the similarity to ABASE)
The birds at de base of the statue debased it with excrement.

decoy
a lure or bait
The coy duck disguised himself as a wooden decoy, but the hunters shot at him anyway.

defenestration
the act of throwing something out the window
It's highly unlikely that this word will be on the SAT, but it's the kind of word everyone should know anyway.

delude
to deceive
De lewd dude deluded himself into thinking he was attractive.

demivierge
a person whose sexual activities stop short of intercourse (from the French, "half virgin")
This word won't be on the test, but think how it will enrich the rest of your life!

demur	to object mildly
demure	reserved; modest The demure poodle demurred at the St. Bernard's drooling in public.
deplete	lessen the supply or content of She de-pleated the skirt by ironing it, thus depleting her stock of pleated skirts.
depraved	morally corrupt; debased; perverted As a prank, the depraved criminal de-paved the highway.
deranged	having a severe mental disorder; being insane The deranged cowboy roamed the streets singing wildly, "Rome, Rome on de range."
derogate	to detract; to take away The effect of the spear protruding from Bob's forehead was to derogate from his usually good-looking face.
descry	to discern; to catch sight of something that is difficult to catch sight of Through the mist they could descry the form of the hungry, one-eyed, one-horned, flying, purple people eater munching on a bag of purple Skittles.
desultory	aimless; disconnected; rambling; haphazard "That speech was so desultory. I could not follow the logic in what you said," she complained.
deter	prevent or discourage from happening The personal trainer tried to deter the dieter from eating all the cookie dough.

Hey! What happened to all the folds in these skirts?

Deplete

devastate | to ruin by violent action
The Blob <u>devastated</u> <u>de vast state</u> of Nevada.

devoid | completely lacking; void; empty; without
<u>Avoid</u> diving into swimming pools that are <u>devoid</u> of water; you could hurt yourself and that would suck.

dexterous | adroit or skillful in the use of hands or body
Houdini was <u>dexterous</u>; he could escape from a straitjacket.

Are you remembering to do the mnemonic thing? Picture yourself watching nine acrobats, each wearing banners across their chests that say *dexterous*. Each contorts into the shape of a letter so they spell out the word *dexterous*. They are all named *Dexter*, except for one who is named *Poindexter*. You lean over to your friend and say, "Wow, are they *dexterous*! I've never seen anyone so *dexterous*. I love *dexterous* people!" Then she looks at you like you're an idiot.

diabolical | fiendish; devilish; nastily scheming
The <u>diabolical</u> demon devised a deadly dungeon.

diaphanous | translucent; gossamer
His <u>diaphanous</u> dinner dress caused much discussion.

discern | to detect by the use of the senses
The watchman <u>dis-earned</u> his pay by not <u>discerning</u> the thieves.

discord | lack of harmony
"I won't use <u>dis chord</u>, 'cause it would create <u>discord</u>," said Mozart.

disparage | to belittle; reduce in esteem
"<u>Dis porridge</u> is too hot," Goldilocks <u>disparaged</u>.

disseminate | to dispense objects such as seeds, newspapers; distribute
While making his stock boy walk the plank, the captain explained, "<u>Dis seaman ate</u> all of the supplies that he was supposed to <u>disseminate</u>."

distraught	anxious; worried; distressed
	Snow White became distraught when the dwarves drank booze and fought.
divers	several
diverse	distinct; varied; differing
	William Shakespeare's divers verses were about diverse subjects.
doleful	sad; mournful
	The thought of watching Bob Dole move into the White House made Clinton doleful.
drastic	severe
	If your swimsuit strap breaks, you are in drastic need of elastic.
dynamic	energetic; vigorous; forceful
	The dynamic duo fell into the Joker's dynamite trap.

And on to a story:

The Distraught Dogcatcher

Dan was distraught. He knew he'd soon have to go up to the dais and declare his candidacy for dogcatcher. He knew he was devoid of charisma and not a dynamic speaker. He wasn't even dexterous at catching canines. Doubtless, he would debase himself by speaking like a deranged fool.

Trying to appear dauntless, he shambled forward with a dearth of enthusiasm.

"Ahem," he began, but was deterred from continuing when he descried the diabolical Great Dane that was rapidly depleting his audience by devouring them. Feeling these events might derogate his speech, Dan's thoughts were thrown into sudden discord, and he felt a drastic need to defenestrate himself.

Later that day, a supporter disparaged Dan's speech. "It was rather desultory. Rumors have been disseminated that he is depraved. We'll have trouble deluding the public into believing the contrary."

E

ebullient — bubbly; overflowing with excitement
The chef took a hefty swig of cooking sherry and then ebulliently tossed bouillon cubes into the soup.

edify — enlighten; educate
Ed defied the edict against education by trying to edify his pupils.

educe — elicit
He tried to educe as much information as possible from the suspects before he deduced who the murderer was.

efface — erase; rub out
I feel an uncontrollable desire to efface the Olsen twins' faces.

effete — tired; barren; decadent
By the time the authors had finished writing the E word list they were effete. (Their readers had been effete ever since aardvark.)

effigy — dummy (mannequin), usually for symbolic torturing
The E words got together to burn F and G in effigy.

emaciated — excessively thin; weak
In May she ate it, but now it's June and she's still emaciated.

emulate — to imitate closely
When the tornado began, Dorothy called out, "Aunty Em, you late. Emulate Toto and hurry up."

epitaph	**memorial text carved on a tombstone** I read the <u>epitaph</u>, "Here lies a politician and an honest man," and wondered how they could fit two people in one grave.
epitome	**something that perfectly represents an entire class of things; embodiment (pronounced eh-pit'-oh-me)** "You're the <u>epitome</u> of stupidity," she screeched after I spilled baloney dip all over her dress.
equestrian	**pertaining to horsemanship; on horseback** The <u>equestrian</u> knights went on <u>a quest</u> to <u>Rion</u>, but were turned away because of a no-horses policy.
equipoise	**equality; balance; equilibrium** (This is one of those words that isn't often seen in print but might be on the test anyway because it is highly decodable.) "equi" = equal + "poise" = balance equipoise = equally balanced An <u>equipoise</u> of speed and comprehension must be acquired in order to succeed on the critical reading section.
equivocal	**capable of two interpretations; ambiguous** **This word is decodable, too.** "equi" = equal + "vocal" = voice equivocal = giving equal voice to two sides "A good meal from this cook is a rare treat," is an <u>equivocal</u> statement.
erode	**to diminish or destroy by small amounts** When <u>a road</u> <u>erodes</u>, there are potholes all over the place.

erudite	scholarly Erudite people say things like, "Ere you diet, would you partake of the torte?" instead of "Want some cake?"
eschew	avoid; shun "Eschew!" he sneezed loudly. "Gesundheit," she replied while eschewing the globules of sneeze juice.
esoteric	known only by a few people Now you are one of the few people who knows this esoteric word.
ethereal	not of the material world The lisping child saw the ethereal ghost and asked, "Ith he real?"
eulogy	praiseful speech at a funeral In Santa's eulogy, the priest explained that Santa had died of high cholesterol because of all those Yule logs he ate.
euphemism	nice way of saying something unpleasant "Moved on to the next world" is a euphemism for "keeled over and bought it," which is a euphemism for "died."
exact	On the SAT, the Serpent will use the secondary definition of this word, which is: to demand The Stamp Act exacted from the colonists taxes they could not afford to pay. So they "X'd" the act.

exhume	to remove from a grave; disinter (see POSTHUMOUS)
	This is decodable:
	      "ex" = out of
	+ "humus" = earth, dirt
	    exhume = remove from earth
	They exhumed the coffin, but there was no cadaver in it.

Ew, GROSS! I'm not going near that guy!

Eschew Eschew

Eschew

exigent

urgent; requiring immediate attention
It is <u>exigent</u> that I find a <u>sexy gent</u> to escort me to the prom.

<u>ex</u>cessively demanding; <u>ex</u>cessively <u>exact</u>ing
I made <u>exigent</u> demands on my fairy godmother to find me a debonair prom date and a diaphanous dress.

Essay on Eggplant

I want to know which <u>erudite</u> vegetable maker invented eggplant. If he is dead I will <u>exhume</u> his coffin and <u>efface</u> the <u>epitaph</u> from his tombstone. If he is alive, I will burn him in <u>effigy</u>. Eggplant is the <u>epitome</u> of bad vegetables. I <u>eschew</u> eating it. I would rather become <u>emaciated</u> than eat eggplant. This is an <u>exacting</u> demand, but would someone please tell me, without being <u>esoteric</u> or <u>equivocal</u>, one good thing about eggplant? It is mushy, it has seeds, it makes my tongue itch, it has a dopey name, and it tastes like the droppings that an <u>equestrian</u> slob forgot to clean up. I wish all of the soil from the world's eggplant farms would <u>erode</u>. Oh, and get this, when eggplants fertilize each other, the round ones with lots of seeds are the female ones and the long, narrow ones are the males. And they do it in public, in front of all the other vegetables. What would happen if humans <u>emulated</u> this behavior?
The <u>end</u>.

fabricate

to invent or make up something (often in order to deceive)
When Michael couldn't remove the stain from the <u>fabric</u>, he <u>ate</u> it and <u>fabricated</u> a story that aliens stole it.

facet

side or aspect; face of something (i.e. faces of gemstones)
"Face it! One of the <u>facets</u> of being a jeweler is sometimes selling flawed <u>facets</u>!

facetious | said in jest
She's so <u>facetious</u> that you should not take what she says at <u>face</u> value.

fallacious | <u>fal</u>se; wrong; incorrect
They used to castigate people who made <u>fallacious</u> statements. (Well, that was a long time ago.)

fastidious | careful about details; impossible to satisfy
Don't be too <u>fastidious</u> when blackening the ovals on the answer sheet of the SAT (see "Little Circles" in Chapter 6).

fatuous | inane; foolish; <u>fat</u>headed
Eating 30 pounds of chocolate a day is a <u>fatuous</u> idea.

fawning | grovelling; overly admiring
The hunter who killed Bambi's mother should have come back and made a <u>fawning</u> plea for forgiveness.

feasible | workable; plausible; possible
Homer's idea of opening a hair salon for bald people was not <u>feasible</u>—who would pay the $30 <u>fee</u>?

fecund | fertile
"<u>Feh! Couldn</u>'t you do without all this smelly manure?" Slick asked Farmer Brown. "No, we need it to make the soil <u>fecund</u>."

fervor | passion
I will fight a ferocious ferret to prove to you the <u>fervor</u> of my love.

That is an INCREDIBLE outfit!

the hat with the earflaps VERY "IN"

and the red checks are so "you"!

Fawning

fetid	smelly I am proud to have <u>fetid</u> feet that smell of <u>feta</u> cheese.
fictitious	false; not genuine Books of <u>fiction</u> have <u>fictitious</u> plots.
filch	steal Since they had zilch, they decided to <u>filch</u>.
flagrant	deliberately conspicuous; glaring After the protestors <u>flagrantly</u> burned the Stars and Stripes, the mayor began a <u>flag rant</u>, condemning the rebels.
flaunt	show off something I flagrantly <u>flaunted</u> my physical <u>flaw</u>lessness to my fawning followers.
fluctuation	irregular variation At the terrifying sight of the nasty analogy question, his heartbeat <u>fluctuated</u> wildly.
foible	weakness, flaw Fergie's <u>foible</u> is her penchant for baubles.
foment	stir up; agitate; incite (think: when you stir something up it <u>foams</u>) When your <u>foe</u> warned you not to <u>foment</u> the army against him, your <u>foe meant</u> he was afraid of getting his ass kicked.
forbearance	patience He played dead with <u>forbearance</u> until the <u>four bears</u> got <u>antsy</u> and went away.
formication	a spontaneous abnormal sensation of ants or other insects running over the skin Some people experience this while taking the SAT.

forte	strong point (think: <u>fort</u>s are strong. Pronounced "for-tay") His <u>forte</u> was sneaking into the <u>fort</u> that was just before <u>Fort</u> B.
frenetic	frenzied; frantic; freaked out When the pilot and the flight attendants became <u>fren</u>zied, the passengers became <u>frenetic</u>.
froward	stubborn (see OBDURATE) The <u>froward</u> guardsmen refused to retreat, so the protestors could not move <u>forward</u>.
frugal	sparing in expense; stingy; miserly They told me that I was <u>frugal</u> Because I bought a plastic bugle.
fulminate	explode; roar; denounce loudly After he bombed the SAT, he <u>fulminated</u> for a <u>full minute</u> against the ETS.
futile	completely ineffective The one-armed floor layer felt his work was <u>futile</u> since he could lay only a <u>few tiles</u> a day.

Fred the Filcher

Freddy had a <u>flagrant</u> <u>foible</u>. He <u>filched</u> fish, sometimes with <u>fervor</u> and sometimes with <u>forbearance</u>, but he never <u>fluctuated</u> from his <u>forte</u>. One day his mother said <u>facetiously</u>, "Freddy, is it <u>feasible</u> that you'll <u>foment</u> a <u>fetid</u> <u>fulmination</u> of fish odor if you continue to <u>frenetically</u> <u>flaunt</u> your <u>filching</u> habits?"

<u>Froward</u> Freddy frowned. "That is a <u>fatuous</u> as well as <u>fallacious</u> suggestion." Then he uttered the following <u>fastidiously</u> crafted verse. "This <u>facet</u> of my abilities provides fish for our otherwise <u>frugal</u> dinner. You should <u>fawn</u> over me, not <u>fulminate</u> against me."

The preceding story was <u>fictitious</u>.

G

gainsay	**deny, dispute; <u>say</u> something <u>against</u> what someone else says** The model <u>gainsaid</u> that she'd <u>gained</u> weight, <u>saying</u>, "The camera always adds thirty pounds."
garbled	**screwed up** The <u>garbled</u> message read, "Please spurgle iceberg before rocking breakfast."
garrulous	**very talkative; loquacious** Even the Serpent would scare you less Than talking to someone <u>garrulous</u>.
genre	**category** It's hard to place *Beavis and Butt-head* in a specific <u>genre</u>. It's a cartoon, a video revue, a satire, and an educational fire-safety show all rolled into one.
germane	**relevant; appropriate** "Germany is not <u>germane</u> to our discussion today," said the history professor. "Today we shall discuss last night's rerun of *ER*."
gestate	**to transform and grow, like a baby inside the womb** Mama Butterfly asked the <u>gestating</u> caterpillar if it wanted something to eat, but it said, "No, I <u>just ate</u>."

But you're a growing boy! Sure you're not hungry?

Naw, I gestate

Gestate

gesticulation	gesture; signal (Somehow <u>gesticulation</u> seems as though it ought to have obscene connotations, but we would certainly tell you if it did.) Igor <u>gesticulated</u> for Dick to hurry up and enter the laboratory, saying, "<u>Yes, Dick, you're late</u> for your brain transplant."
gibberish	rapid, incomprehensible, or nonsensical speaking, drivel The Lewis Carroll poem *Jabberwocky*, which begins "'Twas brillig, and the slithey toves . . ." is written in <u>gibberish</u>.
gibe	to heckle or mock; to taunt; to pick on "Nice <u>jibe</u>," the sailor <u>gibed</u>, after we capsized.
gloaming	twilight If it weren't for the fireflies <u>gleaming</u> in the <u>gloaming</u>, I'd find it <u>gloomy</u>.
gossamer	light, delicate or insubstantial "Let's <u>go somewhere</u> where I can slip into something a little more <u>gossamer</u>," said the Victoria's Secret model.
gourmet	one who appreciates fine food and drink; epicure; connoisseur Wishing he were back at McDonald's, Clinton explained, "I'm not a <u>gourmet</u>, but <u>Gore may</u> be."
grandiose	impressive; <u>grand</u> Barbra Streisand has a <u>grandiose</u> nose.
graphic	vivid; explicit In a sequel to his dinosaur movie, Steven Spielberg left out the prehistoric beasts and kept all the violence, titling it *Graphic* Park.
gratuitous	unnecessary or unwarranted Adding <u>gratuitous</u> sex and violence to this book has been the best thing about writing it.

gregarious	friendly; outgoing; sociable (The ETS loves this word.) My horoscope tells me to be a <u>gregarious</u> Aquarius.
grimace	**(n.) a twisted facial expression** **(v.) to make a twisted facial expression** "Things look <u>grim as</u> long as there's a knife at my throat," the victim thought, <u>grimacing</u> with fear.
grisly	gory The bear made a <u>grisly</u> mess of the Cub Scouts.
gruesome	grisly; gory In the <u>gruesome</u> film, *The Blob*, the Blob <u>grew some</u> more every second.
gruff	**rough or stern in speech or action** Jean Claude Van Damme has made a career of acting <u>tough</u> and being <u>gruff</u>.
gullible	believing anything You don't have to know <u>gullible</u> because they took it out of the dictionary. If you believed the above sentence, you sure are <u>gullible</u>.

Lesser-Known Adventures of the Three Billy Goats Gruff

The Three Billy Goats <u>Gruff</u> met in the <u>gloaming</u> near the bridge.

"I'm really scared of that <u>gruesome</u> troll," Billy Goat #1 said, <u>gesticulating</u> toward the bridge. "Despite her <u>gossamer</u> gown, she doesn't seem too <u>gregarious</u>."

"Yeah, and I heard her <u>gourmet</u> appetite includes a <u>grisly</u> taste for goat's hooves!" #2 added nervously. "I really don't like <u>gratuitous</u> violence.

"Cowards!" #3 <u>gibed</u>. "I don't listen to <u>garbled</u> <u>gibberish</u> that only <u>gullible</u> fools like you would believe. I bet that troll is really a cool gal. Watch me cross that bridge!"

"You have a <u>grandiose</u> opinion of yourself, but you're really pretty dumb. So long, bud," Goat #1 replied with a <u>grimace</u>, anticipating the <u>graphic</u> goat-mutilation horror soon followed.

H

hackneyed

overused; trite
The plot of the movie *Friday the 13th XII* was <u>hackneyed</u>. It was just another horror movie about an axe murderer who <u>hacked knees</u> off.

haggard

unruly; wild; wasted; worn
After a long voyage with the Vikings, <u>Hagar</u> the Horrible looked <u>haggard</u>.

hallowed

holy; sacred
I was hanging out in the cemetery, but I didn't know I was on hollowed <u>hallowed</u> ground until I fell into a grave.

harangue

mean, nasty, angry speech (think: a speech that is so loud it impairs your <u>hearing</u>)
The zookeeper gave us a lengthy <u>harangue</u> about feeding the <u>orang</u>utan.

harbinger

forerunner; something that signals the approach of something; omen
Some words have only one sentence in which they are ever used. The sentence for <u>harbinger</u> is: "The robin is the <u>harbinger</u> of spring."

haughty

proud; vain; arrogant
He thinks he's <u>hot. He</u> shouldn't be so <u>haughty</u>.

hedonism

the philosophy of trying to be happy all the time; a funky state of being in which you do your own thing and don't worry about morality

hedonist | one who follows the philosophy of hedonism
(Compare these words to <u>stoicism</u> and <u>stoic</u>, which are their respective opposites.)
You are being a stoic by studying for the SAT so that you can get into college and spend four years being a <u>hedonist</u>.

heinous | grossly wicked; vile; odious
The scarecrows said, "Since we have <u>hay in us</u> it is a <u>heinous</u> crime to invite us to a bonfire."

hierarchy | social pecking order
As Heather moved <u>higher</u> up the <u>high</u> school <u>hierarchy</u>, she realized popularity was not all it's cracked up to be. (This sentence was based on an after-school special.)

hirsute | hairy (pronounced her-suit)
He was <u>hirsute</u> in his ape costume, which was really just a <u>hair suit</u>. He borrowed it from his girlfriend Rapunzel; it was <u>her suit</u>.

hoary | gray or white from age; old
When someone who is hirsute gets old he is hairy and <u>hoary</u>.

homily | sermon-like speech
The <u>homely</u> preacher delivered a <u>homily</u>.

homonym | a word that sounds like another word but has a different meaning
The German word *sechs*, meaning "six," is a <u>homonym</u> of the English word *sex*, meaning "sex."

The Homily

The <u>hirsute</u> young priest was preparing his <u>homily</u>, but needed advice from the <u>hoary</u> pastor.

"I gotta give a good talk so I can move up in the church <u>hierarchy</u>," he explained. "Can you help me?"

"You speak on <u>hallowed</u> ground," the pastor began, " so don't <u>harangue</u> and be not <u>haughty</u>. Don't forget to condemn <u>heinous</u> <u>hedonism</u>, though. A good public response to your sermon will be a <u>harbinger</u> of your advancement." The priest worked all night, searching for <u>hackneyed</u> expressions and hip <u>homonyms</u>. But when dawn came he just said, "Oh, the heck with it."

iconoclast
destroyer of tradition
When Bob Dylan brought an electric guitar to the Newport Festival, people called him an <u>iconoclast</u> and booed him.

ignoble
not noble
In Orwell's *Animal Farm*, the <u>ignoble</u> <u>pig nobles</u> ruin the barnyard utopia.

ignominious
characterized by <u>ignominy</u>
ignominy
dishonor; disgrace
They suffered an <u>ignominious</u> defeat.
He couldn't bear the <u>ignominy</u> of getting a 400 on the SAT.

Two similar words:

imbibe
drink in; absorb
imbue
to make wet; saturate; to inspire
If you <u>imbibe</u> the meanings of all these words you will be <u>imbued</u> with wisdom.

imminent
about to occur; impending (don't confuse with eminent, which means famous)
<u>I'm in ent</u>ertainment and my curtain call is <u>imminent</u>.

immutable | The best way to learn this word is to learn the root "mut," which means change. Then you can decode <u>immutable</u> to mean "not changeable." You will also realize that <u>mutable</u> = "changeable," <u>mutation</u> = "a change," and trans<u>mute</u> = "to change from one form to another."

"A fat person uses more soap than a skinny person" is one of the <u>immutable</u> laws of physics.

impale | **to pierce with a sharp stake or point**
The <u>imp</u> <u>paled</u> when we took a spike and <u>impaled</u> the mushroom he was sitting on.

impasse | **a dead end (think: impassable)**
If you are trying to pick someone up and none of your <u>passes</u> are working, you have reached an <u>impasse</u>.

impassive | **without emotion; expressionless**
"It looks like I've reached an <u>impasse</u>," Bart muttered <u>impassively</u> as he slammed into the brick wall on his skateboard.

impeccable | **flawless and faultless; not capable of sin**
Woody is not an <u>impeccable</u> woodpecker; he is always making mistakes.

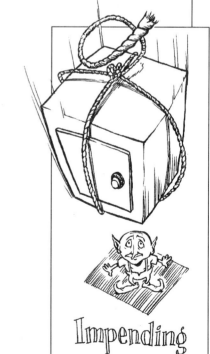

Impending

impending | **about to take place (see IMMINENT)**
The dwarf cowered behind Snow White, sensing <u>imp-ending</u> doom.

imperious	domineering The emperor was imperious.
impropriety	not proper; not displaying propriety Howard Stern was fined by the FCC for his impropriety.

Here are two words that are sure to confuse you:

impugn	to attack as false; criticize
impunity	immunity from punishment "You will not have impunity if you impugn my character with such impudence," shouted Michael at Lisa when she suggested that he was speaking oddly.
incessant	nonstop; ceaseless Her incessant chatter forced me to throw her into a cesspool.
incite	arouse; instigate As soon as Coolio came back in sight, his groupies' cheering incited the crowd to ignite their lighters and demand an encore.
incognito	in disguise, so as not to be recognized Remember the root word "cog"? Well, this is another example of it:

"in" = not
+ "cognito" = known
incognito = not known

The president mingled with the people incognito to find out what they really thought.

incommodious	lacking space; not commodious His apartment was so incommodious, there was no room for a commode.
incontrovertible	indisputable "The evidence is incontrovertible," the lawyer concluded. "The sunburn on your bald head proves that you drive a convertible."

incubus	a nightmare; mental burden (<u>Incubus</u> has another meaning that should help you remember it but, as a matter of taste, we chose not to include it. That ought to entice you into looking it up.) The SAT is an <u>incubus</u> that hovers in the minds of high school students.
indolence	laziness If you study with <u>indolence</u>, they will send you a note of condolence with your score report.
indomitable	unconquerable; impossible to <u>dominate</u> He was the best <u>domin</u>oes player around; he was virtually <u>indomitable.</u>
inept	incompetent The <u>inept</u> astronomy student thought that unicorns live on <u>Nep</u>tune.
infer	conclude based on facts It can be <u>inferred</u> that people dressed <u>in fur</u> are not animal rights activists.

Two more words that will confuse you:

ingenious	original; resourceful
ingenuous	showing childlike simplicity; innocent Remember these words this way: <u>Ingenious</u> has an <u>i</u>, like <u>genius</u>, and it also expresses the main qualities of <u>genius</u>. Baby <u>geniuses</u> frequently discover <u>ingenious</u> ideas in <u>ingenuous</u> ways.
innate	belonging to someone from birth; inherent The malice <u>in Nate</u> is <u>innate</u>. He's been nasty since birth.
insatiable	impossible to satisfy You must develop an <u>insatiable</u> desire to learn more and more vocabulary words.

inscrutable | enigmatic; difficult to understand
The Hungarian table manufacturer's instructions on how to unscrew the table were inscrutable.

insensate | unconscious; lacking sensation
Inhaling too much incense could make you pass out and lie insensate on the floor.

insidious | working or spreading stealthily; sneaking inside to do something bad (not to be confused with INVIDIOUS)
The Evil Testing Serpent uses insidious techniques to torture students.

insipid | lacking excitement; vapid
The insipid innkeeper stayed in, sipped wine, and slept.

intangible | not perceptible to the touch; impalpable
You can't touch the tangent of $\pi/2$; it's intangible.

invective | abusive put-down
On *Cheers*, Carla uses inventive invective ("You have a personality you could store meat in," for example) to insult people.

invidious | making people angry; offensive
The critics of MTV were concerned about the invidious images in videos.

irascible | easily provoked; irritable
The irascible rascal threw her eraser.

Five Irascible Fools

Larry, Lisa, Manek, Michael, and Paul were traveling incognito in the incommodious bus. They had reached an impasse in their indomitable attempts to think of sentences for the I's, and were nearly insensate with indolence.

"Hey, Manek, do you have any ingenious ideas for 'inscrutable,' you inept fool?" Larry inquired.

Manek's face remained impassive. "You know you're just inciting me to anger with your insipid invective. If you continue your invidious behavior, I'll become irascible."

"Are you questioning Larry's integrity by implying that he acted in an <u>ignoble</u> manner?" Paul interjected. "I'm sure he couldn't stand the <u>ignominy</u>."

"If you all don't shut up, I'll be forced to <u>impale</u> you. Especially since you <u>imbibed</u> my iodine," Lisa shouted.

"But what, ho!" Michael exclaimed. "I believe our destination is <u>imminent</u>."

So the bus stopped and they got off, continuing to argue <u>incessantly</u>.

J

jaded	**wearied, especially by too much of the good life** They lived out their <u>jaded</u> existence wearing <u>jade</u> jewelry and driving Ferraris.
jingoism	**extreme patriotism** Francis Scott Key was a <u>jingoistic</u> <u>jingle</u> writer.

These three words all begin with "joc-" and they all mean about the same thing:

jocose	**merry; joking**
jocular	**jolly; joking**
jocund	**merry; jolly**

The <u>jocose</u> jockey did a jig as a <u>joke</u>.
The <u>jocular</u> journalist joined the <u>joker</u>'s club.
The <u>jocund</u> judge joyfully jailed the jolly janitor.

K

ken	**range of knowledge** "<u>Ken's ken</u> is limited," Barbie complained. "He only knows surfboards."

kiosk | pavilion or small open booth where items are bought or sold
The kiosk in Kiev sold cold knishes. (Say this 5 times fast.)

kismet | fate
"Kiss me, baby, it's kismet," slurred the drunk at the singles bar.

kleptomaniac | a compulsive stealer
Old kleptomaniacs never die, they just steal away.

knave | a clever bad guy
knavery | dishonest; mischievous dealing
"Can Avery join the navy?"
"Never, he is always up to some kind of knavery."

Crime Doesn't Pay

The jingoist became jaded. He didn't feel as jocose, jocular, or jocund as he once did. Eventually, he turned to knavery, robbing from kiosks. It was kismet that he got caught. It takes a small ken to be a kleptomaniac. A lesson for us all.

L

labyrinth | a complicated maze or winding series of corridors
You'd be amazed at how easily the laboratory rats get lost in the labyrinth.

lacerate | to rip; maul; tear; mutilate; mangle
Alas, when Arthur ate pickled razor blades, he lacerated his tongue.

lackadaisical | uncaring; lacking in interest or spirit
The florist exclaimed, "I lack a daisy! Call the flower supplier pronto!" But the lackadaisical stock boy didn't pay any attention.

laconic | not saying much; brief; terse; concise; succinct
This sentence is laconic.

There is a Greek story about the war between Laconia and Athens. The Athenians threatened the Laconians by sending a letter to them that said something like, "If we defeat you we will burn your houses, pillage your villages, maul your women and children, etc. . . ." The Laconians sent back a laconic reply that just said, "If."

lambaste | to thrash; maul; beat; whip; bludgeon with big things and other fun stuff; to scold sharply; rebuke
"Baste that lamb or I'll lambaste you!" the cook yelled to his assistant.

Ow, not so hard

Lambaste

languid | lacking energy; weak
languish | to lose strength; waste away
(**Note:** As you will notice, a lot of L words mean either "lazy and lacking energy" or "lusty.") No doubt, learning all of this language is giving you so much anguish that you're starting to languish.

languor | languidness; sluggishness
I can't lie here in languor any longer.

larceny | stealing
Stealing from the cartoonist who created *The Far Side* is Larsony.

lascivious | lusty; lewd
The lascivious lass lusted after Larry.

lassitude | listlessness; a state of exhaustion or weakness
The ship's crew was in such a state of lassitude that they sailed to the wrong latitude.

latent | potential but not yet displayed

He had a <u>latent</u> talent for playing the harmonica, but he didn't discover it until <u>late in</u> his life.

(**Note:** *Latent* is often used in the phrase *latent talent*, which is a handy memory aid because the two words have the exact same letters.)

laud | (v.) to praise (think: "<u>Praise</u> be the <u>Laud!</u>")

(n.) praise

laudatory | (adj.) praiseful

The TV critics did not <u>laud Tori</u> Spelling with any <u>laudatory</u> reviews, so she consoled herself by going on a shopping spree.

lecherous | lewd; lustful; given to sexual activity

The country preacher said to the employees in the brothel, "Yer goin' to Hades 'cause you <u>let yer house</u> be used for <u>lecher-ous</u> activities." They replied, "Don't <u>lecture us</u>."

lethal | deadly

The lisping landlord said, "If you don't sign the <u>leath, I'll</u> thtab you with my <u>lethal</u> thord!"

lethargy | sluggishness; indifference

Are you overcome by <u>lethargy</u> from all this studying? Well, it's time to wake up, so:

STOP STUDYING

1. Go to the nearest store.
2. Buy four cups of coffee and a six-pack of Jolt cola.
3. Rapidly consume everything you just bought.
4. Go back to work (and relax!).

lewd | indecent; obscene

It is <u>rude</u>

To be <u>lewd</u>.

licentious

immoral; morally wild or sexually unrestrained
"I've got my driver's <u>license</u>," Terry proudly exclaimed. "Now we can be <u>licentious</u> in the back seat of my car."

limacine

pertaining to or resembling a slug (see PACKWOOD)
This word won't be on the test but it's really useful.

lithe

graceful; supple; limber; moving <u>lightly</u>
When the <u>lithe</u> dancers at the ballet studio spread rumors that the lisping prima ballerina was getting fat, she responded, "<u>Lithe, lithe</u>, they're all <u>lithe</u>!"

loathe

hate (The last four letters of <u>loathe</u> can be reorganized to spell <u>hate</u>.)
"Pick up some bread at the store, okay?" she asked.
"No, I'll buy tortillas," he replied. "You know I <u>loathe loaves</u>!"

lucubration

hard, scholarly studying (see COGITATE)
Readers of this book won't have to do any <u>lucubration</u>.

lugubrious

mournful or sad
When Lou the undertaker's friends died, he was too <u>lugubrious</u> to bury them. Finally, they got so tired of waiting to be buried that they came back to life and said, "<u>Lou, go bury us.</u>"

An Open and Frank Note from the Authors

With words in this list like <u>lewd</u>, <u>licentious</u>, and <u>lecherous</u>, you're probably looking forward to a great story. Well, you won't find one here, but not because we were too <u>lackadaisical</u> or <u>languid</u>. We actually did write a pretty <u>lascivious</u> one, but the publisher <u>loathed</u> it. After she read it, she <u>lithely lambasted</u> us with <u>lethal</u> cans of lima beans, <u>lacerating</u> our upper torsos. When she <u>laconically</u> called us "<u>limacine</u> idiots," we left. And so, in protest, we didn't do an L story. Humblest apologies. We hope you'll forgive us.

M

macabre — gross; ghastly; suggestive of horrible death and decay
You will always find this word on the back covers of worthless horror novels.
"This macabre story is about a psychotic farmer who chokes people with corn on the cob."

magnanimous — noble; generous; forgiving; magnificently kind
The magnanimous king allowed the prisoner to live on one condition: that he take the SAT every day for the rest of his life. The prisoner chose death.

Note: The root "mal-" means bad. The next few words all begin with "mal-":

malaise — a feeling of illness or depression
After I ate the jar of mayonnaise, I had a feeling of malaise that made me lazy.

malediction — a spoken curse
The male chauvinist's remarks earned him a malediction from the feminists.

malevolent — wishing evil on others; malicious (the opposite of benevolent)
All year I am malevolent. But I repent for my life on Lent.

malice — the desire to do bad to others; spite
malicious — having malice
The Queen of Hearts felt malice toward Alice.

malign — say bad things about; slander
He maligned me by saying that I couldn't remember my lines.

malignancy	**a malevolent and malicious act (also, a malignant tumor)** In an act of extreme <u>malignancy</u>, the bully was trying to break my leg. Suddenly, the doorbell rang. I said to him, "Get off <u>my leg'n see</u> who's at the door."
malodorous	**smelling bad; having a bad <u>odor</u>** The air in the testing center will be <u>malodorous</u>.
maneuver	**a skillful or clever move** The captain used a tricky sailing <u>maneuver</u> to rescue the <u>man</u> <u>over</u>board. The man thanked him, "<u>Man, you very</u> clever."
maritime	**near the sea; concerned with shipping or navigation** We had a <u>merry time</u> when we vacationed in a <u>maritime</u> resort. Mnemonic time again: You're out at sea on the U.S.S. *Maritime*. The crusty old captain, whose facial hair is in the shape of the word *maritime*, orders you to swab the deck. In only two days you will reach the *maritime* resort where you will party until you pass out on the beach, your body leaving the word *maritime* imprinted in the sand. You are woken up by the lulling sound of the waves, "*Maritime, maritime. . .*"
meander	**to wander around aimlessly** <u>Me and her</u> <u>meandered</u> down the path.
melancholy	**sadness; depression; pensiveness** When he finds out that she <u>can't elope</u>, he'll be <u>melan-choly</u>.
mellifluous	**sweet sounding; flowing with honey or sweetness** <u>Mel is fluent</u> in the <u>mellifluous</u> lines of *Hamlet*.

Don't be sad, we can still get married

we just can't elope

Melancholy

mendacious	untruthful; lying Men who say they don't fear commitment are probably being <u>mendacious</u>.
mendicant	**(n.) a beggar** <u>Men dat can't</u> get jobs often become <u>mendicants</u>. **(adj.) practicing begging** The bum lived a <u>mendicant</u> existence.
meticulous	**extremely careful and precise** He was so <u>meticulous</u> that he used the <u>metric</u> system to measure the diameter of his navel lint.
miasma	**a poisonous atmosphere or cloud (often in swamps)** Deep in the swamp, Eugene cried: "This <u>miasma</u> is bad for <u>my asthma</u>."
minuscule	**very tiny** <u>Minuscule</u> students go to <u>mini-schools</u>.
misnomer	**an inappropriate or wrong name** "My name is Miss Troller!" screamed the teacher. "To call me <u>Miss Gnomer</u> is a <u>misnomer</u>!"
monotonous	**always at the same pitch; boring; repetitious** This word is easy if you break it up into its parts:

Misnomer

"mono" = the same, one

 "tone" = sound

 + "ous" = <u>having the qualities of</u>

monotonous = having the same sound

The concerto played on the one-keyed piano was <u>monotonous</u>.

moo | the low, deep sound that a cow makes
In a low, deep voice the cow said "<u>Moo</u>."

mordant | bitingly sarcastic or nasty
She <u>mordantly</u> told him that he needed <u>more dental</u> adhesive.

morose | sullen; depressed
<s>If you love learning vocabulary words, you will be <u>morose</u></s> when you get to the word *overt* because after it there are no <u>more Os</u>.

myriad | many; a lot; a very large amount
<u>Mary had</u> only one little lamb, not <u>myriad</u> lambs.

Manek's Problems

In a small <u>maritime</u> village, there lived a <u>morose</u> review-book author named Manek. Most of the citizens were <u>magnanimous</u> to him because he was a <u>mendicant</u>, but there was a <u>malevolent</u> gang in town (led by Michael) who <u>maliciously</u> <u>maligned</u> him. "Hey, Manek," they would yell. "You're more <u>malodorous</u> than a <u>moo</u>-cow."

Manek bore the <u>mendacious</u> gang no <u>malice</u>, though he wished he could <u>meander</u> through the town's <u>myriad</u> streets without these <u>monotonous</u> comments. He grew <u>melancholy</u> and suffered from a great <u>malaise</u> as he <u>morosely</u> contemplated his problem.

N

nadir | absolutely lowest point (The word *zenith* is the opposite of <u>nadir</u>. If you ever get these two confused, just remember that no one would name their brand of TV "<u>Nadir.</u>")
She knew their relationship had reached its <u>nadir</u> when she asked him to have sex and he said "<u>Nah, dear</u>."

naive	lacking in worldly wisdom or experience After God expelled them from Eden, Adam said, "The time is <u>nigh, Eve</u>. We can no longer be <u>naive</u>."
nascent	coming into being; emerging (see RENASCENT) Your <u>nascent</u> vocabulary will cause <u>an ascent</u> in your verbal score.
nefarious	evil <u>No fairy is</u> <u>nefarious</u>.
nemesis	a vengeful enemy In the book of Genesis the Serpent is Eve's <u>nemesis</u>.

neologism	a newly coined word, phrase, or expression
	    "neo" = new
	+ "<u>logism</u>" = idea, word
	  neologism = new word
	Whoever made up the word <u>neologism</u> created a <u>neologism</u>.

neophyte	a beginner ("neo" = new) The <u>neophyte</u> boxer was <u>new</u> to <u>fight</u>ing.
nexus	the bond or link between things A <u>nexus</u> is a bond that co<u>nnects us</u>.
noisome	offensive; disgusting; filthy; malodorous (Don't be fooled; this word has nothing to do with noise.) My parents get angry when I don't clean my <u>noisome</u> room. It really an<u>noys 'em</u>.
nonchalant	appearing casual; cool; indifferent; chilled-out Because the hare considered the race against the tortoise a <u>non-challenge</u>, he was <u>nonchalant</u> about it and ended up losing.
nonplussed	perplexed; baffled She had expected to get an A-<u>plus</u> on the test; when she received an A-minus, she was <u>nonplussed</u>.

notorious

famous for something bad; infamous
The nefarious noteperson was <u>notorious</u> for leaving nasty <u>notes</u> on people's doors.

novel

On the SAT this won't refer to a literary genre, but rather mean **new; unusual; different**
Years ago there was <u>no Velc</u>ro. Then someone had the <u>novel</u> idea of inventing it.

novice

beginner; a person new to something
He was a <u>novice</u> when it came to carpentry—he had <u>no vise</u>.

noxious

harmful to health or morals
In industrial cities, the water can be <u>noxious</u>, and the people ob<u>noxious</u>.

PUNCH ME! uh.. I mean HIT ME!

I was like that, once

Novice

nuance

a subtle variation in color, meaning, or some other quality
I could tell by the subtle <u>nuance</u> in her voice that my <u>new aunt</u> thought I was being a <u>nuis</u>ance.

A Villain's Death

The <u>nefarious</u> villain had reached the <u>nadir</u> of his <u>notorious</u> career. He had run into his <u>nemesis</u>, Nice Ned, the sheriff, after stealing some counterfeit cash (he often didn't notice the <u>nuances</u> of forged bills). Now he lay dying from two fatal earlobe wounds near a <u>noisome</u> junkyard in the desert.

Looking back, he recalled his <u>nascent</u> life as an outlaw. He had started as a <u>naive</u> <u>novice</u> in New York, but when the <u>noxious</u> city fumes got to him, he headed west where a <u>novel</u> future awaited him. In later years, no longer a <u>neophyte</u>, his <u>nonchalant</u> attitude had left him <u>nonplussed</u>. Now nearly dead, he wanted to establish a <u>nexus</u> with his lost youth, but it was too late.

O

obdurate — hardened against good influence
I can't en<u>dure it</u> when I try to reason with you and you're <u>obdurate</u>.

oblivion — the state of being totally forgotten
Lincoln will never fall into <u>oblivion</u>. No, <u>Abe'll live on</u> in our memories forever.

obsequious — fawning; too easily compliant
"May I polish your toenails and peel you some grapes?" asked her <u>obsequious</u> attendant.

obsolete — out of style; outdated
The vinyl LP is virtually <u>obsolete</u>.

obstreperous — unruly; defiant; boisterous
High school librarians always say things like, "Let's keep the noise level to a minimum," "Cut the chatter," and "Don't be <u>obstreperous</u> in the library."

obtrude — to force oneself or one's ideas on others; <u>intrude</u>; to stick out
You gotta be some kinda social sl<u>ob t' rude</u>ly <u>obtrude</u> your opinions on others.

obtuse — You may remember that in math an angle is called <u>obtuse</u> if it is greater than 90 degrees. However, the meaning that would be on the SAT is: **stupid, thick-headed (think: an <u>obtuse</u> angle is "thick" and so is an <u>obtuse</u> person)**
(**Note:** An acute angle is less than 90 degrees and an acute person is sharp-minded—the opposite of <u>obtuse</u>.)
The <u>obtuse</u> man could not draw an <u>obtuse</u> angle.

occult	**pertaining to supernatural phenomena** A cult holds occult rituals.
odious	**offensive; hateful** The drug dealer was odious—he was trying to "O.D." us.
officious	**obnoxious and pushy in giving opinions** "Swimming in the lake is prohibited!" yelled the lifeguard to the drowning people. To which they replied, "Oh, fish us out and don't be officious!"
ogle	**to stare at** The skier ogles through her goggles whenever any cute ski instructors whiz by.
olfactory	**pertaining to the sense of smell** The stench of that ol' factory was offensive to the olfactory sense.
omnipotent	**all-powerful** This word is totally decodable. "omni" = all + "potent" = powerful omnipotent = all-powerful Lex Luthor desires to be the omnipotent ruler of the Earth, but Superman always defeats him.
omniscient	**all-knowing** Again, this is decodable: "omni" = all + "scient" = knowledge, knowing omniscient =all-knowing He read every issue of _Omni_ science magazine in the hope that he would become omniscient.
onerous	**burdensome** Would you honor us by helping us carry this onerous box of lead?

opulent	rich

<u>Opulent</u> Oprah always wore <u>opals</u>—and diamonds and rubies and emeralds and . . .

orifice	a small hole, opening, or vent

"I've had a hard day at the <u>orifice</u>," said the dentist.

oscillate	to swing back and forth

"His behavior <u>oscillated</u>," the babysitter reported. "He would be <u>docile eight</u> hours and then go crazy!"

ostensible	apparent; seeming (but usually not really)

The <u>ostensible</u> reason that <u>Austin is able</u> to bench press 300 pounds is his daily workout routine. The real reason is anabolic steroids. (This could also account for his breasts.)

ostentatious	showy; pretentious

Glittering Emerald City is <u>Oz-tentatious</u>.

ostracize	to banish or exclude

The <u>ostracized ostr</u>ich stuck its head in the sand.

overt	open and observable, not hidden (see COVERT)

Meg <u>overtly</u> knocked <u>over T</u>eddy's crystal toothbrush holder in order to attract attention.

A Fairy Tale

I went to the king, seeking to marry his daughter, but he was <u>obdurate</u> in his refusal. I was <u>obsequious</u>, but he was an <u>odious</u> and <u>obstreperous</u> man who kicked me out of the <u>opulent</u> palace because I was not pleasing to his <u>olfactory</u> senses. I went away, determined to <u>obtrude</u> my marital aspirations on him by raising an army and assaulting his <u>omnipotent</u> forces. However, my own forces were blown to <u>oblivion</u>.

HARD DAY AT THE
Orifice

I then went to see <u>Omniscient</u> Olga, an old one-eyed witch who dealt in the <u>occult</u>. When I arrived at the <u>orifice</u> that led to her cave, she <u>ogled</u> me with her one eye. She advised me to go and be of service to the king, to offer to carry out every <u>onerous</u> task, <u>ostensibly</u> out of the kindness of my heart, but really to penetrate the castle and elope with the princess.

I made my way to the <u>ostentatious</u> royal city. As I <u>overtly</u> approached the gate, however, a guard informed me that I had been <u>ostracized</u> from the kingdom. Heartbroken, I left and went to seek my fortune selling doorknobs to nomads.

P

Packwood	**an old politician with quite a diary** Chances are this won't be on the test.
palatable	**acceptable to the taste; sufficiently good to be edible (think: <u>plate</u>-able)** The cannibal found his <u>pal edible</u> and quite <u>palatable</u>.
palliate	**to moderate the severity of, abate** "He looks <u>pale; he ate</u> something poisonous," the doctor said. "We'll have to <u>palliate</u> the poison with an antidote."
pallid	**having an extremely pale complexion** He was so <u>pallid</u> that even his eyes had <u>pale lids</u>.
palpable	**capable of being touched or felt (see TANGIBLE); real** I pinched my <u>pal Pablo</u> to see if he was <u>palpable</u>.
paragon	**a model or example of perfection** Batman and Robin were a <u>pair of goners</u> but Robin, that <u>paragon</u> of digital dexterity, managed to reach his utility belt and foil the Riddler's evil trap.

parch	to make very dry, especially by heating When things heat up playing board games, my throat sure <u>parches easy</u>, and I have to get a drink. (If you don't get the joke in this sentence, consult your local board game dealer.)
parsimonious	stingy The man was so <u>parsimonious</u> that he would not share his <u>persimmon with us</u>.
pathos	a quality in something that makes you pity it; a feeling of sympathy or pity (remember "pathy" = feeling) Feel <u>pathos</u> for me as I wander down this <u>path oh so</u> pitiful.
paucity	smallness in number; scarcity (see DEARTH) Remember, never name your pet store "<u>Paw City</u>." The <u>poor city</u> has a <u>paucity</u> of rich people.
pecuniary	relating to money "I seem to be lacking <u>pecuniary</u> support" is a euphemism for "I'm broke."
pedagogue	schoolteacher or educator; a boring, dry teacher The teacher was such a <u>pedagogue</u> that <u>Peter gagged</u> at the thought of listening to another one of her boring lectures.
pedant	a boring person who knows a lot but has little practical experience; dweeb Melvin, the six-year-old <u>pedant</u>, brought his <u>pet ant</u> to show-and-tell and droned on about it until all the kids fell asleep.
pedestrian	You already know that this means a person traveling on foot. However, when it's used on the SAT it means: **commonplace; ordinary** Compared to being a neurosurgeon, being a <u>pediatrician</u> is <u>pedestrian</u>.

penchant
a strong liking; an inclination
Baseball teams have a penchant for pennants.

pensive
engaged in deep, often sad, thought
After much deep, often sad, thought, William Penn decided to call his new state Pensive-ania.

(**Note:** Don't get the next two words confused. They have the same first five letters and they both have to do with money, which you can remember because of the word penny. However, penurious has two very different definitions, and only one of them relates to penury.)

WELCOME TO PENSIVE~ANIA

Pensive

penurious
parsimonious; stingy
Scrooge was penurious.
extremely poor
Tiny Tim was penurious.

penury
poverty; destitution
Tiny Tim lived a life of penury.
Penury is a poor word that doesn't have as many letters as penurious. Penurious is a stingy word with lots of letters but it won't give any of its letters to penury.

perfunctory
done routinely, carelessly, and listlessly
If you are beginning to study in a perfunctory manner, it's time for a break. Put on some funk music and let it permeate your room. But you can't do that, because you don't know what permeate means yet. So you'd better forget the break and continue studying.

permeate
to spread or flow through
permeable
capable of being permeated
Your hair must be permeable to Clairol if you want a perm.

perspicacious	perceptive; understanding If you look at things from all <u>perspec</u>tives, you are <u>perspicacious</u>.
petulant	unreasonably irritable or ill-tempered That <u>pet you lent</u> me barked and snapped and was generally <u>petulant</u>. I'm giving it back.
philanthropy	improving the world through charity; love of humanity in general We did not write this book out of a penchant for pecuniary matters, as that would have been parsimonious and penurious of us. Instead, <u>philanthropy</u> was our motive.
pillage	to rob violently SATilla the Hun <u>pillaged</u> the village.
pithy	laconic; concise and meaningful <u>Pyth</u>agoras was the first person to approach this triangle from the right angle, when he came up with his <u>pithy Pyth</u>agorean theorem: $a^2 + b^2 = c^2$.

(**Note:** The root "plac-" in the next two words means calm.)

placate	appease; pacify; calm 7 tried to <u>placate</u> gossip-starved 8 by telling her that 9 had 6 with 5, but instead of appeasing her, the news seemed to <u>plague 8</u>.
placid	calm; composed; undisturbed "<u>Pla</u>!" <u>Sid</u> said, spitting out a mouthful of water. "This lake is calm and <u>placid</u>, but it tastes disgusting."
plaintive	sad; melancholy (think: com<u>plain</u>) When she realized that Judge Wapner was going to rule against her, the <u>plaintiff</u> became <u>plaintive</u>.
plethora	superabundance; <u>plenty</u>; excess (opposite of DEARTH) In case you haven't noticed yet, there is a <u>plethora</u> of terrible puns in this book.

plunder

to rob (usually violently); pillage

SATilla the Hun rode in like th<u>under</u> to <u>plunder</u> our village. I escaped because I hid <u>under</u> my mattress.

politic

shrewd; clever

<u>Politic</u>ians must be <u>politic</u> in order to win votes.

posthumous

continuing or done after one's death

"post" = after

\+ "humus" = earth

posthumous = after in earth

Suppose the five of us died of "<u>pun</u>"icillin poisoning. Our book would have to be published <u>posthumously</u>.

pragmatic

practical (think: "pragtical")

The Craft<u>matic</u> adjustable bed is <u>pragmatic</u> because it is <u>prac</u>tically auto<u>matic</u>.

precipice

cliff; steep overhang

The <u>precipi</u>tation, combined with the <u>ice</u>, was responsible for his driving off the <u>precipice</u>.

precocious

characterized by unusually early development

The high school basketball coach hoped that there would be some <u>precocious</u> basketball players in our elementary school, so he <u>pre-coached us</u>.

precursor

predecessor, what came before

Although Mickey might disagree, many would say the <u>precursor</u> to the mouse was the computer keyboard.

You mean, you have to type in all your commands? What about the "mouse"?

This is before all that

Precursor

presage

to give an indication or warning of something that will happen in the future

"pre" = before

\+ "sage" = a smart person who tells people things

presage = tell before

When the economists <u>presaged</u> that the economy was going to get worse, Hillary watched the <u>prez age</u>.

prevalent	**commonly occurring or existing** Before knights were <u>prevalent</u>, the world was in its <u>pre-valiant</u> period.
prevaricate	Prevaricate means to, ah—it's from the French *prevaricat*—it means to, um, to win the lottery. Yeah, that's it—win the lottery. We <u>prevaricated</u> in the above definition. <u>Prevaricate</u> really means: **avoid the truth; equivocate; lie**
proboscis	**a long, hollow snout** The bumblebee's <u>proboscis</u> <u>prob</u>ed for nectar in the flower.
profuse	**abundant; overflowing** Our <u>prof</u> <u>use</u>d <u>profuse</u> amounts of profane language. Then he got fired.
proliferate	**to increase or spread rapidly** The <u>pro-life</u> movement <u>proliferated</u> in the fundamentalist part of the state.
prolific	**producing lots of offspring or fruit; fertile; producing lots of work or results** The guy who writes *Cliffs Notes* is <u>pro-Cliff-ic</u>; he's got hundreds of titles in print.
puissant	**powerful, mighty** Even though it's a compliment, you shouldn't call the school bully "<u>puissant</u>" because he might think you called him something else.
pulverize	**to grind to bits** If I asked nicely, could I <u>pulverize</u> your gerbil?

WHAT'D you call me?

Uh... puissant..?

Puissant

pusillanimous

timid; cowardly; wimpy
The lion in *The Wizard of Oz* was <u>pussyllanimous</u>.

putrid

decomposed; foul-smelling (pukey)
<u>P.U.! Try</u> disinfecting this <u>putrid</u> sneaker.

The Plumbers

Mario and Luigi walked up to the door and <u>perfunctorily</u> rang the bell. When someone answered, they promptly introduced themselves.

"We haven't come to <u>plunder</u>," said Mario.

"And we haven't come to <u>pillage</u>," said Luigi.

"We're just two <u>pedestrian</u> plumbers. We've come to fix your john," they both added, smiling.

After rushing immediately to the bathroom, they <u>pusillanimously</u> turned <u>pallid</u> and swore <u>profusely</u> at the sight of the <u>putrid</u> mess.

"I never had a <u>penchant</u> for plumbing," Luigi whined <u>plaintively</u>. "But it's better than living in <u>penury</u>."

"Oh, don't be <u>petulant</u>," Mario responded, <u>placidly</u> starting his work. "Just think of your work as <u>philanthropic</u>. Without plumbers, bad smells would <u>proliferate</u> everywhere."

"Don't <u>placate</u> me. I mean, try to be <u>perspicacious</u>. Plumbing is not the <u>paragon</u> of professions," Luigi continued. "And we only get paltry <u>pecuniary</u> sums."

Suddenly, a <u>plethora</u> of black goop <u>permeated</u> a crack in a valve and Mario, now very dirty, became <u>pensive</u>.

"You may be right," he said. "It may not be <u>politic</u>, but let's terminate this porcelain pot."

So together they <u>pulverized</u> the toilet and left.

Q

"The world would be a better place if there were more Q-words."
—ANONYMOUS

quagmire

literally: a swamp. However, the definition that would be used on the SAT is: **a difficult situation that's hard to get out of.** (**Note:** This definition is a figurative use of the first definition.) Batman was in a quagmire when the Penguin tried to drown him in swamp muck, but he escaped by using the anti-quagmire Bat-spray.

quail

to draw back in fear
The country quailed when Dan Quayle became president.

qualm

doubt; uneasiness; a sudden pang of sickness or faintness
Normally calm, Cindy had some qualms when the photographer asked her to pose atop a volcano in Guam.

quandary

a state of uncertainty; dilemma
He was in a quandary about whether to do his laundry; he liked the grunge look but his clothes were beginning to smell.

> But, what if I rain and no one's even planned a picnic?

THE Qualm BEFORE THE STORM

qualitative
quantitative

having to do with a quality
capable of being expressed as, or having to do with, a number or quantity
(Quantitative comparison questions are a part of the math SAT, in which you have to decide which of two numbers is bigger.)
"I did really well on my SATs" is a qualitative description of how you did on the SAT.
"I got a 1580 on my SATs" is a quantitative description of how you did on the SAT.

quarantine | isolate because of a disease
We had to ⌐quarantine⌐ this word so that it wouldn't infect its neighbor and make it queasy.

queasy | nauseated; uneasy
<u>Uneasy</u> and queasy rhyme. So does the following poem:
When on the boat it got breezy
I began to feel <u>queasy</u>.
Drug dealers are sleazy.
(A public service message from the authors.)

querulous | complaining; peevish
The characters on MTV's *The Real World* are <u>querulous</u>. They're always complaining about each other.

quip | a snappy response
Quip = QUIck + Point (i.e., a <u>quip</u> is a quick and witty point made during a conversation)
I said to him, "Be careful with those detergents." He <u>quipped</u>, "Yeah, I know what you mean. I put some spot remover on my dog the other day and he disappeared." (from comedian Steven Wright)

quixotic | having the same foolish, impractical, romantic idealism as Don Quixote (Really, this isn't a pun.)
Nestle's CEO had the <u>quixotic</u> notion of making <u>Quik exotic</u> by offering flavors like sundried tomato.

quorum | the minimum number of people that have to be at a meeting in order for the meeting to be official (It sounds like a video game, doesn't it?)
Before the council can begin the boredom, it's required that they have a <u>quorum</u>.

A Quick Meeting of Minds

"<u>Quorum</u>, <u>quorum</u>, we must have a <u>quorum</u>!" shouted the leader.

"Why?" asked an idiot. "<u>Qualitatively</u> speaking, it's quicker to quantify the quarks in a quarter."

"Ahh, we are indeed in a <u>quagmire</u>. We need a <u>quantitative</u> estimate of how many quacks are here."

"Yes, it is a bit of a <u>quandary</u>," spoke another idiot. "I know, why don't we vote on whether or not to begin the meeting?"

"I have <u>qualms</u> about doing that," said the first idiot.

"Quiet, you idiots!" quoth the leader.

They <u>quailed</u> before his wrath, and both felt a bit <u>queasy</u>.

"Now then," said the leader, "don't be <u>querulous</u>. I have a plan. You may think me somewhat <u>quixotic</u>, but I truly believe that if we burst forth with enough clever <u>quips</u>, we might be recognized as not being quite so stupid as we really are. And with that thought in mind, I'd like to close this meeting of the village idiots."

R

rampage
(n.) a course of wild behavior
The guy who was supposed to bring us a male sheep went on a <u>rampage</u>, then moved to Hawaii.
(v.) to move wildly
Grandma said, "No one at <u>Gramp's age</u> should <u>rampage</u>."

rampant
unrestrained
The <u>ram panted</u> after it ran <u>rampant</u> around the field for two days.

rant
rave; speak wildly
My p<u>arents</u> always <u>rant</u> and rave when I don't wear socks. So I will buy bright orange socks to appease them.

rapacious | plundering; ravenous; greedy
The <u>rapacious</u> veloci<u>rap</u>tor attacked the children while they were still in the car, eating the fat kids first.

Are you still remembering to do the mnemonic thing? Okay, we'll walk you through it one more time. Picture the velociraptor deep in the jungle, wearing a sweatshirt that says *rapacious*. It opens its frightening mouth and exhales its foul-smelling breath, and you see that its teeth spell out *rapacious*. Hear the wild shrieks ("*rapacious! rapacious!*") as it pounces on the baby brontosaurus, using its sharp claws to tear the word *rapacious* into the tender flesh. Blood flows from the disemboweled bronto onto the ground, where it forms the word *rapacious*.

Yes, we know we're sick and twisted. But we also know our vocab words.

rapprochement | reconcilation (think: re-approachment)
Julie <u>approached</u> her estranged little brother carrying a Gameboy as a peace offering, but her attempt at <u>rapprochement</u> failed when he shot her with his squirt gun.

ratiocination | logical, methodical thinking
Through a process of <u>ratiocination</u>, you could have figured out this word because it sounds like <u>rational</u>.

rationalize | to make <u>rational</u>; justify
It is impossible to <u>rationalize</u> the senseless crime of cat juggling.

ravage | plunder
SATilla the Hun <u>ravaged</u> the countryside.

ravenous | hungry
The raven was so ravenous he ate his own wing.

raze | to tear down; demolish
The striking cereal workers used an enormous razor to raze the raisin bran factory to the ground.

realm | kingdom
The king promised me half his realm if I would take his verbal section for him, but I knew he was lying.

Sir, you've demolished my house!

You asked for a Raze, didn't you?

Raze

recalcitrant | stubborn
I adamantly and obdurately refuse to admit that I am recalcitrant.

recapitulate | to repeat, or state again, in a form that is more laconic and much briefer than the manner in which it was initially stated
Now we are going to recapitulate the above definition: to repeat concisely.
Think: When a sportscaster recaps the game, she gives a brief summary of what has happened.

reciprocal | mutual
We have a reciprocal agreement not to spit watermelon seeds at each other.

recondite | abstruse; profound
If this story wasn't so recondite, I reckon I'd understand it.
concealed; hidden from sight
He kept his pet condor recondite for fear that his environmentalist sister would set it free.

rectify | to cor<u>rect</u>; set right
Tim had to visit the proctologist to <u>rectify</u> recurrent rectal problems.

recumbent | lying down
With both legs broken and his th<u>umb bent</u>, he spent most of the day <u>recumbent</u>.

redolent | fragrant
I use Pep<u>sodent</u> because it's so <u>redolent</u> of peppermint.

redoubtable | frighteningly awe-inspiring; formidable
Un<u>doubtedly</u>, the prospect of serving 100 hungry murderers a Thanksgiving dinner with<u>out a table</u> is <u>redoubtable</u>, but we think you can do it.

redress | set right; remedy; compensate
When Cinderella arrived at the ball wearing only a slip and glass slippers, the prince suggested it was time to <u>redress</u> the situation.

redundant | repetitious; done over and over many times; repeatedly repetitive
The above definition is <u>redundant</u>.

refractory | disobedient; stubborn
The <u>refractory</u> prism refused to <u>refract</u> the light rays, so they sent it back to the factory.

refulgent | shining; radiant
"It's time to <u>refuel, gents</u>" said the driver, who loved gas stations, with a <u>refulgent</u> smile.

refute	disprove "Ref, you'd better listen up while I refute your call" said the irate player. "That ball was in."
reiterate	repeat (note: iterate also means repeat) I would like to reiterate my accusation—I truly believe that you are a noodlehead.
relevant	having significant importance Peanuts are relevant to our elephant's development.
remorse **remorseless**	bitter regret; guilt having no remorse When the remorseless spy catcher took away our telegraph machine for the second time, we were re-Morse-less.
renascent	coming into being again (see NASCENT) During the Renaissance, classical culture was renascent.
reticent	silent; restrained in behavior Scarlett said to Rhett, "Why are you so reticent?" He did not respond. "Is it because I didn't write you a letter?" she asked. He nodded. "But Rhett, I sent you a postcard."
retrograde	moving backwards to an earlier, usually inferior, position After receiving an A grade in history first semester, Michael's B grade second semester was retrograde.
Retsyn	We're not sure what this is, but there's a glistening drop of it in every little Cert.
rhubarb	This won't be on the test, but try repeating it five times quickly out loud.

I can't believe I've slipped back down to a C-

REPORT CARD

Retrograde

rob | **filch; pilfer; loot; purloin; peculate**
You know that <u>rob</u> means steal, but do you know all the words in the above definition? Each is a different kind of stealing. Go filch a dictionary and look up the different connotations of each word.

ruddy | **having a healthy, reddish color (<u>ruddy</u> rhymes with bloody)**
When you get a facial, the beautician makes your face muddy so that it will be <u>ruddy</u>.

ruminate | **to chew cud (this definition won't be on the SAT)**
to think a lot about; cogitate
(Note how the definitions are related. "To think a lot about something" is kind of like "chewing something over in your mind." Also, when cows are chewing their cud, they look like they're thinking.)
The physicist went into the laboratory <u>room 'n' ate</u> cupcakes while <u>ruminating</u> about how to put the filling inside Twinkies.

A Romance

He was <u>recumbent</u> on his bed, <u>ruminating</u> on his <u>renascent</u> affair with the countess. She had left him and then she had returned, and they had reached a <u>rapprochement</u>. Now that she was <u>reciprocating</u> his love he was once again the happiest man in the <u>realm</u>. Or was he?

There was a rap on the door and the air was suddenly <u>redolent</u> of her perfume. "Darling," she said opening the door, her face <u>refulgent</u> with rapture. He frowned as she kissed him and she laughed. "Really. Don't be such a <u>recalcitrant</u> child. You're being altogether too <u>reticent</u>." She kissed him again.

He remained <u>refractory</u> and refused to smile. She came over and reclined next to him. "I'm sorry I left you. I had to, I needed room . . ." She began <u>recapitulating</u> the explanation she had given when she left. He did not respond.

Suddenly there was an explosion on the street below. Riotous sounds reverberated through the air. The countess strode swiftly to the window.

"It's the Roman army. They've been threatening to <u>raze</u> the city and now they're on a <u>rampage</u>." A group of soldiers began battering the front door. "Our only recourse is to run to the roof as rapidly as we can," she <u>ratiocinated</u>. She climbed to the roof and crept over to the neighboring building. He hesitated at the gap between the buildings, momentarily paralyzed by the <u>redoubtable</u> distance to the ground. Then he leapt across, and they raced over the roofs, with the <u>rapacious</u> soldiers running <u>rampant</u> through the streets below, <u>ravaging</u> the city. "<u>Remorseless</u> rogues," she muttered. "They'll change their tune later when they'll have to <u>rectify</u> all the damage they're doing."

"Undoubtedly they've <u>rationalized</u> their behavior by saying it was the only route left open for them," he replied.

They rested a moment, trying to recover from the exertion. Their faces were <u>ruddy</u>.

"You're wonderfully quick," he remarked.

"I can't <u>refute</u> that. I'm also <u>ravenous</u>. We'll have to risk a reappearance."

The outskirts of town were quiet. They slipped into a restaurant. They were led to a table and gratefully sat down. "Now listen here," he scolded, sipping his red wine. "I want some assurance that you won't run off again and leave me rueing the day I met you."

"Whatever are you <u>ranting</u> about?" she retorted.

He <u>reiterated</u> his request, becoming riled. She laughed. "Darling, you're being ridiculous as well as <u>redundant</u>. It's such a bore, really. Waiter, there's a drop of <u>Retsyn</u> in my soup. Please be good enough to remove it." She turned to him again.

"Relax. I'm here now, and so is our repast, at last."

S

saga a long adventure story
Waterworld is the <u>soggy saga</u> of a futuristic planet where it costs a ridiculous amount of money to make movies.

salacious	lecherous; erotically stimulating "Ooooo, that's <u>so luscious</u>," he said, licking his lips <u>salaciously</u>.
sanguine	reddish, blood-colored The bull's hopes <u>sank when</u> he saw his <u>sanguine</u> wound. **optimistic; cheerful** "I'm so glad to be an arctic bird," <u>sang Gwen</u> the <u>sanguine</u> penguin.
scanty	insufficient; small (often used in expressions like, "The <u>scantily</u> clad models were displaying the fall line of underwear.") Food is <u>scanty</u> in the <u>shanty's</u> pantry.
scrutiny	inspection; study; careful searching An inspection of Canadian police is a <u>scrutiny</u> of the Mounties.
sedate **sedative**	to soothe, calm, or tranquilize something, usually a drug, that <u>sedates</u> In *One Flew Over the Cuckoo's Nest* they give <u>sedatives</u> to <u>sedate</u> patients who are seditious.
sedition	conduct or language inciting rebellion against authority Karl Marx's publisher rejected Marx's first manuscript of *The Communist Manifesto* saying, "This <u>edition</u> does not contain enough <u>sedition</u>."
Seinfeld	A state of doing nothing, talking about nothing, and watching a TV show about nothing.
sequester	to separate; set apart; isolate Tired of having his SAT studies interrupted, Larry hired a boat and went on a <u>sea quest</u> for a desert island where he could <u>sequester</u> himself for a semester.
servile	humbly yielding; submissive The <u>servants</u> were <u>vile</u> and <u>servile</u>.

shiftless

lazy; showing lack of motivation; incompetent
The <u>shiftless</u> secretary couldn't type capital letters. (Get it?)

simultaneous

happening at the same time
I will now attempt to rub cheese on my chest while <u>simultaneously</u> drinking salsa through a straw and juggling ostrich eggs.

Shiftless

sinister

foreboding of evil
(Sinister means *left* in Latin. In ancient times the left side was considered unlucky—the side from which evil would approach. This notion survives today in phrases such as "right-hand man," "left-handed compliment," or gauche [French for "left"], meaning uncool or really tacky.)
Six <u>sinister</u> sisters scared seven silly senators. (Say this 10 times fast.)

skeptical

doubting; disbelieving
You think you can <u>escape tickle</u> torture? I'm <u>skeptical</u>.

sloth

indolence; inactivity
"I'm at a loss to explain my <u>sloth</u>," confessed the lazy, two-toed furry animal hanging languidly in the tree.

slovenly

messy; characteristic of a <u>slob</u> (remember, whenever "love" gets in the middle of anything, it gets messy)
Unless you're Martha Stewart, your <u>oven</u> may look <u>slovenly</u> after you make Sweet and Tasty 800 Bars (see page 271).

somber	dark; dull; gloomy The remorseful <u>bomber</u> was <u>somber</u> when he realized what he had done.
soporific	sleep-inducing The other SAT books are <u>soporific</u>; ours is sophomoric.
sparse	**thinly spread or distributed; not crowded** I was still hungry after eating at the fancy restaurant. They arranged the food <u>sparsely</u> and filled in the gaps with <u>parsley</u>.
stagnant **stagnate**	**not moving or flowing; motionless, <u>stationary</u>** **to be stagnant** The air in SAT testing halls is often <u>stagnant</u>, which perhaps explains why the proctors look stale and crusty.
static	On the SAT, this probably would not refer to the fuzzy white dots that show up on your TV when your antenna screws up, nor to the effect produced when you rub a balloon across your head, but instead to: **having no motion; at rest; <u>stationary</u>** The contents of our <u>attic</u> is <u>static</u>; it hasn't changed in years.
steadfast	**fixed or unchanging** No matter how many times we tried to fix the clock it <u>stayed fast</u>. It was <u>steadfast</u>. **faithful** One must be <u>steadfast</u> on Yom Kippur, and not eat. In<u>stead, fast</u>.
stinkhorn	Look up this word in an *American Heritage Dictionary, New College Edition* (not the second edition). The picture is the most phallic image you will ever see in a venerable reference book.
stolid	**showing little emotion or pain; emotionally <u>solid</u>** Even though I loved my pet <u>stinkhorn</u>, I tried to be <u>stolid</u> when they <u>stole it</u>.

submission	the act of yielding to the authority of another The submarine captain demanded the <u>submission</u> of the sailors on the <u>sub-mission</u>.
subvert	to overthrow or undermine the power of The poet was accused of <u>subversive</u> behavior when he wrote a revolutionary poem.
succulent	juicy; interesting Eve <u>sucked</u> on the <u>succulent</u> forbidden fruit.
suffrage	the right to vote; franchise Before 1920, women <u>suffered</u> from a lack of <u>suffrage</u>. But the <u>suffragettes</u> changed all that and now women can rock the vote along with men.
summon	to call forth; to call together The king <u>summoned</u> his advisor. When his advisor's footsteps could be heard in the hall, the king's submissive assistant exclaimed, "<u>Someone's</u> <u>comin'</u>."

Following are four superior words beginning with "super."

supercilious	haughty; conceited; disdainful The <u>supercilious</u> person said, "You are a <u>super silly ass</u>."
superfluous	beyond what's necessary; extra Superman once <u>flew us</u> home without his cape. This suggests that his cape is just a <u>superfluous</u> item and not something that he needs in order to fly.
superlative	the most; of the highest order; surpassing all others We're going to be <u>super late if</u> the car breaks down, and Mom is going to be <u>superlatively</u> pissed off.

supersede

to take the place of
After Farmer Clark planted the new tomato <u>super seed</u>, it completely <u>superseded</u> the regular seeds.

surreptitious

done clandestinely (secretly) **or by stealth**
Afraid that the public might see, Daniel stroked the cow's udder <u>surreptitiously</u>.

sweat gland

a small secretory gland in the skin that excretes water and body salts
Are you awake?

swindle

to cheat or defraud
This airplane doesn't really work, but thi<u>s wind'll</u> keep it up in the air long enough for me to <u>swindle</u> the customer into buying it.

sycophant

a servile person who follows and flatters another person in the hope of winning favor
After the concert, the rock star was surrounded by <u>sycophants</u>. Suddenly he screamed, "I'm <u>sick of fans</u>. You guys are crazy. You're nothing more than a bunch of <u>psycho fans</u>."

synthetic

not real; man-made; fabricated
"<u>Synthetic</u> fabric is one thing—I like my polyester and rayon gowns," cried Cruella DeVil, wrapping her white coat with black dots around her. "But <u>synthetic</u> Dalmatian fur? Never!"

Boy, did I get left in the dust!

NEW SUPER SEED

OLD REGULAR SEED

Supersede

A Shocking Trial

My <u>sweat glands</u> were working overtime in the <u>stagnant</u> air of the courtroom as I <u>stolidly</u> continued my un<u>scrupulous</u> questioning of the defendant on trial for <u>sedition</u>. Although he remained <u>steadfast</u> in proclaiming his innocence, the jury was obviously <u>skeptical</u>. Compared to my <u>superlative</u> arguments, the other lawyer's points were <u>soporific</u>; his <u>scanty</u> arguments were <u>sparsely</u> filled with <u>synthetic</u>-sounding facts and his words <u>stagnated</u> as he spoke. The judge just sat <u>somberly</u> in the shadows. I was confident. All further speech was <u>superfluous</u>. I know you'll think me <u>shiftless</u>, but I thought I could afford to be <u>slothful</u>. So, <u>superciliously</u> I said, "The State rests, your Honor," and the jury was <u>sequestered</u>.

Two hours later the jury was <u>summoned</u>, and I waited, drooling <u>salaciously</u>, expecting the <u>succulent</u> word, "Guilty." So I was surprised when I heard the word "not" as well. "I've been <u>swindled</u>!" I yelled. Then the bailiff hit me over the head and I <u>submissively</u> accepted a <u>sedative</u>.

Now I cultivate <u>stinkhorns</u> and lead a much quieter life.

T

table
On the SAT they would not use this word or refer to the four-legged household object. Rather, the SAT definition is:
to postpone thinking about; to put off until later
The legislature <u>tabled</u> the amendment that would have made Doc Martens the national shoe.

taciturn
untalkative; uncommunicative
The normally chatty billionaire was <u>taciturn</u> when the IRS asked what his <u>assets earn</u>.

tact
skill in dealing with people in difficult situations (think: good social <u>tactics</u>)
When at a funeral, it is not <u>tactful</u> to say, "Damn, she owed me money."

tangible
existing materially; palpable; able to be touched
Compare with in<u>tangible</u>: Love, fear, and hope are in<u>tangible</u>. <u>Tangerines</u>, antelopes, and pencils are <u>tangible</u>.

| **tedious** | boring; tiresome; trivial |
| | The other team scored so many touchdowns that it became tedious to watch them <u>TD us</u>. |

| **temerity** | recklessness; wild craziness; lack of regard for danger |
| | "Linda's <u>temerity</u> in facing the Terminator was nothing compared to ours facing the ETS," boasted the brash review-book authors. |

temperance	the quality of being temperate
temperate	showing self-restraint by not doing things to excess; moderate
	She was <u>temperate</u>: She rarely lost her <u>temper</u> and never <u>ate</u> too much.

| **tempestuous** | stormy; turbulent; like a <u>tempest</u> (violent windstorm) |
| | When we lose our <u>tempers</u>, <u>eschew us</u> because we behave <u>tempestuously</u>. (If you forgot what eschew means, we "<u>sugg-eschew</u>" go look it up.) |

| **tenacity** | persistence; tending to hold on firmly |
| | The student took <u>ten SATs</u> with <u>tenacity</u> until she scored a 1600. It took her so many tries because she hadn't read *Up Your Score*. |

| **tenet** | a principle or doctrine |
| | The Ten Commandments are <u>ten eternal</u> <u>tenets</u>. |

tepid	lukewarm; a little warm
	(Did you ever try the one where you put a sleeping person's hand in tepid water and . . .)
	Tom's tea was <u>tepid</u>, so he nuked it in the microwave.

terrestrial	of the earth
	Often when I gaze celestial,
	I forget all things <u>terrestrial</u>.
	In other words, when I think of space,
	I always fall flat on my face.

terse | concise; free of superfluous words
This verse
is <u>terse</u>.

thwart | to prevent from taking place; challenge
"We must <u>thwart the wart</u>," the dermatologist decided.

tirade | a long and vehement speech
The dean gave the sorority girls a <u>tirade</u> for responding to the fraternity's panty raid with a <u>tie raid</u>.

torrid | parched by the sun; hot; burning
I plan <u>to rid</u> myself of this <u>torrid</u> climate by moving to Alaska.
passionate
Soap opera previews always talk about "<u>torrid</u> love affairs."

treachery | betrayal of trust; traitorousness
When <u>Treach</u> left his rap group Naughty by Nature to embark on a solo career, the group called him <u>treacherous</u>.

trepidation | fear; a state of anxiety or fear that makes you <u>tremble</u>
We couldn't think of a good sentence so we made up a bunch of bogus words:
prepidation—fear of clothes from J. Crew
strepidation—fear of getting a sore throat
stripidation—fear of taking off your clothes
trapidation—fear of getting stuck
tripidation—fear of vacations and falling
troopidation—fear of getting drafted or of watching *Sgt. Bilko*.
(This should be enough to remind you that <u>trepidation</u> means fear.)

tribute | a gift expressing gratitude or respect
I paid tribute to the Tribune by papering my bathroom with it.

triskaidekaphobia

fear of the number 13
If you have triskaidekaphobia, you'll always leave #13 on the SAT blank. (This word won't be on the test, but you should use it as much as possible.)

truncate

to shorten by chopping off the end
The elephant's trunk was truncated when his friend ate his trunk.

Truncate

U

ubiquitous

being or seeming to be everywhere at the same time; omnipresent
The Serpent is ubiquitous. He tortures students all over the nation at the same time.
Take five of those yellow "Post-It" notes and write ubiquitous on each one. Then stick them all over your house. The stickers will then be ubiquitous.

There are a lot of SAT words that start with "un-." However, since "un-" usually means *not*, most of these words just mean the opposite of what they mean without the "un-." For example: unabashed = not abashed

However, some "un-" words aren't direct opposites. Others aren't even words without the "un-" (for example, uncle).

unassuming

not pretentious; modest
Although they were rich enough to pay off the federal deficit, they were unassuming, and lived in a tent.

unawares	unawares doesn't mean not <u>aware</u>, but: by surprise; unexpectedly (note: it's an adverb) We came up behind him <u>unawares</u> and saw him in his <u>under</u>wear.
uncouth	crude; unrefined; awkward (think: uncool) The <u>uncouth</u> <u>youth</u> hit people in the tooth (then scratched his hairy pits and grunted).
unruly	difficult to govern; impossible to discipline They were used to living without <u>rules</u>, so they were <u>unruly</u>.
unscrupulous	unprincipled; lacking ethical values After the church robbery, the minister lamented, "It takes an <u>unscrupulous</u> criminal to <u>unscrew</u> the seats and leave us <u>pewless</u>."
unwitting	unaware, not knowing The Evil Testing Serpent fiendishly devours <u>unwitting</u> students.
upshot	outcome; result (This word was originally archery terminology. The last shot of an archery tournament was called the <u>upshot</u>, and it often determined the result or outcome of the tournament.) Bart was hit in the rear by an <u>upshot</u> at the archery tournament. The <u>upshot</u> of this was that he had to take the SAT standing up.
usurp	to illegally seize the power or rights from another Yusef <u>usurped</u> Boris's position by staging a coup.
usury	the lending of money at outrageously high interest; loan-sharking When the 250-pound loan shark practiced <u>usury</u>, his creditors <u>usually</u> paid him back pretty quickly.

Tutu Story

"Don't be <u>taciturn</u>!" urged the talkative twerp wearing a tutu. "Look at me—I have great <u>tact</u>, and no one could accuse me of <u>trepidation</u>. In fact, it's often been said that my <u>temerity</u> pays <u>tribute</u> to my <u>torrid</u> soul."

His <u>temperate</u> companion held <u>tenaciously</u> to his <u>tenets</u> and tried to tune out his <u>tempestuous</u> tutued friend's <u>tirade</u>.

The situation was entirely too <u>tedious</u>, so I turned to someone else at my table and asked, "Do you think that Congress will <u>table</u> the discussion about the Doc Martens?"

There was an almost <u>tangible</u> silence. Then a sandaled young man put an ice cube in his <u>tepid</u> tea and said, "That's a touchy subject here. We're all upset about our senator's <u>treachery</u> in supporting the bill."

"We're going to try to <u>thwart</u> him," said the <u>temperate</u> companion <u>tersely</u>. "If that bill passes, I'll <u>truncate</u> his term and the <u>upshot</u> of this will be that I will <u>usurp</u> his power."

His words caught me <u>unawares</u>. The guy had seemed to me to be polite and <u>unassuming</u>, but instead he was an <u>uncouth</u> and <u>unruly</u> youth.

V

vacillate	**to waver from one side to the other; <u>oscillate</u>** While the skier <u>vacillated</u> about whether to use Vaseline or Chapstick his lips got chapped.
vacuity	**emptiness; vacuum** The scientists were amazed by the utter <u>vacuity</u> in the proctor's brain—there was not a trace of brain matter anywhere.
vainglorious	**<u>vain</u>; boastful** <u>Vainglorious</u> <u>Gloria</u> boasted about her vocabulary in <u>vain</u>—she got a 210 on the verbal section.

valor	courage; bravery Val Kilmer showed valor when he did his own stunts in *Batman*.
vehement	with ardor; energetically or violently forceful They fed the sedatives to the vehement protesters via mints.
ver-	**The motto of Harvard is "Veritas" and the motto of Yale is "Lux et Veritas." Since these two schools may be knocking down your door once you get your 1600, you might as well know that "veritas" is Latin for truth. ("Lux" means light.) When you see the root "ver-" in an SAT word, that word probably has something to do with truth.** For example: veracity—truthfulness; accuracy verdict—conclusion; judgment verification—proof that something is true verisimilar—appearing to be true or possible verisimilitude—the quality of being verisimilar veritable—unquestionable; actual; true verity—a statement or belief considered to be the permanent truth vermicide—anything used to kill worms (Well, it doesn't always work.)
verbose	excessively wordy (this word has nothing to do with truth) They wrote and transcribed and copied down on to paper and composed and thought of and typed a sentence that would be verbose because it had excessive verbs.
vex **vexation**	to irritate or bother the act of vexing His vexing habit of reciting vocabulary words during sexual activity ruined his sex life.
vilify	**to slander; defame (think: make vile)** Joe McCarthy's villainous lies vilified many innocent people.

Although the next two words have the same first six letters and are related, they are not at all synonymous.

vindicate

to clear of blame or suspicion
The lawyers will <u>vindicate</u> their client by displaying evidence
that they ha<u>ve indicating</u> that he didn't mean to steal the
adult diapers from the grocery store.

vindictive

vengeful
The <u>vindictive</u> Witch of the West wanted to kill Dorothy in
order to avenge the death of the Wicked Witch of the East.

vivacious

animated; full of energy
Sleepy the Dwarf took some <u>Vivarin</u> and became <u>vivacious</u>.

vocabulary

**What you need to be successful in life, according to the
ETS. However, this isn't true—look at Dan Quayle.**

vociferous

loud; obnoxious as hell
The <u>vociferous</u> student demanded in a loud <u>voice</u> that the
proctor turn on the lights before handing out the tests.

voluble

**fluent in speech (especially in the derogatory sense of
someone who talks too much)**
The professor was so <u>voluble</u> that we had to take volumes of
notes.

voracious

eager to consume mounds of food
We were so <u>voracious</u> that we even ate the Tupperware.

vulcan — a pointy-eared alien, devoid of warmth and emotion, who thinks logically
Come on! Don't fall asleep. Only a few more pages to go.

vulnerable — unprotected
The Evil Testing Serpent is <u>vulnerable</u> to the tricks in *Up Your Score*.

wanton — immoral; unchaste; cruel
His blowing up the <u>one-ton</u> truck was an act of <u>wanton</u> destruction.
They had a <u>wanton</u> night of passionate entanglement in a vat of <u>won-ton</u> soup.

whim — a capricious, freakish idea
On a <u>whim</u> the tournament directors decided to let the <u>wimp</u> play at <u>Wim</u>bledon.

wily — crafty
<u>Wile E</u>. Coyote uses <u>wily</u> methods of sneaking up on the Roadrunner <u>while he</u> isn't looking.

wistful — yearning; <u>wishful</u> with a hint of sadness
As he thought of his lost love, he <u>whistled</u> a <u>wistful</u> melody and drank a bottle of her perfume.

wow — of or pertaining to golly-gee-whillikers

wrath — anger; rage
Elmer Fudd is full of <u>wrath</u> at that <u>wrath</u>cally wrabbit that keeps eating his garden.

X

Sorry, there are no SAT words that begin with X.

Y

yummy | delicious
Well, we didn't want to cop out for two letters in a row!

An Avuncular Vendetta

My uncle was <u>valorous</u>, yet he was inclined to be quite <u>voluble</u> when faced with danger. His <u>verbose</u>, <u>vacuous</u> speeches terrified and bored his enemies. Certain <u>vindictive</u> individuals have attempted to <u>vilify</u> his reputation by insisting that he was a wimp, but he has always managed to <u>vindicate</u> himself by <u>vehemently</u> <u>verifying</u> the <u>veracity</u> of his claims of courage.

Anyway, one day while my uncle was <u>vacillating</u> over a choice of beverages, the <u>vainglorious</u> Victor Ventura burst in on him, extremely <u>vexed</u>. He voiced his message <u>vociferously</u>: "I consider you a vile swine, and in the future I will not hesitate to spray you with <u>vermicide</u>."

"Pray tell," said my uncle <u>vivaciously</u>, "what is the cause of your <u>vexation</u>?"

"I came here with a <u>voracious</u> appetite," replied Victor, "and on a <u>whim</u> you <u>wantonly</u> denied me any food, you wretched worm."

"<u>Wow</u>," said my <u>wily</u> uncle <u>wistfully</u>, "you may as well spare me your <u>wrath</u>, because I haven't got anything <u>yummy</u> to offer you."

Z

zany	crazy; insane On the advertisement for *Tiny Toon Adventures*, the voice says, "Tune in and watch the zany antics of the Tiny Toons every Thursday at 3:30." But you'll be studying at that time.
zeal **zealous**	enthusiasm full of zeal The zealous seal spun the ball with zeal.
zenith	peak; summit; acme (see NADIR, zenith's antonym) If the Zenith company could invent a TV that would change channels automatically whenever a show started getting stupid, that would be the zenith of television technology.
zest	gusto; happy and vivacious enjoyment If you use Zest soap, you will feel full of zest for the rest of the day. You will also feel Zestfully clean.
zyzzyva	any of various tropical weevils of the genus Zyzzyva, often destructive to plants Who cares about zyzzyvas? You are done with the word lists. Congratulations! Think of all the words you know now that you didn't used to know. Good work. You are going to rock on the verbal section.
A Final Poem	A zany, zealous Zyzzyva Zestfully Zig-zagged up to the Zenith.

USEFUL SYNONYMS

The following are lists of synonymous SAT words. Actually, they aren't exact synonyms, but they are closely related. When one of these words shows up on the test, it is usually enough to recognize that it's one of the *Slander* words, for example. However, sometimes you have to know the word's specific connotations. Use these lists only as aids; you should know the particular meaning of each word.

Stealing/Plunder
depredation
kleptomania
larceny
filch
loot
peculate
pilfer
pillage
plunder
purloin
ravage
rob
swindle

Slander
calumniate
be captious
denigrate
make innuendo
insinuate
malign
vilify

Soothe/Make Better
allay
alleviate
ameliorate
appease
assuage
mitigate
mollify
palliate
sedate

Brief/To the Point
concise
laconic
pithy
terse

Lusty
bawdy
concupiscent
lascivious
lecherous
lewd
licentious
salacious

Stingy/Greedy
avaricious
frugal
parsimonious
penurious

Wealth
affluence
opulence
ostentation
superfluity

SIMILAR-LOOKING WORDS

The following is a list of pairs of words that look similar and are easily confused with each other. Make sure you know the difference between them.

1. adulate and adulterate
2. adverse and averse
3. anachronism and anarchism
4. antipathy and apathy
5. ascetic and aesthetic
6. baleful and baneful
7. censure and censor
8. capitulate and recapitulate
9. disparate and desperate
10. divers and diverse
11. elicit and illicit
12. heterogeneous and homogeneous
13. illusion and allusion
14. imbibe and imbue
15. imminent and eminent
16. ingenious and ingenuous
17. mendicant and mendacious
18. penury and penurious
19. pestilence and petulance
20. qualitative and quantitative
21. zyzzyva and aardvark

THE MATH SECTION

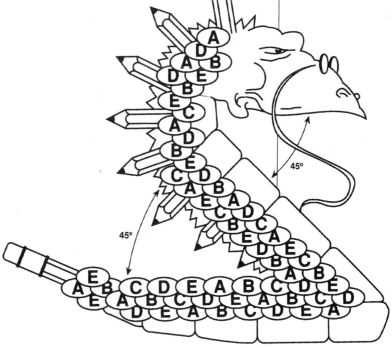

THEORY OF STUDY

Why was six afraid of seven?
Because seven ate nine.

With this lame joke as an introduction, we welcome you to the wonderful world of SAT math.

As most people know, the most appropriate place for doing math is in the bathroom. First of all, there are many geometric shapes in the bathroom: square tiles, round drains, cylindrical toilet paper rolls. Second, there is generally ample time for even the most freakish discoveries—an ancient Greek calculated π to 70 digits while relaxing on a pay toilet in fourth-century Ithaca. Einstein himself concluded that space is bent while trying to catch a slippery bar of soap during an excursion in the tub. And everyone knows that Doc Brown from *Back to the Future* came up with the flux capacitor when he fell off the can.

What we mean to say is that when you go to the bathroom, you're not doing anything else useful, so you might as well study math.

This was Larry's idea, by the way.

On every SAT, there are 60 math questions—35 standard multiple-choice questions, 15 quantitative comparisons, and 10 grid-in questions, all of which will be explained later.

This chapter covers eight main issues calculator use, fractions/units, word problems, equations, geometry problems, quantitative comparisons, funny symbol problems, and grid-in problems. We do not intend to teach you the fundamentals of mathematics—instead we're showing you test-wise problem-solving techniques. If you have trouble with very basic things, then you ought to talk to your math teacher: Direct contact with a good teacher is far more useful than anything we could tell you, but be sure to use a condom.

Sometimes in this chapter, we will discuss some relatively advanced subjects. If you are shooting for a math score of above 550, we recommend that you learn the material in these sections. Even if you are not a math guru, you should still read the advanced sections. If you can follow what's going on in the advanced part, great. Otherwise, if you're not shooting for a great math score, don't worry about it.

Quick and accurate are the operational words for the math section. If you run out of time, you lose points. And if you do certain things wrong, you lose points. Either way, your grandmother won't be able to brag about your scores (and you wouldn't want that, would you?).

A note before we begin: As on the verbal section, we suggest that if you skip a question because you don't know the answer, make a mark in the margin. Put an X next to the questions you don't think you'll be able to figure out. Put a ? next to the ones you think you could figure out with more time but don't want to spend the time on right now.

CALCULATORS

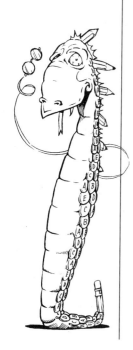

"**W**ow!" yelled Jimmy. "I get to use a calculator on the SAT! I'm going to ace this test!" Jimmy assumed he could get by on the math section of the SAT with only a calculator, blew off all his math classes, and didn't bother to study at all. When test time came, Jimmy realized that there was a lot more to the test than calculators. Jimmy now walks the streets wearing only a garbage bag and bowling shoes.

What is the moral of this sad tale? Don't put too much faith in your calculator. The ETS says that students who use them do slightly better than those who don't, but no problem can be completed solely by knowing how to push buttons and every math problem can be answered *without* using a calculator. While we're not going to discourage the use of a calculator, we want you to know that if you're good at arithmetic, you'll do fine without it. So, the trick is knowing when to use it. In addition, make sure you:

1. Know how to use your calculator.

You're going to feel pretty stupid if halfway through the test you realize you don't know where the equal sign button is.

2. Know your arithmetic.

The only thing your calculator will be able to help you

with is arithmetic: adding, subtracting, multiplying, and dividing. But most of the math problems will not involve complex calculations, and it may be quicker to do them in your head than to use your calculator. For instance, if a problem calls for you to add 21 and 13, your head will move a lot quicker than your fingers to tell you the sum is 34. If you find yourself trying to multiply 3,425 by 9,461, you're probably doing the problem wrong.

Some problems will ask you to decide if something is a factor. Knowing your dividing rules will help a lot. Here's a list:

a. any positive integer is divisible by 1 (we hope you already know this one).

b. even numbers are divisible by 2 (we hope you know this one, too).

c. numbers whose digits add up to multiples of 3 are divisible by 3.

Example: 186. Add the digits: $1 + 8 + 6 = 15$ (a multiple of 3). So 186 is divisible by 3.

d. numbers whose last 2 digits form ("form," not "add up to") a number that is divisible by 4 are divisible by 4.

Example: 103,424 is divisible by 4 because 24 (last 2 digits) is.

e. numbers that end in 5 or 0 are divisible by 5.

f. numbers divisible by 2 *and* 3 are divisible by 6.

g. no rule for 7. Sorry, we don't make the rules!

h. numbers whose last 3 digits form a number that is divisible by 8 are divisible by 8.

Example: 10,496,832 is divisible by 8 because 832 (last 3 digits) is.

i. numbers whose digits add up to multiples of 9 are divisible by 9.

Example: 304,164. Add the digits:
$3 + 4 + 1 + 6 + 4 = 18$ (a multiple of 9)

j. numbers that end in 0 are divisible by 10.

If you find yourself trying to multiply 3,425 by 9,461, you're probably doing the problem wrong.

We tried the following problem using these rules and then again using a calculator. We got the answer faster the first time.

What is the *least* positive integer divisible by the numbers 2, 3, 4, and 5?
(A) 30
(B) 40
(C) 60
(D) 90
(E) 120

You can immediately tell they're all divisible by 2 and 5, because they end in 0. You can use rule c to cross out (B), and rule d to cross out (A) and (D). That leaves (C) and (E), and since we want the smallest number, (C) is the answer. That wasn't that bad, was it?

3. Know your squares.

In addition to the above rules, you should also know your squares and square roots. Questions usually don't directly ask for squares and square roots, but sometimes you can see short-cuts if you know them. Here's a table of the squares of numbers 11 to 20. Learn them so that you can save time on your calculations.

Number	Square	Number	Square
11	121	17	289
12	144	18	324
13	169	19	361
14	196	20	400
15	225		
16	256	(Also memorize $25^2 = 625$)

If you see one of these squares in a problem, chances are you'll have to take the square root.

Here's another arithmetic trick that might come in handy: Check the last digits. If you're multiplying two numbers together, you can figure out what the last digit of the answer is without multiplying them completely: Multiply the end numbers together and take the last digit of this product.

Example: 23 × 257 = (A) 5,911
(B) 5,312
(C) 4,517
(D) 6,417
(E) 5,118

Without multiplying it out, let's do a last-digit check: 3 × 7 (the two last numbers) = 21; last digit = 1. Only choice (A) ends in 1, so the answer is (A).

4. Calculators and fractions don't mix well.

If you see a problem with fractions in both the question and the answer, drop your calculator. Changing fractions to decimals can be confusing, and there's no need for it.

As you may already know, some calculators are also mini-computers that can store information, such as vocab definitions. But if you were planning to use these to cheat, don't count on it. According to the College Board, no hand-held computers or anything with a lettered keyboard will be allowed for the test. Also, you can't keep your calculator on your desk during the verbal section.

One last word on calculators: If you're bored during the test, you can always punch in 58008 and turn your calculator over. We realize it's not politically correct, but it makes us laugh every time.

Real mature, guys.

— Lisa

FRACTIONS/ UNITS

You've done a lot of fractions in math class, so you know, more or less, how to work with them. But do you know what a fraction *means*? Do you completely understand that ⅗ not only means *three-fifths*, but also means 3 *divided by* 5? Also, do you completely understand that miles/hour means *miles divided by hours*? If not, read this section extra carefully. Fractions and units are the most important things to master for the math SAT.

The Meaning of a Fraction

The following problem will illustrate why *three-fifths* and *3 divided by 5* are the same thing.

The Quiche Problem

Charles Barkley, Shaquille O'Neal, Arnold Schwarzenegger, Steven Seagal and Jean-Claude Van Damme are having dinner together. They order 3 quiches, which they plan to divide equally. How much quiche does each person get?

Here's a three-step solution to this problem:

Step 1: Cut the first quiche into 5 equal pieces (i.e., into fifths) and give 1 piece to each person.

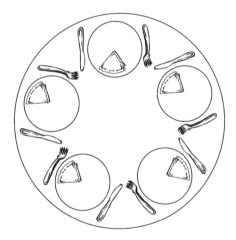

Step 2: Do the same thing to the second quiche:

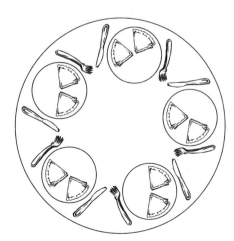

Step 3: Do the same thing to the third quiche:

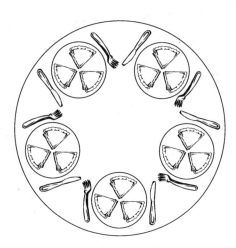

Now, as you can see, everyone has 3 slices of quiche. Each slice is a fifth of a quiche, so everyone has three-fifths (⅗) of a quiche. So, 3 quiches were divided equally among 5 people to give each person ⅗ of a quiche.

This is what this problem was designed to demonstrate—that 3 divided by 5 and ⅗ are the same thing: 3 quiches divided by 5 people = ⅗ of a quiche per person. Read this paragraph over and over again until you understand it. Then go eat some quiche.

Complex Fractions

The Serpent loves testing your ability to work with fractions by creating problems that contain complex fractions. A complex fraction is a regular fraction divided by another regular fraction. Here are some examples of complex fractions:

$$\dfrac{\frac{3}{5}}{\frac{7}{13}} \quad \text{or} \quad \dfrac{\frac{a}{b}}{\frac{c}{d}} \quad \text{or} \quad \dfrac{\frac{\text{hours}}{\text{mile}}}{\frac{\text{wombat}}{\text{person}}}$$

Since complex fractions are a pain in the neck, you want to make them into regular fractions. There is a simple rule for simplifying complex fractions.

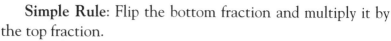

Simple Rule: Flip the bottom fraction and multiply it by the top fraction.

Simple? Well, actually it is. You just have to recognize each individual fraction. Label the complex fraction like this:

$$\text{upper }\{\ \cfrac{\text{top of the upper}}{\text{bottom of the upper}} \\ \text{lower }\{\ \cfrac{\text{top of the lower}}{\text{bottom of the lower}}$$

What the Simple Rule says is that you can simplify any complex fraction by flipping the bottom fraction and multiplying it by the top fraction. This is what the Simple Rule looks like:

$$\frac{(\text{top of upper})}{(\text{bottom of upper})} \times \frac{(\text{bottom of lower})}{(\text{top of lower})}$$

Here's an example:

$$\cfrac{\dfrac{a}{b}}{\dfrac{c}{d}} = \frac{a}{b} \times \frac{d}{c} = \frac{ad}{bc}$$

You may want to draw arrows: $\cfrac{\dfrac{a}{b}}{\dfrac{c}{d}}$

Another way to think of this is $\cfrac{\dfrac{a}{b}}{\dfrac{c}{d}} = \frac{a}{b} \times \frac{1}{\frac{c}{d}}$

Using real numbers: $\cfrac{\dfrac{2}{3}}{\dfrac{7}{6}} = \frac{2}{3} \times \frac{1}{\frac{7}{6}} = \frac{2}{3} \times \frac{6}{7} = \frac{12}{21}$

Here are some problems. Make each complex fraction into a simple (regular) fraction. Practice the Simple Rule.

1. $$\dfrac{\dfrac{3}{5}}{\dfrac{4}{7}} = ?$$

You should immediately rewrite this as:

$$\dfrac{3 \times 7}{5 \times 4}$$

2. $$\dfrac{\dfrac{\text{kumquats}}{\text{person}}}{\dfrac{\text{brains}}{\text{oat bran}}}$$

You should immediately rewrite this as:

$$\dfrac{\text{kumquats} \times \text{oat bran}}{\text{person} \times \text{brains}}$$

Word Fractions

Miles per hour is a way that we measure speed. You've probably seen miles per hour written as a fraction: miles/hour. Using the quiche problem, we just confirmed that *fractions* mean "division." So *miles per hour* must mean "miles divided by hours." But what does that mean? How do you divide a mile by an hour? What does it mean to travel 400 miles divided by 8 hours? The following problem will attempt to answer all of these questions.

The Frozen Yogurt Problem

After our quiche-eaters have finished eating, they get in the car to go to a frozen yogurt shop. The yogurt shop is 500 miles away. If it takes them 10 hours to get there, what was their average speed?

Answer: The key is to realize that if they drive 500 miles in 10 hours then they have 500 miles to divide among 10 hours of driving. (It's just like having 3 quiches to divide among 5 people.) So rewrite it as:

$$\frac{500 \text{ miles}}{10 \text{ hours}} = \frac{50 \text{ miles}}{1 \text{ hour}} = 50 \text{ miles/hour}$$

Now you know why *miles per hour* is the same thing as miles/hour.

Units

Anything that you can count or measure will have a unit associated with it. *Pounds* are units, *miles* are units, *hours* are units, *miles/hour* are units, even *noodles* can be units if you are counting or measuring with noodles.

Knowing the tricks of working with units can help you do problems faster and can show you how to do problems that you otherwise wouldn't know how to do. The rule for working with units is that you can multiply and divide them just as you would numbers. For example, when you multiply (or divide) fractions containing units you can cancel units in the numerator with units in the denominator:

$$\frac{10 \text{ miles}}{1 \text{ hour}} \times 5 \text{ hours} = 50 \text{ miles}$$

$$\frac{10 \text{ pizzas}}{3 \text{ people}} \times 7 \text{ people} = \frac{70}{3} \text{ pizzas}$$

And you can divide using the Simple Rule:

$$\frac{\dfrac{5 \text{ pounds}}{\text{chicken}}}{\dfrac{3 \text{ chickens}}{10 \text{ McNuggets}}} = \frac{50 \ (\text{pounds} \times \text{McNuggets})}{3 \ (\text{chickens})^2}$$

After some practice, multiplying and dividing units will be as simple and as natural to you as multiplying and dividing numbers.

We will now do a few practice problems from real SATs that show the procedure for doing units problems.

A gasoline tank on a certain tractor holds
16 gallons. If the tractor requires 7 gallons to
plow 3 acres, how many acres can the tractor
plow with a tankful of gasoline?
(A) 6⁶⁄₇ (B) 7⅙ (C) 7⅓ (D) 10⅔ (E) 37⅓

There are two steps to all units problems:

1. Figure out what information they give you.
2. Pick, from only three options, what to do with that information in order to get the correct unit in the answer.

Step 1: Figure out the information given.

a. "7 gallons to plow 3 acres" = $\dfrac{7 \text{ gallons}}{3 \text{ acres}}$

b. "A gasoline tank holds 16 gallons" = 16 gallons
c. "How many acres?" means . . . answer in *acres*.

Step 2: Do the right thing with the information given.

In all units problems, you have three options for what to do with the given information. You can:

1. Multiply the first thing × the second thing.
2. Divide the first thing/the second thing.
3. Divide the second thing/the first thing.

The great thing about units problems is that it is not necessary to understand what's going on in order to know which of the three options to use. You automatically know which one to choose because only one of the options will give you the answer in acres (the unit you want). Look at the three options:

1. $\dfrac{7 \text{ gallons}}{3 \text{ acres}} \times 16 \text{ gallons} = \dfrac{(16 \times 7) \text{ gallons}^2}{3 \text{ acres}}$

Nope! The answer has to be in terms of acres, not in terms of $\dfrac{\text{gallons}^2}{\text{acres}}$.

2. $$\dfrac{\dfrac{7 \text{ gallons}}{3 \text{ acres}}}{16 \text{ gallons}} = \dfrac{7 \text{ gallons}}{3 \text{ acres} \times 16 \text{ gallons}}$$

Nope! We want acres in the numerator.

3. $$\dfrac{16 \text{ gallons}}{\dfrac{7 \text{ gallons}}{3 \text{ acres}}} = \dfrac{16 \text{ gallons} \times 3 \text{ acres}}{7 \text{ gallons}} = 6\dfrac{6}{7} \text{ acres}$$

Yes! This is the right answer. Notice that we didn't even have to figure out what the problem was all about; we just manipulated the information so that the answer would be in the correct unit.

Let's do another one:

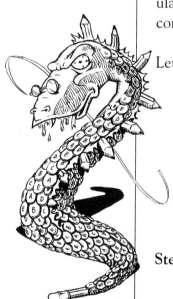

> A mechanic can install carburetors in 3 cars every 4 hours. At that rate, how long will it take the mechanic to install carburetors in 5 cars?
> (A) 6 hrs. 20 min.
> (B) 6 hrs. 40 min.
> (C) 7 hrs. 15 min.
> (D) 7 hrs. 30 min.
> (E) 7 hrs. 45 min.

Step 1: Figure out the information given.

$$\text{``3 cars every 4 hours''} = \dfrac{3 \text{ cars}}{4 \text{ hours}}$$
$$\text{``install in 5 cars''} = 5 \text{ cars}$$

Because the answer choices are in terms of hours and minutes, and because the question asks, "How long will it take?" the answer will be in terms of hours and minutes.

Step 2: Do the right thing with the information given.

Try the three options. Remember, all we care about is that the answer be in terms of the unit "hours."

1. $$\frac{3 \text{ cars}}{4 \text{ hours}} \times 5 \text{ cars}$$

Nope. Gives answer in cars²/hour.

2. $$\frac{\dfrac{3 \text{ cars}}{4 \text{ hours}}}{5 \text{ cars}}$$

Nope. Gives answer in $\frac{1}{\text{hours}}$. We want the hours in the numerator.

So, sure enough, the third option works:

3. $$\frac{\dfrac{5 \text{ cars}}{3 \text{ cars}}}{4 \text{ hours}} = \frac{5 \text{ cars} \times 4 \text{ hours}}{3 \text{ cars}} = \frac{20}{3} \text{ hours} =$$

6 hrs. 40 min. (B)

Sometimes units problems require more than one operation. For example, if you want to calculate how many seconds there are in a day, you would do the following set of operations:

$$\frac{60 \text{ sec}}{1 \text{ min}} \times \frac{60 \text{ min}}{1 \text{ hour}} \times \frac{24 \text{ hours}}{1 \text{ day}} = \frac{60 \times 60 \times 24 \text{ sec}}{\text{day}}$$

Note that even if you hadn't known that the right way to do this problem was to multiply these quantities together, you could have figured it out by trying all the possibilities of dividing and multiplying. Only one of those possibilities would have given an answer in terms of seconds/day.

And now we break for a commercial . . .

Don't you hate it when rabid elephants attack you and steal your pencils? I do. On the crucial day of my test, I was carrying no fewer than eight number 2 pencils and this tremendous elephant, foaming at the mouth, lunged out of the test center and grabbed my writing implements. I was ticked off.

But then I decided to try new improved Oxford Anti-Elephant soap. It not only cleans and softens my skin but also keeps those pesky pachyderms away. Now I can carry as many pencils with me as I like, and it's improved my whole life.

Well, some of my life. Actually, the point of this message is to remind you to have enough number 2 pencils around when you take your test. Also, we wanted to give you a break from reading about math—after all, math is not the most exciting material available for perusal.

Now, get back to work!

WORD PROBLEMS

You really don't need to know much more than the basics of math to get through the word problems—but you do need to know how to think. It turns out that a lot of the math questions deal more with words than with straight math. Often the hard part is translating the words into math. You see,

$$\frac{(378,614 \times 2) + 4}{136,319} = y$$

looks like a hell of a problem. But it isn't that bad because it's just numbers and you can do it knowing only how to add, multiply, and divide. You don't really have to think—you just have to apply the skills you've (supposedly) known since second grade. In fact, you could solve it on your calculator effortlessly.

The really hateful questions are the word problems:

> Bill has four apples and is 18 years old. Sue has 25% more apples than Bill and is 1/3 as old. Alex had twice as many apples as Sue (and is 3/2 as old), but he gave one of his apples to Bill (and that's why Bill has four instead of three).

> For which individual is the ratio of apples/age the greatest?

Not only do you need to know about ratios and percentage

and addition, but you also need to know how to translate the words into math. (The answer is Alex, by the way.)

So let's start with words—Okay? (Put the Doritos away and pay attention.)

Key Words

The following are a bunch of rules for how to change confusing words into easy-to-understand numbers and mathematical symbols.

Rule #1: *Of* usually means multiply. Like "½ *of* y" means multiplying ½ times y.

Rule #2: *Exceeds* by or *is greater than by* means subtract (or add).

Examples:

x exceeds y by 7   means $x - y = 7$ or $y + 7 = x$

x is greater than y by 7   means $x - y = 7$ or $y + 7 = x$

Rule #3: *Percent (%) usually goes with of.* Remember that *per cent* means *per hundred,* so a percent problem is really just a problem with fractions. They tell you the numerator and give you the "%" sign, which you translate into meaning "over one hundred." For example, 25% is really $^{25}\!/_{100}$, which is a fraction.

25% of y becomes $^{25}\!/_{100}$ of y (remember *of* means multiply), so it's $^{25}\!/_{100} \times y$ or, if you're using a calculator, $.25 \times y$.

Do the same thing for percentages greater than 100%. For instance, 250% means $^{250}\!/_{100}$, or 2.5.

Rule #4: But wait, there's *more*. Percent can be made trickier with the word *more.*

If Sue has 25% *more* apples than Bill, then she has as *many* apples as Bill *plus* 25% more.

So the word *more* can be broken down into: *As many plus ———.*

But we can do better than apples:

> Bill has exactly 8 pairs of underwear, all of which are sexy. Sue has 50% more pairs of underwear than Bill. 75% of Sue's total collection of underwear is sexy.

> Who has more sexy underwear? (Don't get distracted.)

Here's the answer:
By Rule #4, Sue has *as many* pairs as Bill *plus* 50%.
So, Sue has 8 pairs + $\frac{50}{100}$ of 8.
Sue has 8 + 4 = 12 pairs of underwear.
75% of her 12 total pairs of underwear is sexy.
Using Rule #3, this becomes $\frac{75}{100}$ of 12.
And finally, using Rule #1, this becomes $\frac{75}{100} \times 12 = 9$.
Sue has 9 pairs of sexy underwear and Bill has 8, so Sue has more. But they both have about as much fun.

Rule #5: *Ratio*—Okay, so what's a ratio? A ratio is a comparison (yep—just like in the analogy questions).

If you say $y > x$ then you're comparing y and x and finding out that y is larger than x. (And, you might ask, who really cares?) But $y > x$ is not a ratio. Ratios involve "division comparisons":

> "the ratio of y to x is 5" means $y/x = 5$

Here, y is being compared to x. Again y is bigger—but now we know that y is 5 times bigger. (Wow. Excitement.) This expression could also be written as:

> "y is to x as 5 is to 1" or $y{:}x$ as $5{:}1$

Okay, well, how *is* 5 to 1? 5 *is* five times as big as one (obviously). So y is five times x, get it?

It's probably easiest to think of this as a fraction:

$$\frac{y}{x} = \frac{5}{1}$$

Rule #6: *Chance* or *probability* is a type of ratio.

When a problem asks what the chance or probability is that a particular thing will happen, all it's really asking you to do is to set up a ratio like this:

$$\frac{\text{number of times the particular thing could happen}}{\text{number of times any of the things could happen}}$$

Here's an example going back to the sexy underwear:

If there are 12 pairs of sexy underwear and 36 pairs of not-so-sexy underwear in a huge laundry bag, what is the probability that, at random, Bill will grab a pair of sexy underwear?

Number of times Bill could grab any pair of underwear = 12 pairs of sexy underwear + 36 pairs of not-so-sexy underwear = 48 total pairs of underwear.

12 / 48 = .25

Bill has a 25% chance of grabbing a pair of sexy underwear. Good luck, Bill!

Rule #7: *Average*—an average is a number that summarizes or represents all the numbers in a group.

There are three types of averages: mean, median and mode.

Arithmetic mean is the most commonly used average, and if you are asked to simply find the average, you should find the mean.

Arithmetic mean = (a + b + c + d . . .)/n where a, b, c, d . . . are the numbers, and n is the number of numbers being averaged. For example, the mean of 3, 5, 6, 7 is:

$$(3 + 5 + 6 + 7) / 4 = 5¼.$$

Notice that $n = 4$ since there are four numbers in the group. Sometimes figuring out what n is can be tricky: Here's an example of such a problem:

Larry's average for the first three tests was 90%; his average for the next two was 80%. What was his overall average?

To find n in this problem you have to notice that there are *five* test scores to average: the first three can be thought of as 90s, the next two as 80s, and the average becomes:

$$\text{mean} = \frac{(90 + 90 + 90 + 80 + 80)}{5} = 86\%$$

If you tried to do this by averaging 80% and 90% you'd be wrong. And Larry would have been upset because you gave him an 85% instead of an 86%.

Median is the middle value of a group. It's the number that would be right in the middle of the list if you arranged the numbers from smallest to largest. The median of:

$$1, 4, 56, 59, 342, 697, 3455$$

is 59. If the number of values are even (which would mean there are two "middles"), then the median is the mean of these two middle values. The median of:

$$3, 8, 45, 67, 107, 156, 223, 1032$$

is the mean of 67 and 107, or 87. (If you are given a list of numbers that is not in numerical order, put it in order before looking for the median.)

Mode is the value or values that appears the greatest number of times. The mode of:

$$3, 24, 95, 24, 56, 74, 61, 74, 74$$

is 74. The modes of:

$$34, 46, 27, 1, 83, 46, 90, 1, 63$$

are 1 and 46.

Sample Problems

1. The ratio of tattoos to nose rings in this room is 3 to 1. The number of nose rings is 12. How many tattoos are there in total, and what can we do to curb society's fascination with bodily mutilation?

Sorry, but we can only help you on the first part of the question. Let's set it up like a *math* problem:

a. By Rule #5 (ratio): $\dfrac{\text{tattoos}}{\text{nose rings}} = \dfrac{3}{1}$

b. number of nose rings = 12

c. Replace the words *nose rings* in the first step with the number 12 to get: $\dfrac{\text{tattoos}}{12} = \dfrac{3}{1}$

Now, solve for tattoos. Tattoos = 36.
Why? Because $\dfrac{36}{12} = \dfrac{3}{1}$ right? Or 36:12 = 3:1.

2. 5 is what percent of 10?

"Wait—I haven't done this!" you moan. Just relax—you can do it with what you already know. Change the question around to read:

What percent of 10 is 5?

Of means multiply—so something *times* 10 is 5. You should be able to figure out that the something is ½. (Right? ½ × 10 is 5, isn't it?) And ½ is 50%, so that's the answer: 5 is 50% of 10.

Another way to set this up is using a ratio:

5 is to 10 as x is to 100

$5 : 10 :: x : 100$

$$\frac{5}{10} = \frac{x}{100}$$

And solve for x by multiplying both sides by 100:

$$\frac{5}{10} \times 100 = x = 50$$

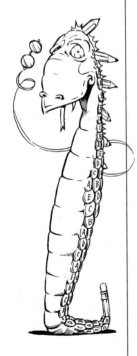

3. On a map, if one inch represents thirty miles, then how many inches represent 75 miles?

This is a thinly disguised ratio problem—the key word here is *represent*. The problem can be translated to look like this:

$$1 \text{ inch} : 30 \text{ miles} :: x \text{ inches} : 75 \text{ miles}$$

$$\frac{1}{30} = \frac{x}{75}$$

Solving for x gives us $x = 2\frac{1}{2}$ inches.

However, it might be easier if you just think in your head, "Okay, the problem is asking how many times 30 goes into 75. That's easy! $2\frac{1}{2}$! God, I'm smart!" Sometimes problems are easier than they look.

4. Mary's average salary for her first 6 years of work was \$15,000; her average salary for the next 2 years was \$16,000. What was her average salary over the entire 8 years?

Notice that n for this problem is 8; the average is:

$$A = \frac{(6 \times 15,000 + 2 \times 16,000)}{8} =$$

$$\frac{(90,000 + 32,000)}{8} = \$15,250$$

5. If Paul ate 300% more pizza than Manek ate, and Manek ate an entire pizza, then how many pizzas did Paul eat?

Paul ate *as many* pizzas as Manek *plus* 300%.

So Paul ate ONE pizza PLUS 300% of one.

So Paul ate FOUR PIZZAS! (Paul, you glutton.)

6. Suppose Michael took the SAT 8 times and his combined scores for each time were 1490, 1490, 1520, 1530, 1550, 1600, 1600, 1600. What was his median score? What was the mode of his score?

Well, 1530 and 1550 are the 2 in the middle, so average them and you'll see that the median equals 1540. And since 1600 shows up the most times, 1600 is the mode.

Another thing to watch out for in word problems is common

sense. Make sure you don't pick an answer that says that Chris travels 200 miles an hour on his bike, or that Amy ate 3000 cookies in one day. The SAT doesn't have outlandish answers.

Advanced Math for Word Problems

The Moving People Problem

These questions are famous. They have no relevance to anything, really, but involve people making work for themselves by going places and coming back again for no apparent reason.

> A man in a bus travels 4 miles in 3 minutes. Then he gets out of the bus and walks back to his starting point, taking $\frac{9}{20}$ hour. What was his average speed for the whole trip?

Answer: 16 miles/hour

The best way to deal with this type of word problem is to plot it out, with distances and times (like this):

4 miles in 3 min by bus + 4 miles in 27 min walking
= 8 miles in 30 minutes total

Get it? Add up total miles, divide by total time, and you'll like, totally get the answer. (Remember to convert 30 minutes to ½ hour in order to get the answer in miles/hour.)

Example:
> A boat travels 3 miles north, 4 miles east, and then sinks. If it sank to a depth of 1 mile, then how far is it from its starting point?

Use the Pythagorean theorem and a picture to get the answer.

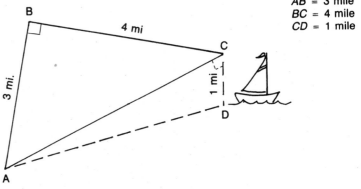

AB = 3 mile
BC = 4 mile
CD = 1 mile

Point A is where the boat began. It sailed 3 miles north to point B, then 4 miles east to point C. It then sank 1 mile, to point D. The distance of the boat from its starting point is AD. So you must solve for AD, but first you must figure the distance of the hypotenuse, AC, of the triangle ABC.

$$AC^2 = AB^2 + BC^2$$
$$AC^2 = 3^2mi + 4^2mi$$
$$AC^2 = 25mi$$
$$\sqrt{AC^2} = \sqrt{25mi}$$
$$AC = 5 \; mi$$

Now you're ready to solve for AD, the hypotenuse of triangle ACD:

$$AD^2 = AC^2 + CD^2$$
$$AD^2 = 5^2mi + 1^2mi$$
$$AD^2 = 26 \; mi$$
$$\sqrt{AD^2} = \sqrt{26 \; mi}$$
$$AD = \sqrt{26} \; mi$$

So, the distance of the boat from its starting point is $\sqrt{26}$ miles, or 5.1 miles.

Here's another:

A man's goldfish swims around the edge of its cylindrical fishtank, which has a radius of 1 meter (it's a big fishtank), at a rate of 1 lap per 30 seconds. How long does it take the fish to swim 32π meters, if after every 4 laps the fish takes a 5-second break to eat some McNuggets? (Include the final break.)

(A) 16 minutes

(B) 500 minutes

(C) 8⅓ minutes

(D) 32 minutes

(E) $30/32\pi$ minutes

Since the circumference of a circle is π times diameter, then each lap is 2π meters. The fish swims 32π meters, or 16 laps:

$$16 \text{ laps} \times \frac{30 \text{ sec}}{1 \text{ lap}} = 480 \text{ seconds} = 8 \text{ minutes}$$

However, we also need to add the breaks. Since there are 16 laps, the fish must take 4 breaks.

$$4 \times 5 \text{ seconds} = 20 \text{ seconds}$$

Answer: 8 minutes, 20 seconds =
$8\frac{1}{3}$ minutes = (C)

End Advanced Math

Enough of this math stuff—the SAT requires fast thinking in difficult situations. So here's a scenario—you have three seconds to come up with the appropriate response.

A psychotic iguana with a bottle of dishwashing detergent is chasing you and gaining every second. The soft grass you're running on barefoot suddenly ends and you're faced with the option of treading on a minefield strewn with broken glass or walking across a river of flowing lava. Which do you choose?

Answer: Neither. What are you, stupid? I'd much rather face an iguana (even a psychotic one with detergent) than deal with a minefield or hot lava. So remember, if you really *don't* like any of your choices, then, "it cannot be determined from the information given" may be an option.

EQUATIONS

The rule for equations is *do it to both sides*. We don't care what *it* is, but do it to both sides. That keeps everything nice and equal. So if your lover is your enemy:

(lover = enemy)

and you want to kill your enemy, you must kill your lover too:

(kill your lover = kill your enemy)

There. Nice and equal. Well, equal, anyway.
So if you have:

$$x + 36 = 40$$

and you want to solve for *x*, then do it like this. Subtract 36 from the left *and* subtract 36 from the right to get:

$x + 36 - 36 = 40 - 36$ which means that $x = 4$.

Now check it by substituting 4 for x in the original expression:

$$4 + 36 = 40$$
$$40 = 40 \quad \text{Bingo!}$$

Here are some examples:

1. $12x = 24$ Divide both sides by 12 to get $x = 2$

2. $3x + 4 = 28$
   Subtract 4 from both sides to get $3x = 24$
   Divide both sides by 3 to get $x = 8$

3. Solve for fish:

3 × (fish + grapefruit) = college
Divide both sides by 3:

$$\text{fish} + \text{grapefruit} = \frac{\text{college}}{3}$$

subtract grapefruit from both sides:

$$\text{fish} = \frac{\text{college}}{3} - \text{grapefruit}$$

Okay. "Number 3 was a moronic question," you might say to yourself. Yes. It was. But they ask similar questions on the SAT just to see if you know these rules. They use x, y, and z more than they use fish and grapefruit, but it's the same basic idea.

4. $x - y = 17$
What is $y + 12$?
(A) x
(B) $x + 5$
(C) $x - 5$
(D) $x - 7$
(E) It cannot be determined from the information given.

Answer: $x - y = 17$
$x - y + y = 17 + y$
$x = y + 17$
$x - 5 = y + 17 - 5$
$x - 5 = y + 12$

(C) is correct.

5. $x + 3 - y = 10$
Solve for x in terms of y.
(A) $y + 7$
(B) $y + 3$
(C) $y - 7$
(D) $10 - y$
(E) $13 - y$

Answer: $x + 3 - y = 10$
$x + 3 - y + y = 10 + y$
$x + 3 = 10 + y$
$x + 3 - 3 = 10 + y - 3$
$x = 7 + y$

(A) is correct.

GEOMETRY PROBLEMS

Basic Math for Geometry

First off, familiarize yourself with the following symbols, definitions, laws, and formulas.

Symbols: $\parallel$ means "is parallel to."

l_1 ———————
l_2 ———————

$l_1 \parallel l_2$

$\perp$ means "is perpendicular to."

l_1
——+——l_2

$l_1 \perp l_2$

Congruent angles have equal numbers of degrees. (They fit perfectly over each other.)

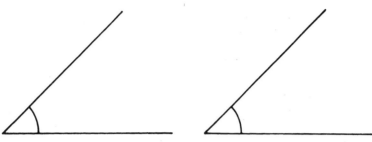

Complementary angles add up to 90 degrees of arc. (If they look complementary, and it doesn't say "not drawn to scale," they probably are complementary. Don't bother proving it to yourself if you're pressed for time.)

Supplementary angles add up to 180 degrees of arc. (If they look supplementary, they probably are.)

Parallel lines cut by another line: These things are full of congruent and supplementary angles. You could try to memorize which pairs of angles are congruent and which pairs are supplementary, but why bother? The ones that look supplementary are supplementary, and the ones that look congruent are congruent.

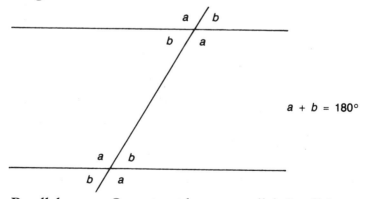

$a + b = 180°$

Parallelogram: Opposite sides are parallel. Parallelograms have two pairs of *equal* (or *congruent*) angles and four pairs of *supplementary* angles. In the diagram, the ones that look equal are equal and the ones that look supplementary are supplementary.

General Note: Here's a tip that may help you with geometry problems and possibly with other parts of the math test as well. If the caption for a diagram says "not drawn to scale," then the first thing you should do is make a quick sketch that is to scale. One of the reasons they don't draw things to scale is to obscure the answer. So, if possible, draw it to scale—nothing elaborate, nothing time-consuming. Just a quick sketch. Maybe it will reveal the answer immediately.

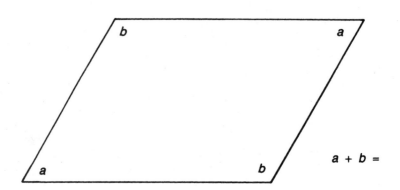

$a + b =$

Similar triangles: Well, boys and girls, now it's time to give you some exciting insights into similar triangles. But after extensive research, we've decided that there is nothing exciting about similar triangles. In fact, there's been nothing *new* in similar triangles for something over 2,000 years—but (and this is the incredible part) they're still in fashion with the ETS. So don your toga and get psyched for a bacchanalian triangle party!

What are similar triangles? Similar triangles are two or more triangles with angles of the same measure in different sizes. Here, for example, are two similar triangles:

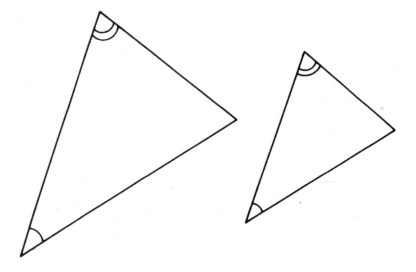

Continuing along this line of thought, here are two similar fish:

Same shape, different sizes (size 6 and size 10).

The technical way to think about similar triangles is that the two triangles have three angles of corresponding measures. And if you think about it, knowing that *two* of the three angles are the same is enough to ensure that *all three* are the same, since the angles of a triangle always add up to 180°.

So, to jump right in here, what is the measure of angle x if A and B are similar triangles?

A.

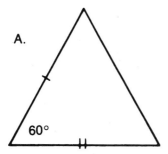

60°

B.

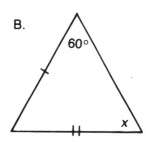

60°

x

Answer: $x = 60°$. Why? Because all three angles are 60° (since $60 + 60 + 60 = 180°$).

Here's another one:
If AB ∥ CD, then what is ⊖ ?

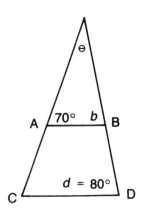

Answer = ⊖ = 30°. The key here is the parallel lines. Remember the congruent angles involved with parallel lines? Sure you do. So think of them when looking at the picture: Angle *b* must be the same as angle *d*, namely 80°. Which brings us to a **Similar Triangle Rule**:

The top triangle is similar to the big triangle if their bases are parallel (see picture).

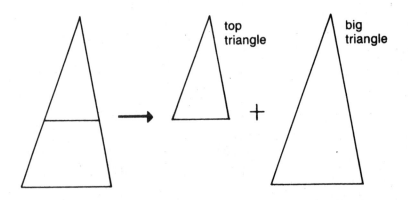

Got it? So if you see a triangle intersected by a line parallel to its base, the two triangles are similar.

Here's some more important information on triangles:
- Pythagorean theorem for right triangles: $a^2 + b^2 = c^2$

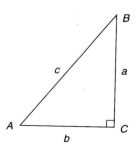

- In a 30°-60°-90° triangle, the ratio of the sides is $1: \sqrt{3}: 2$

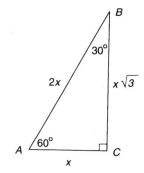

- In a 45°-45°-90° triangle, the ratio is $1: 1: \sqrt{2}$

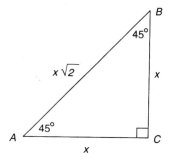

Circles:

$area = (\pi \times r^2)$

$circumference = (2 \times \pi \times r)$

arc = measure of central angle

arc also = 2 × measure of inscribed angle

Well, what the hell is all this *arc* stuff? Let us show you:

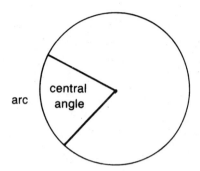

So if the central angle = 30°, then the arc would also equal 30°.

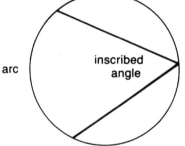

As you can see, an inscribed angle is an angle made by drawing two lines from a point on a circle. The degree of the arc is always 2x that of the angle, so if the angle was 35°, the arc would be 70°.

Area: In general, area is a length times a width.
Circle: area = $\pi \times r^2$ (r is radius)
Rectangle: area = $b \times h$ (b is base and h is height, or vice versa)
Triangle: area = $\frac{1}{2} \times b \times h$. (The $\frac{1}{2}$ comes in because a triangle is $\frac{1}{2}$ as large as a rectangle with the same base and height.)

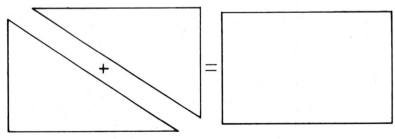

Another important thing to remember about triangles is that the sum of any two sides of a triangle must always be larger than the other side.

Volume: In general, volume is an area times a height.
Rectangular solid: volume = length × width × height

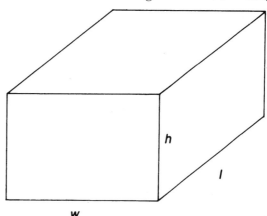

Surface area, or the amount of area on the surface of the solid, is often seen as lots of little areas added up.

Rectangular solid: surface area = (2 × l × w) + (2 × h × w) + (2 × h × l). Why? Because there are three different pairs of sides.

Cylinder: surface area = (2 × π × r²) + (2 × π × r × h). The 2 × π × r² are the two ends (circles), and the 2 × π × r × h is the rectangle you get if you unroll the side.

Important Note: Most of the geometrical formulas are actually printed in the SAT exam instructions. So, if you draw a blank, scan the instructions for the formula you need.

Now, solve these sample problems:

1. Jennifer wants to build a fence (God knows why people are always building fences in questions like these) to enclose a circle with an area of 144 × π. How much fencing will she need? (Draw a picture. It usually helps.)

Amount of fence = circumference
Circumference = 2 × π × r

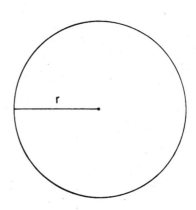

Well, we can't solve it without knowing the radius. So, find the radius from the known area ($144 \times \pi$).

$$144 \times \pi = \pi \times r^2$$

$$r^2 = 144$$

$$r = 12$$

So she needs $2 \times \pi \times r = 2 \times \pi \times 12 = 24 \times \pi$ fence. She also needs a psychoanalyst.

2. Which angles are equal in this picture?

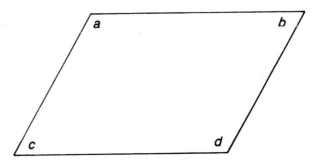

Answer: (a, d) and (c, b), because in a parallelogram, opposite angles are equal.

Which are supplementary?

Answer: (a, c); (b, d); (a, b); and (c, d), because consecutive angles are supplementary.

But don't prove it each time. Just know it by looking.

3. What is the measure of angle *x*?

Notice that angle *y* and 150° form a straight line, so they are supplementary. Since *y* + 150° = 180°, *y* = 30°. Now use the sum of the angles of the triangle to solve for *x*.

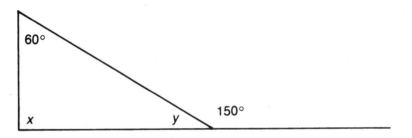

Answer: 90°

4. What is the measure of angle *x*?

The 40° angle is *inscribed*, so the arc shown is 80°, as is, therefore, central angle *x*.

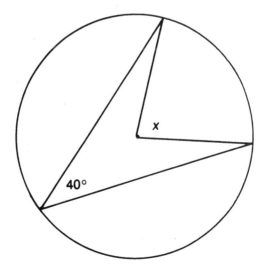

Answer: 80°

5. What is the measure of angle *x*?

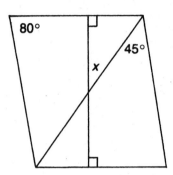

Break down the figure into the following components to find *x*.

First:

These angles are supplementary, therefore: y = 100°

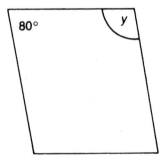

Second:

$z + 45° = y = 100°$

$z = 55°$

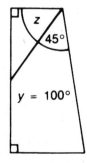

Finally:
$x + 55° + 90° = 180°$
$x = 35°$

Answer: 35°

The above three questions were worded the same, yet they dealt with different geometric shapes. It's important that you learn to deal with angle measures in a variety of geometric figures.

Advanced Geometry

The advanced geometry involves a little more thinking and a whole bunch of tricks.

The Weird Geometry Questions

Some of the nastier questions involve weird geometry—geometry that is hard to figure out at first from the diagrams—but which turns out to be really easy if you look hard enough. The main strategy is to separate the big shape into lots of little shapes, and then solve them one by one.

1. What is the area of the shaded thing?

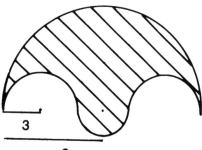

Well, what the hell is it? There's no formula for shapes like this, but don't panic.

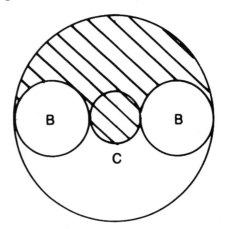

This shape is actually a bunch of circles—the big one (A), two medium ones (B), and the small one (C). You know the formula for the area of a circle ($\pi \times r^2$), so you can solve this problem by subtracting the two medium circles from the big circle, adding the small circle, and dividing everything by 2. The answer is $\frac{1}{2}(64\,\pi - 18\,\pi + 4\,\pi) = 25\,\pi$. Pretty cool, no?

2. Again, find the shaded area.

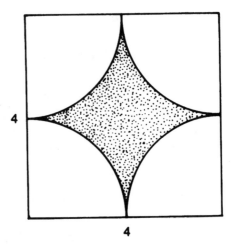

The shaded part is what's left over when you cut quarter circles out of a square. So you can solve for the area of the

square minus 4 × △. Four quarter circles equals one whole circle, therefore the area of the shaded area equals the area of the square minus the area of a circle with a radius of 2.

Answer: $16 - 4\pi$

3. Yet again, what's the shaded area?

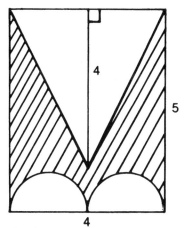

Here's how to do this one:

The area of the rectangle is $5 \times 4 = 20$.

The area of the two semi-circles = area of 1 whole circle. Since the whole side of the rectangle = 4, then the radius of the circle is 1, so the area of the circle is π.

The triangle can be rearranged into a rectangle whose sides are $2 \times 4 = 8$.

Answer: shaded area = $20 - \pi - 8 = 12 - \pi$

End Advanced Geometry

COORDINATE GEOMETRY

Usually there are some problems that require you to know some coordinate geometry (graphs). We'll go over the stuff you need to know, but if this doesn't sound familiar or if you've forgotten it, we recommend you get a brand new pad of graph paper and go visit your math teacher at lunch time. Math teachers love students who come to them for help eagerly carrying their own graph paper.

This is the basic graph with some points on it:

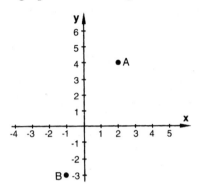

The y-axis goes down-to-up. The x-axis goes left-to-right. The origin is the point where they meet.

Any point on a graph has two coordinates. For example, point A above has coordinates (2,4), which means that if you start at the origin and want to get to A, you have to go 2 units to the right and 4 units up. For point A, 2 is called its "x-coordinate" and 4 is called its "y-coordinate." The origin has coordinates (0,0) and point B has coordinates $(-1,-3)$.

Distance Between Two Points

For any two points, say (a,b) and (c,d), the distance between them is given by the following formula which looks fancier than it is:

$$\text{Distance} = \sqrt{(a - c)^2 + (b - d)^2}$$

For example, to get the distance between point A and point B on the graph above, you would plug them into the formula (it doesn't matter which you call (a,b) and (c,d)) and get:

$$\overline{AB} = \sqrt{(2 - (-1))^2 + (4 - (-3))^2}$$
$$= \sqrt{3^2 + 7^2}$$
$$\text{Answer} = \sqrt{58}$$

(If you care why the distance formula works, just draw a right triangle using $\overline{AB}$ as the hypotenuse, and you'll see that the formula is just another version of the Pythagorean theorem.)

Slope

The slope of a line is an indication of how "steep" it is. To figure out the slope of a line that connects two points (a,b) and (c,d), you use the formula:

$$\text{Slope} = \frac{\text{change in } y}{\text{change in } x} = \frac{b - d}{a - c}$$

The following two questions relate to this graph:

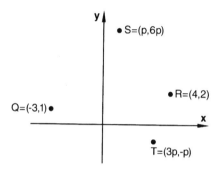

1. What is the slope of the line that would connect point Q and point R?

Just plug the coordinates of the two points on the line into the formula:

$$\text{Slope} = \frac{\text{change in } y}{\text{change in } x} = \frac{1 - 2}{(-3) - 4} = \frac{-1}{-7} = \frac{1}{7}$$

2. What is the slope of the line that would connect point S and point T?

$$\text{Slope} = \frac{\text{change in } y}{\text{change in } x} = \frac{6p - (-p)}{p - 3p} = \frac{7p}{-2p} = \frac{-7}{2}$$

The Formula of a Line

We have not yet seen an SAT math question that requires you to know the formula for a line: $y = mx + b$. Still, it can't hurt to understand that this formula describes a line with a slope of m and a y-intercept of b. (*The y-intercept* is the y-coordinate of the point where the line hits the y-axis.) This means

that for any point on the line, you can figure out the y-coordinate by multiplying the slope by the point's x-coordinate and then adding the y-intercept. Here's an example:

> 3. The equation of a line is $y = 3x + 5$. If the x-coordinate of a point on the line is 1, what is the y-coordinate of that point?

Answer: $y = (3 \times 1) + 5 = 8$

Note: The SAT will not require you to know the formulas for curves such as parabolas or hyperbolas.

Bar Graphs and Pie-Charts

Since the SAT is big on practical reasoning ability, they have included lots of bar graphs and charts of real-world information which you have to interpret. The charts might indicate profits of a company on the y-axis and months on the x-axis, or amount of energy used on the y-axis and five different cities on the x-axis, or any two related things. These questions are usually pretty easy if you know the principles of coordinate geometry we have just reviewed. Start reading the graphs and pie-charts in the bottom corner of the front page of the *USA Today*. They're incredibly inane but if you get used to reading them, you'll do fine when you get to questions about similar graphs on the SAT.

QUANTITATIVE COMPARISONS

Okay, the idea behind quantitative comparison questions is that you've never seen them before—the Serpent made up something so ridiculous that no one else would ever use it.

Quantitative comparisons work like this:

For each problem you are given two expressions: *stuff* A and *stuff* B. The object is to pick which is bigger (A or B). Pick (C) if they are equal and (D) if you can't tell (meaning Einstein couldn't tell).

Note: Don't be a dope and choose (E). Even if (E) is on your answer sheet, it is not a choice in this section.

The trick is that you don't always need to *solve* A or B; all you have to know is which one is bigger. For example:

$$\begin{array}{cc} A & B \\ 23{,}160 \times (400{,}306{,}124 + 936{,}124{,}131) & 456/3 \end{array}$$

It doesn't take much to figure out that A is bigger, so using your calculator would be a waste of time. Try this:

$$\begin{array}{cc} A & B \\ \frac{1}{2} + \frac{1}{17} + \frac{1}{7} & \frac{1}{20} + \frac{1}{5} + \frac{1}{8} \end{array}$$

Again, A is bigger. Without solving, notice that:

$$\frac{1}{2} > \frac{1}{5}$$
$$\frac{1}{17} > \frac{1}{20}$$
$$\frac{1}{7} > \frac{1}{8}$$

So every fraction on the left is bigger than a corresponding fraction on the right and therefore the sum on the left side is bigger.

Note: Never select choice (D) if there is no unknown variable, such as x, in the question, because if there is no unknown in the problem, then there must be enough information to decide which is bigger.

Plugging In

As we pointed out earlier, you don't have to find answers for everything in the quantitative comparison section; all you have to do is figure out if A or B is bigger. If the things that you're comparing are algebraic statements, then sometimes the fastest way to do this is to plug in numbers and see which statement comes out bigger. The Evil Testing Serpent wants you to do this. But he wants you to do it wrong. For example:

$$\begin{array}{cc} A & B \\ x^2 & x^3 \end{array}$$

The ETS wants you to choose (B), because he thinks you'll say to yourself, "Hmmm . . . which is bigger, 10^2 or 10^3? I guess

10^3 is bigger, so the answer is (B)." The correct answer is actually (D). Why? Because although B is bigger when x is greater than 1, A is greater when x is less than 1. For example, if $x = \frac{1}{2}$, then:

$$(\tfrac{1}{2})^2 = \tfrac{1}{4} \qquad\qquad (\tfrac{1}{2})^3 = \tfrac{1}{8}$$

The moral of the story is: ~~If you're using the plug-in method, always plug in a number greater than 1, a number between 1 and 0, 1 itself, 0, and a negative number. Always means always.~~ Make sure that you do this ~~every time you plug in!~~

THE FUNNY SYMBOL QUESTION

As if the SAT didn't already have enough ridiculous things on it, the Serpent came up with the funny symbol question. Here's how funny symbol questions work.

The Serpent gives you some symbol like this:

@

He tells you what it does and you're supposed to apply it. Easy. *Don't freak out* and say, "Oh, no! We never went over @ in my math class, I guess I can't do this one." The fact is that no one has ever seen that symbol in his math class. The Serpent just dreamed it up. (Yes, he loses sleep at night thinking up funny symbols and how to make them exceptionally cruel.)

And he will tell you exactly what it means.

The Evil Testing Serpent defines the symbol, usually using x and y (or a and b, or whatever) in terms of arithmetic commands ($+$, $-$, $\times$, $\div$), which you know how to use.

You take the numbers they give you in the question and do the arithmetic that the funny symbol represents. Be careful that you do it in the ~~same order as in the definition of the funny symbol~~.

Okay, here are some examples:

1. If $x \diamond y = x^2 + 2y$ then what is $3 \diamond 4$?
    (A) $6x$
    (B) 42
    (C) 3
    (D) 11
    (E) 17

Answer: (E). Plug in 3 and 4 where x and y were in the definition.

2. $\boxed{n} = 2(n^2 + n) / (n + 1)$. What is $\boxed{35}$?
    (A) 70
    (B) 64
    (C) 32
    (D) $35n$
    (E) 1

Answer: (A)
Note: $2(n^2 + n) / (n + 1) = 2n (n + 1) / (n + 1) = 2n$.

Take it from here.

3. $L @ K = L + {}^K\!/\!_L$. What is $L @ (L @ K)$?
    (A) $L + 2K + {}^K\!/\!_4$
    (B) $2L + {}^K\!/\!_4 + 1$
    (C) L
    (D) $L + 1 + {}^K\!/\!_{L^2}$
    (E) ${}^L\!/\!_K$

Okay. We know you're tired of this, so we'll give it to you:

$$L @ (L @ K) \quad = L @ (L + \tfrac{K}{L})$$

$$= L + \frac{(L + \tfrac{K}{L})}{L}$$

$$= L + \tfrac{L}{L} + \tfrac{K}{L^2} = L + 1 + \tfrac{K}{L^2}$$

Answer: (D)

Remember: Always do the stuff in the parentheses first.

4.

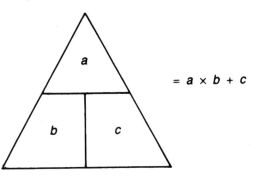

$= a \times b + c$

If

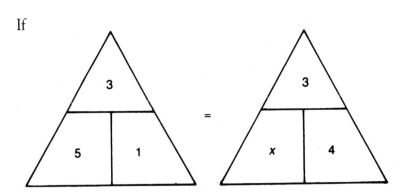

What is x?
(A) 1½
(B) 3
(C) 4
(D) 5
(E) 8

Answer: (C)

GRID-IN PROBLEMS

The SAT also has 10 math questions for which *you* produce the answer. No more of that stinking multiple choice—here's a chance for some creativity!

On the test, these problems will be called "Student Produced Answers." However, the ETS informally calls them "grid-in problems," and many of the questions will ask you to "grid" a number. Well, get this: **The ETS screwed up!** Let's say that again; it feels good. **The ETS screwed up!** You see, in every dictionary we've looked at, the word *grid* is only used as a noun. It doesn't exist as a verb! The ETS made up a word! We think it's pretty downright disgusting that the ETS will nail you if you don't know the meaning of the word *supercilious*, yet it has no qualms about making up its own word. **The ETS screwed up!**

Don't be thrown off by these problems: They test you on the same subject matter as in the rest of the test. The only difference is in the way you answer them.

In fact, because the content is the same as the rest of the test, there aren't any special hints we can give you. The only tricky part of this section is knowing how to fill in the answers. There are directions for this on every test, but because you probably won't have time to read them, we've provided a summary.

First of all, take a look at the grid below:

Notice that on the top is space to write in your answer. However, this is not required—the computer only scores what's in the ovals. So don't bother to write in the answer unless you have trouble filling in the ovals otherwise.

You can start your answer in any column. Either of these positions is correct:

Both fractions and decimals are accepted. If the answer is ¼, you can use either ¼ or .25. But remember to make decimals as accurate as possible. For instance, ⅔ can be filled in as .666 or .667, but not .66 or .67. Because of this we think it's easier to stick with fractions.

Important: You can't state your answer in mixed fractions. For instance, 2½ would look like ²¹⁄₂ (twenty-one halves). So, you have to use ⁵⁄₂ or 2.5.

For some reason, there is a decimal point in the last column: Ignore it. There is no possible answer that would use it.

If for some reason you forget, the largest possible answer on the grid is 9,999; the smallest answer is 0. There are no negative answers. If you get a negative number or a five-digit answer, try the problem again.

Here are two real SAT questions to whet your appetite (have you ever seen *whet* used in a sentence without *appetite*?):

1. If $(a/6)(12b) = 1$, what is the value of ab?

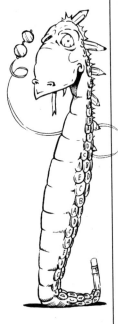

Answer:

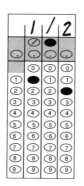 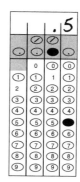

(Remember: You don't have to write in the answer on top; we just did it for clarity.)

2. The lengths of the sides of a triangle are a, 9, and 17, where a is the length of the shortest side. If the triangle is not isosceles, what is one possible value of a?

Answer:

In this case, you could have written any number greater than 8 and less than 9. If a were 9 or greater, it wouldn't be the shortest side anymore. And if it were smaller than 8, you couldn't make a triangle out of it (just try drawing it).

What else do you need to know for the math section of the SAT? Not a whole lot, actually. Many of the questions just involve common sense. Notice that in some of the questions you don't have to waste time doing mathematical computations. Sometimes the choices they have listed aren't simplified—so why in the world should you simplify your answer? Look over the choices before you work the problem all the way out.

If you have time at the end of a math section to check your answers, here's a little trick: Use a different method to get the answer than the one you used the first time. That way you won't make the mistake of doing it wrong the same way twice.

And remember, a good command of really basic things will make you work faster, and as we said earlier, speed and accuracy are essential to doing well on the math section.

Now go do the math sections on some practice SATs from *Real SATs*. And make your grandmother proud!

GUESSING, OR THE ETS STRIKES BACK: IMPOSTORS FROM HELL

IMPOSTERS FROM HELL

The Serpent decided to include among the answer choices the wrong answers a student would be most likely to come up with.

Just when you thought it was safe to go back into the testing hall . . .

One day, soon after his self-inauguration as Supreme Commander of the High School, the ETS woke up in his comfortable and slimy bed and realized that he was dissatisfied with his SAT. Apparently, his torturous questions didn't always fool students. Scores were *much* higher than he wanted them to be. He felt very sad, as well as lugubrious, melancholic, despondent, downcast, doleful, woebegone, and disconsolate.

So, later that afternoon, he decided to pay a visit to one of his testing halls to see what the problem was. He actually overheard a student say, "Gee, this SAT really isn't that difficult." The Serpent felt his scales quiver in humiliation. Drastic action was necessary. The flaw in his SAT had to be discovered and corrected, and fast.

The ETS knew he had made the questions as mean and nasty as he possibly could. But after weeks of re-reading his Slimy and Atrocious Torture and eavesdropping on students taking it, he realized what the matter was. Sometimes students would get math problems wrong and find that *their wrong answer* wasn't one of the choices. So they tried the problem again and got it right the second time. At other times, when they couldn't do one of his cruel math or verbal questions, they would guess randomly and, out of sheer luck, get it right. This sort of thing just wouldn't do. But how could he possibly correct this flaw?

Then he had a brilliant idea. It was also sagacious, discerning, perspicacious, and acute. He decided to put, within the list of answer choices, the wrong answers that students would be most likely to come up with if they made an error in figuring out the question or if they had to guess. That way, if a student made a mistake or had to guess, the student would choose one of the Serpent's wrong answers.

He decided to call these tricky wrong answer choices Impostors. With this concept incorporated throughout his SAT, students would once again live in fear. The Evil Testing Serpent chuckled hideously to himself and his scales shone with proud energy because he knew that his delicious years of tyranny would continue . . . forever.

Okay, don't get frightened. We didn't mean to scare anybody. Actually, the plain truth is that the Evil Testing Serpent was mistaken. He didn't plan on *Up Your Score*. We've psyched out his system of Impostors and discovered that, if you use them properly, they actually make the SAT easier. In this section we illustrate several techniques that we have developed to recognize Impostors, to avoid them, and to trick the Serpent by using them to help you find the right answer.

Impostors are used in both the verbal and math sections. For an example of a type of verbal Impostor, look at this analogy question from an actual SAT:

COVEN : WITCHES ::
(A) tavern : bartenders
(B) altar : clergy
(C) amulet : vampires
(D) castle : royalty
(E) choir : singers

This is the eighth question out of ten in a sub-section, so you know that it's a hard question that most students get wrong. The Serpent puts in an Impostor so that people who don't know the word "coven" will get the wrong answer. Choice (C) is the Impostor here. Someone who doesn't know what "coven" means will see the word "vampires" and immediately connect it with "witches." But in analogy questions, you don't have to connect the *words* in the example given and in the answer choices; you have to connect the *relationships between the words* in the example given and in the answer choices. If you knew that a coven was a group of witches, you would have chosen (E), because a choir is a group of singers. (Remember: This example was at the end of the section, so the obvious choice was wrong; for questions at the beginning of a section sometimes the obvious answer is right. For more on this see Rule 2 on page 203.) Here's another example:

AIR : GRIEVANCE ::
(A) ventilate : room
(B) divulge : secret
(C) breathe : oxygen
(D) wander : path
(E) fertilize : plant

To get this one right, you have to realize that in this question "air" is a verb (you can tell this because the words in the answer choices are always the same parts of speech as the original pair and the first words here are all verbs.) In this question, *air* means "tell, publicize," so the correct answer is (B), because to divulge a secret means to tell it. The Imposters here are (A) and (C) because they both try to lure people into answer choices that relate to the kind of air that is in their heads.

On the math section, the ETS puts in Impostors that are the answers a student would get if she used the wrong method to solve a problem. He makes sure that if you screw up in the way that he hopes you will, the answer that you get with your blunder is one of the answer choices. For instance, the first question on one SAT math section reads:

If $x + y = 2$, then $x + y - 4 = ?$
(A) -2 (B) 0   (C) 2   (D) 4   (E) 6

The correct answer is (A), but the Serpent made sure that (C) was one of the choices in case some airhead left the minus sign out of the answer. He also made sure that (E) was there just in case some pasta brain added the 4 instead of subtracting it. He also made sure that (B) was there in case some goo-head decided that x and y were each equal to 2. So, in this example, the Impostors are (B), (C), and (E).

After the following dramatic interlude on the value of guessing in general, we will show you how to use Impostors to your advantage.

GUESSING, THE SAT, AND THE SPECTER OF WORLD DESTRUCTION

A Deep and Moving Play

T*he Cast:*

A sagacious guru who has read *Up Your Score*
His naive disciple who has not

Disciple: To guess or not to guess? That is the question.
Guru: Guess, my son, guess.
Disciple: But they take off a fraction of a point for each wrong answer, whereas they don't take off any points if I just leave it blank. So if I guess wrong, it's going to hurt my score.
Guru: Ah, silly lad, how foolish you are. Even if you guess completely randomly, you should get a fifth of the questions correct just by the laws of chance (in the sections where there are five choices). So, the quarter of a point that the ETS takes off for each wrong answer is cancelled out on the average by the number of lucky guesses you make.
Disciple: I'm so confused. Give me an example.
Guru: I would be honored. Imagine that there were 100 questions on the test and five answer choices for each question. If you guess randomly you should get 20 questions correct by the laws of chance. But then the cruel SAT graders take off a quarter of a point for each of the remaining 80 questions that you missed. In other words, they'll subtract ($\frac{1}{4}$) × 80, or 20 points from the number of correct answers that you have. You have 20 correct answers, so you have a final score of 20 − 20 = 0, which is exactly what you should get if you didn't know anything and were guessing randomly. It is also exactly what you would have gotten if you left everything blank. So, my child, you see that guessing didn't hurt you.
Disciple: Yeah, but it didn't help me either.
Guru: Right you are. But you were guessing randomly. If you can make educated guesses, or eliminate even one of the answer choices, then the odds will be decidedly in your favor and guessing can significantly increase your score.
Disciple: What about four-choice questions in the math section? Should I guess there?
Guru: Yes, you should. On the four-choice questions, the

ETS takes off ⅓ of a point for every wrong answer. Therefore, you're in exactly the same situation as with five choices.

Disciple: And on the grid-in math questions?

Guru: That is a different situation, my son. There is no penalty for wrong answers on those questions. However, that does not mean that you should automatically guess on every one. On the other questions, there are only four or five answer possibilities but on the grid-ins, there are around 14,000. Therefore, you will probably be wrong if you guess randomly, and you will have wasted valuable time filling in all those circles. On these questions, guess if you have the slightest idea of what the answer is. Then, if you have plenty of time at the end, go back and fill in the blank ones with a number between 1 and 10, where the answer's most likely to be.

Disciple: Are there any secrets to being a sagacious guesser like you?

Guru: It's a good thing you asked. I can recommend an invaluable book that has an incredible section about guessing. It's called *Up Your Score*. It's a masterpiece, really. Buy some copies for your friends and family.

> **On the grid-ins there are around 14,000 possible answers, so if you guess randomly, you'll probably be wrong.**

So, not counting that pathetic excuse for a play, just how valuable is this guessing stuff, anyway?

Incredibly valuable. We did two experiments to prove that guessing really works. First, we took the test by only looking at the answer choices without reading any of the questions. We got an average combined score of 660. Although that's not going to get anyone into Harvard, it is 260 more points than would be expected from someone with no knowledge of the questions. In our second experiment, we had 10 kids take the test and leave blank all the questions that they couldn't do. Next, we had them read this chapter and then guess on all the ones that they had left blank. Their scores were increased, by an average of 35 points, and they guessed correctly on 40 percent of the questions that they had left blank. Ay caramba! Pretty good improvement for a simple application of the six basic guessing rules, which we'll now discuss.

THE SIX RULES OF GUESSING

Rule #1: One of these things is most like the others.

If you have no idea what the correct answer is, choose the one that looks the most like all the other answers. This works because the Evil Testing Serpent is going to make his Impostors look as much as possible like the correct answer. Use the Impostors to show you the path to the correct answer.

For example, if the answer choices are:

(A) $\frac{\sqrt{3}}{7}$ (B) $\frac{\sqrt{3}}{2}$ (C) $\frac{-\sqrt{3}}{2}$ (D) $\frac{3}{2}$ (E) $5\frac{\sqrt{3}}{2}$

You should choose (B). Why? Because four out of five choices have a $\sqrt{3}$ in them, the correct answer probably has a $\sqrt{3}$ as well, so you can eliminate choice (D). Since four out of five choices have a 2 in the denominator, the correct answer probably does, too; so eliminate (A). Since four out of five answers are positive, the answer probably is, too; eliminate (C). None of the answers (A) through (D) has a 5 in it, so (E) is probably wrong. This leaves (B) as the best guess.

Rule #2: Problems increase in difficulty as you go along.

We have repeatedly pointed out that each sub-section of a math or verbal section gets progressively more difficult as it goes along. The first problem in the sub-section should be easy; the last problem should be hard. This should be taken into account when you guess. If, on one of the questions near the end of a sub-section, the Serpent puts in an answer choice that can be arrived at through a simple calculation, it is probably an Impostor. Look at the following problem:

> What is the ratio of the area of a rectangle with width w and length $2w$ to the area of an isosceles right triangle with hypotenuse of length w?
>
> (A) $\frac{8}{1}$ (B) $\frac{4}{1}$ (C) $\frac{2}{1}$ (D) $\frac{1}{2}$ (E) $\frac{1}{4}$

If you do not know how to do this problem, or you don't have time to do this problem, or you have a personal grudge against

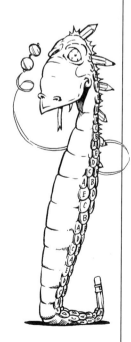

the word *hypotenuse*, you should keep in mind Rule #2. This was problem number 25—the last question in the section and therefore the hardest. According to this rule, you would eliminate answers (C) and (D) because they are both simple ratios of the two numbers that are in the problem (i.e., *2w/w*, or *w/2w*). If that was all that you had to do to solve this problem, it would have been easy and therefore it wouldn't have been the last question in the section.

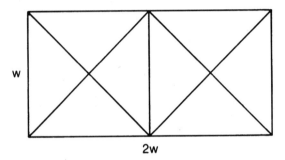

You could actually solve this problem by drawing the following sketch:

The sketch immediately shows you that 8 isosceles right triangles with hypotenuse *w* fit in 1 rectangle with width *w* and length *2w*. In other words, the rectangle is 8 times as large as the 1 triangle. So the answer is (A).

Rule #3: Three's a crowd.

You know how you freak out when, for a couple of multiple-choice questions in a row, you keep getting the same letter for your answer? Well, the Serpent has been watching you and knows this. You'd think that he would use this information to be cruel to you, and just to blow your mind make all the answers for the whole test (D). Yet he does not do this. Although it may seem that the Serpent decided to show some mercy to his victims, he knows that if nine times in a row the correct choice were (D), the students taking the SAT would panic and die from heart failure. That wouldn't be any fun for the Serpent because then they could never again be subjected to his torturous exams. Nice reptile, don't you think?

So, he deliberately makes sure there aren't many "runs"—three or more answers in a row that are the same letter. In a sample of 20 tests, there were only nine triples; statistically there should have been about 24. Also, there were no runs of four or more and there should have been about nine according to the laws of chance.

So if you pick (C) for two questions in a row that you think you got right, and you're not sure about the next one, don't guess (C). This rule should also be applied if, for instance, you chose (D) on question 15, skipped question 16, and then chose (D) again on question 17. When you go back to guess at number 16, don't guess (D).

Note: If somewhere in the test your answers form a triple but you are confident that they are correct, don't change them. It might, however, be wise to pay special attention to those questions if you have time to recheck your answers.

Rule #4: Choose an answer that contains the number represented in most answer choices.

This rule pertains to a type of question that comes up occasionally in math and critical reading questions in the following nasty format:

> Based upon what you read in the passage, which is true?
> I.   Bart Simpson will be the class valedictorian.
> II. Babe the pig will elope with Simba the lion king.
> III. Jim Morrison is alive and living in the body of Roger Clinton.
> (A) I only
> (B) II only
> (C) I and II only
> (D) I and III only
> (E) I, II, and III

Following Rule #4, in this example you should pick an answer that has a I in it because I shows up four times in the answer choices, whereas II only shows up three times and III

only twice. This works because, if indeed I is true, the Serpent considers any wrong answer with a I in it to be an Impostor. If you have no idea at all about whether the other statements are true, select *I only*. However, if you have a hunch that statement II is correct as well, then you would go with (C) because that contains both I (which shows up the most) and II, which you think might be correct.

Sometimes there is a tie between two numbers. Say I and III showed up three times each. In this case, choose an answer that has both I and III in it, whichever one you think is correct.

Of course if you think the best answer is one that I doesn't appear in, go with that. Don't use any of these rules against your better judgment.

Rule #5: Pick "non-answers" at the beginning, not at the end.

On the math section, there will always be a few questions that have as an answer choice, "It cannot be determined from the information given." *The Princeton Review* has devised a good rule for guessing on this type of question. They say that if "It cannot be determined . . ." is offered at the *beginning* of a math section, then it has about a 50-percent chance of being correct. However, if it is offered near the *end* of the test, it's probably wrong. (Probably, but not *always* wrong; if you think it's probably right, then choose it.)

Why does this work? Well, the Evil Testing Serpent knows that most students will not be able to do the last couple of questions. He wants to make sure that there is a tempting answer choice for those students. So he makes one of them "It cannot be determined from the information given." Many students are conned into selecting this sort of answer at the end, when the problems are hard, because they are usually rushed for time and don't see a way to solve the problem right away, even though there is one. In other words, when a "non-answer" is offered near the end of a section, it's probably a trick.

Rule #6: On the reading section, beware of answer choices that express an opinion too strongly, or that make an absolute statement.

For example, without even reading the passage, we can make a good guess on this SAT question:

The author's attitude toward Aristotle's writings is best described as one of

(A) unqualified endorsement
(B) apologetic approval
(C) analytical objectivity
(D) skeptical reserve
(E) scholarly dissatisfaction

Choice (A) is making too absolute a statement. While the authors of SAT reading passages usually take a positive stance toward their subject, they almost never make an "unqualified endorsement." You might also eliminate choice (C) and choice (D) because they are redundant. To be "analytical" is pretty much the same thing as to be "objective"; to be "skeptical" is pretty much the same thing as to show "reserve." You can tell that the Serpent had to find two-word Imposters that would match the real answer, so he used redundant words in these choices. If "reserve" or "objectivity" had been the right answer, he wouldn't have bothered making any of the choices have two words. So that leaves (B) and (E), but you can eliminate (E) because it is saying something negative about Atistotle, so the correct answer is (B).

A FINAL WORD ON GUESSING

Before we move on to the next section, you should know that guessing on a question is really no substitute for knowing the answer. Formally, we call this the Sponge Brain Rule, which says: "If you know the right answer, don't guess a different answer."

CHAPTER 5

SAT II WRITING TEST

THE STORY OF LITTLE-READ WRITING SERPENT

Around the same time that the ETS revised his SAT, educators began to complain that there should be an essay on it. But the stubborn Serpent didn't feel like putting an essay on his trusty SAT. Instead, he looked around his malodorous cave at the various rusty instruments of torture he had collected over the years and dug up the one he had once called "The English Compositions Achievement Test With Essay." Brushing off the remnants of decaying student flesh that coated it, the Serpent drooled, "Yes! This is it! This old test already has an essay on it. I'll rename it the SAT II Writing Test! And I'll make a big fuss about it so most colleges will require it! And the high school students will continue to writhe in eternal agony!"

You can stop trembling. There's no need to be frightened. We have once again caught the Serpent by the short curlies and have sent him whimpering back to his cave. *Up Your Score* will now show you how to outsmart his puny excuse for a writing test and you will all live happily ever after. . . .

The SAT II Writing essay section supposedly tests you on how well you can write, and the multiple-choice section (usage, sentence correction, and revision-in-context questions) tests you on your ability to recognize and correct mistakes in grammar, sentence structure, and word choice. The test is an hour long: You are allowed 20 minutes for the essay and 40 minutes for the 60 multiple-choice questions. It's scored like an SAT I, on a scale of 200 to 800. Many colleges require that you take this test.

In this chapter, we will explain the three types of multiple-choice questions and suggest strategies for attacking them. Then, we will cover the 13 most important grammatical rules to know. Finally, we will tell you how to write a kick-butt essay. If you really want to kick butt on this test, it will help to find some practice tests, but since the Serpent is pretending that this is a new test, he hasn't made too many practice ones available. So, first of all, get a copy of the *Taking the SAT II Subject Tests* booklet from your high school guidance coun-

ENGLISH COMPOSITION ACHIEVEMENT TEST WITH ESSAY

selor, and while you're there ask if there are any practice tests in the guidance office. Then buy a book called *The Official Guide to SAT II Subject Tests* and take the Writing Test. (This book will also be useful if you are planning to take any other SAT II tests.) If you want to take any of the practice tests in the other review books (those not put out by the College Board), do so at your own risk. Most of the ones we looked at were stupid and quite different from the real thing.

As with the verbal sections of the SAT I, a good way to prepare is to read a lot. The more you read, the more you will develop a sense for what sounds right and what doesn't.

THE THREE QUESTION TYPES

Type #1: Usage Questions

These questions take less time than the other multiple-choice questions. A typical usage question looks like this:

The <u>children</u> would <u>giggled</u> <u>as</u> they smeared
        A   B   C
applesauce on <u>each other</u>. <u>No error</u>.
                    D   E

You are to assume everything that isn't underlined is the way it's supposed to be, and then find the error in one of the underlined portions. The answer to the example above is (B), because *giggled* should be *giggle*.

Follow this procedure when doing usage questions:

1. Read the *whole* sentence quickly but carefully.
2. If you're positive that you see the error, mark it on the answer sheet and go on to the next problem.
3. If you don't see the error, look at each underlined portion very carefully; see if it follows 13 of the rules listed later in this chapter (Rule #8 doesn't apply to usage questions) or any other rules you might know. Something that sounds wrong probably is.
4. If you still don't find an error, mark (E).
5. If you have time left at the end of the test, go back and check all the questions for which you chose (E).

Type #2: Sentence Correction Questions

These questions take more time than the usage questions, but less time than revision-in-context questions. They also play with your mind. A typical sentence correction question looks like this:

> The doctor warned the students that <u>it are a myth that one cannot</u> get pregnant for 24 hours after taking the SAT.
> (A) it are a myth that one cannot
> (B) it are a myth, that one cannot
> (C) it is a myth that one cannot
> (D) it is a myth which one cannot
> (E) its myths are that one cannot

Your job on this type of question is to select the answer choice that would best replace the underlined part of the question. The correct answer to the above question is (C). Choice (A) is always exactly the same as the underlined portion of the sentence and is the correct answer whenever the original sentence is okay.

This is the procedure you should follow when doing sentence correction questions:

1. Read the *whole* sentence, not just the underlined part. Often the underlined part is grammatically correct by itself but is wrong when put in the context of the whole sentence.
2. Never read choice (A). Remember, choice (A) is always the same as the original sentence. Why read it again?
3. Even if you think that the original sentence is correct, check each one of the different answer choices to see if one of them is better than the original sentence.
4. If you still think that the original sentence is cool, then pick choice (A).
5. If you think that the sentence is wrong, look for the choice that will make it right.

6. If you can't decide which is the right answer, choose the one that is phrased the most like Dan Rather would phrase it.

7. If you can't figure out the answer, choose *the shortest one*. English is a relatively efficient language. Good writing often involves short, to-the-point sentences that don't go on for ever and ever talking about all sorts of things, and getting redundant, and being just generally too long, when they could be short but aren't because they're long, in fact much longer than they have to be (like this sentence). So choosing the shortest answer works on an extraordinary percentage of questions. Take a look at this question:

Mr. Howe's class has organized a special program for our <u>school: the purpose being to</u> help us increase our understanding of Japanese culture.

(A) school: the purpose being to
(B) school and the purpose is to
(C) school, the purpose is to
(D) school, being to
(E) school to

The answer is (E).

Type #3: Revision-In-Context

These questions are sort of a combination of sentence correction questions and the reading questions from the SAT. A revision-in-context passage is a short essay full of flaws. It's supposed to be like an early draft of an essay that you would revise in school. Whatever.

The first thing you should do is read through the passage quickly, just to get a sense of what it is about. As you read it you will notice mistakes, but don't bother marking them down because any question that refers to a mistake will tell you where the mistake is.

Here's an example:

1. The jellator is unlike most animals. 2. It is known mainly for what it cannot do. 3. It is known less for what it can do. 4. It cannot reproduce. 5. It cannot hunt for its food. 6. It cannot walk on hind feet. 7. The one thing it can do is stop its own heartbeat.

8. When placed under dire conditions, such as when under attack, the jellator curls itself into a little ball and makes its heart stop beating. 9. The attacker, sensing that its prey is no longer alive, loses its desire to hunt and runs away. 10. The jellator then goes back to its own business of doing nothing in particular. 11. Scientists have many ideas about this unique skill.

12. Some believe that the jellator, possessing no other defense methods, evolved this ability over thousands of years. 13. Others believe that a meteor crashed eons ago, imbuing a jellator with magical skills. 14. However, the most common belief about the jellator's ability is that there is a little elf that lives inside the jellator's chest and holds the heart still when a predator is nearby.

Here are examples of three types of questions that would follow a passage like this:

1. Which of the following is the best way to combine sentences 1, 2, and 3?
   (A) The jellator is known mainly for what it cannot do, unlike most animals, and less for what it can do.
   (B) Known less for what it can do and mainly for what it cannot do, the jellator is unlike most animals.
   (C) Knowing what it can and cannot do, the jellator is unlike most animals.
   (D) Unlike most animals, the jellator is known more for what it cannot do than for what it can do.
   (E) The jellator is more like a dessert topping than an animal.

The correct answer is (D).

2. Which of the following is the best revision of the underlined portion of sentence 9 below?

The attacker, sensing that its prey is no longer alive, <u>will lose its desire to hunt and ran away.</u>

(A) will have run away and desired to hunt.

(B) will lose its desire to hunt and run away.

(C) will have lost; its desire to hunt and ran away.

(D) will have lost it, and desired to have run away.

(E) will lose, desire, hunt and run away.

The answer to this question is (B).

Note: This type of question, which asks you to fix one sentence, is just like the sentence correction questions, except that choice (A) is *not* the same as the underlined portion of the sentence.

3. In relation to the passage as a whole, which of the following best describes the writer's intention in the third paragraph?

(A) To summarize the rest of the passage

(B) To illustrate an example

(C) To provide theories for explaining the information in the second paragraph

(D) To prove the existence of jellators

(E) To titillate the reader with lewd, lascivious tales of bawdy lechers

The answer is (C).

Notice that while on the surface these questions look like the reading passage questions on the SAT I, these questions will never ask you questions about facts and ideas in the passage. Still, you will have to more or less understand the passage, because fixing the mistakes requires knowing what the passage is trying to say.

THE 13 RULES OF THE WRITING TEST

These are the rules most consistently tested for on the SAT II Writing Test. We won't give any in-depth explanations or use any fancy grammatical terms in this section. For each rule, we will simply make you aware of the concept and then give examples. Instead of being "textbookish" and going into the grammatical theory behind our rules, we will depend on your ability to "hear" when something "sounds" right or wrong.

Nevertheless, you will have to understand the following basic grammatical terms that you probably already know. Sorry.

noun
A word that denotes a person, place, thing, idea (joy), quality (stickiness), or act (drooling).

pronoun
As Homer Simpson said when he was studying for his high school diploma, "A noun that has lost its amateur status." Actually, a word that takes the place of a noun. (Example: The Serpent is evil. *He* is cruel. *He* is a pronoun because it takes the place of *Serpent*.) *It, they, we, who,* and *them* are some examples of pronouns.

verb
A word that expresses action (jump) or a state of being (be). A verb tells what's happening in the sentence.

subject
The noun that "does" the action of the verb in the sentence. (Example: *He* drooled. *He* is the subject because *he* is the thing that drooled.)

object
The noun that the verb acts upon. (Example: He tickled *me. Me* is the object because *me* is the thing that got tickled.)

preposition
Prepositions are words like *to, at, in, up, over, under, after, of.* They go with objects. (For example, in the phrase "in the house," *in* is a preposition and *the house* is the object.)

singular
Having to do with a single thing or single unit. (Example: noodle.)

plural
Having to do with more than one thing. (Example: noodles.)

Rule #1: Subject-Verb Agreement Screw-ups

Subject and verb must agree in number, so isolate the subject and the verb and make sure that they match. If the subject is singular, the verb should be singular; if the subject is plural, the verb should be plural.

Example 1:
The proctor, as well as the students, were overcome by the tedious ticking of the timer and fell asleep.

| *Isolate:* | subject: | proctor |
| | verb: | were overcome |

Combine: "The proctor were overcome."
This should sound wrong to you. The verb should be singular—*was overcome.* Don't be tempted by the plural word *students*; it is set off by a pair of commas, so it's not part of the subject.

Correct: The proctor, as well as the students, was overcome by the tedious ticking of the timer and fell asleep.

Three expressions that are similar to the *as well as* in the above example are: *in addition to, along with,* and *together with.* When you see one of these expressions on the test, chances are the Serpent is trying to make you think that the subject is plural.

Example 2:

The anguish of the students have been a source of pleasure to the ETS.

Isolate: subject: anguish
verb: have been

Combine: "The anguish have been a source of pleasure."

This should sound wrong to you. Don't get confused by the plural word *students*, because it isn't the subject. *Students*, in this sentence, is an object. You can tell because it comes after a preposition, *of*. Whenever a word comes after a preposition, it is an object, not a subject.

Correct: The anguish of the students has been a source of pleasure to the ETS.

Example 3:

Each of the streets were painted green.

Isolate: subject: each
verb: were

Combine: "Each were painted green."

This one is a little trickier. You have to realize that the subject of the sentence is *Each* and not *of the streets*. (*Streets* is an object of the preposition *of*.) Anytime you see "of the _____," the word that goes in the blank is an object, not a subject. Although *streets* is plural, the subject of the sentence, *Each*, is singular.

Correct: Each of the streets was painted green.

If you replace the "of the _____" part of the sentence with the word *one*, it is easier to see why the subject is singular:

"Each one was painted green" sounds much better than "Each one were painted green."

There are 13 singular subjects like *each* that you should memorize: *each, every, either, neither, one, no one, everyone, everybody, someone, somebody, anyone, anybody,* and *nobody*.

Whenever you see one of these words as the subject of a

sentence on the test, pay careful attention to whether the verb is singular. For example:

Incorrect: Neither of the streets *were* painted green.
Correct: Neither of the streets *was* painted green.

Again, it helps to replace the "of the _____" part of the sentence with the word *one:* "Neither one was painted green" should sound better to you than "Neither one were painted green."

Incorrect: Either this street or that street *were* painted green.
Correct: Either this street or that street *was* painted green.
Incorrect: One of the streets *were* painted green.
Correct: One of the streets *was* painted green.

Rule #2: Singular Subjects Take Singular Pronouns

Singular subjects take singular pronouns; plural subjects take plural pronouns. You know the list of singular subjects that you just memorized (*each, every, either, neither, one, no one, everyone, everybody, someone, somebody, anyone, anybody,* and *nobody*)? Well, it also applies to pronouns. Whenever one of the words on the list is the subject, the pronoun that refers to that word has to be singular. This is a hard rule to "hear" because so many people break this rule that we're used to hearing it the wrong way.

Example 1:
Not one of the boys read their SAT study guide.
Isolate:　　subject:　　one
　　　　　　　pronoun:　　their

The above sentence doesn't sound awful to most people, but it's wrong. The subject *one* is singular, but the pronoun *their* is plural. (*Boys* is plural, but it's an object. You can tell it's an object because of the "of the _____" construction.) The correct pronoun would be *his*.

Correct: Not one of the boys read his SAT study guide.

Example 2:

Each of the girls ate their lunch.

Isolate: subject: Each
                 pronoun: their

Each is singular, but *their* is plural. Try replacing the *of the girls* part of the sentence with *one* and you should see why the pronoun *her* sounds better than *their*.

Correct: Each of the girls ate her lunch. (Again, think "each one.")

Rule #3: Pronoun Subjects and Objects

You must know when to use the words in the column on the left and when to use the words in the column on the right:

Subjects	Objects
I	Me
He	Him
She	Her
They	Them
We	Us
Who	Whom

The words on the left are subjects, the words on the right are objects:

I like hot dogs, but hot dogs don't like *me*.

He goosed Susie, so Susie kicked *him*.

She is good enough for Grape-Nuts, but are Grape-Nuts good enough for *her*?

We all hate the ETS, because the ETS hates *us*.

Who killed Bozo? Bozo killed *whom*?

Example 1:

Julio and me were down by the schoolyard.

Always simplify these sentences. Does "Me was in the schoolyard" sound right? No. "I was in the schoolyard."

Correct: Julio and I were down by the schoolyard.

Example 2:

The dog and him are eating pizza.

Does "Him is eating pizza" sound right? No. "He is eating pizza."

Correct: The dog and he are eating pizza.

Example 3:

The SAT II was easy for Huey and he because they read *Up Your Score.*

"The SAT II was easy for he" should sound wrong to you. If it doesn't sound wrong, then recognize that the word *he* is an object in the sentence and therefore should be *him.*

Correct: The SAT II was easy for Huey and him because they read *Up Your Score.*

Rule #4: Pronoun Consistency

Pronouns should be consistent throughout a sentence. When *one* starts with a particular pronoun, *one* should continue to use that pronoun, or a pronoun that is consistent with it, throughout *one's* whole sentence.

Example:

The more you study for the SAT, the more one thinks about moving to Mongolia.

This sentence starts with the pronoun *you* and then ends with the pronoun *one.* This is inconsistent. It should be either:

The more *you* study for the SAT, the more *you* think about moving to Mongolia.

or:

The more *one* studies for the SAT, the more *one* thinks about moving to Mongolia.

Rule #5: Correct Tense

Make sure the time of an action is consistent. Look for key "time words" such as *when, while, as, after,* and so forth, and make sure the tenses make sense.

Example 1:
After he ate the newt and brushed his teeth, I will kiss him.

The problem here is that the verbs *ate* and *brushed* happened in the past, whereas *will kiss* is going to happen in the future. Change it to either:

After he eats the newt and brushes his teeth, I will kiss him.

Or to:

After he ate the newt and brushed his teeth, I kissed him.

Example 2:
While I was painting his feet, he had tickled me.

Presumably, he *interrupted* the feet painting with his tickling, and so the sentence should read:

While I was painting his feet, he tickled me.

This makes the sentence consistent. Never mind that it's weird—consistency is all that matters on the SAT II. So, as the people in these sentences carry on with their mildly deviant activities, just go through and make sure everything is done in the proper time sequence.

Rule #6: Adjectives and Adverbs

Remember the difference between an adjective and an adverb? If not, your sixth-grade teacher will hunt you down and pinch you. The ETS likes to mix these two up.

Adjectives describe nouns. An adjective will always make grammatical sense in the phrase:

The _____ wombat. (Example: The *lascivious* wombat.)

Adverbs describe verbs or adjectives or other adverbs. They usually, but not always, end in "-ly." An adverb will always make grammatical sense in the sentence:

The wombat did it _____. (Example: The wombat did it *lasciviously.*)

Example 1:

I ran slow.

The word *slow* is an adjective. You can tell because it makes sense in the phrase, "The slow wombat." However, in Example 1, it is being used to describe the verb *ran*. This is impossible. Adjectives only describe nouns. *Adverbs* describe verbs. Use *slowly* instead.

Correct: I ran slowly.

Example 2:

Poindexter juggles good.

Poindexter has problems. The word *good* is an adjective, but it's being used to describe the word *juggles*, which is a verb. Again, you have to use the adverb:

Correct: Poindexter juggles well. (Notice that *well* is an adverb even though it does not end in "-ly.")

Example 3:

I hate lumpy fish on soporific afternoons.

The sentence is grammatically correct, not to mention worthy of analysis from a psychological perspective. If you immediately jumped on this sentence and tried to correct it, it means you're too tense. Eat some frozen yogurt.

Another tricky aspect of adjectives and adverbs is comparison between more than one person. Take the adjective *juicy*.

If you're talking about only one object, you would use *juicy*: "This fruit is juicy." If you're comparing two objects, you would use *juicier*: "This apple is juicier than that pear." If you're comparing more than two objects, you would use *juiciest*: "Of the three fruits, the orange is juiciest."

Example 4:

Dan is the older of the four athletes.

Since there's more than two objects being compared, we can't use *older*.

Correct: Dan is the oldest of the four athletes.

Rule #7: Parallel Construction

Ideas that are parallel (related) should be expressed in the same way.

Example 1:

I like spitting, drooling, and to slurp.

Spit, drool, and slurp are parallel activities. They should be expressed in the same way:

Correct: I like spitting, drooling, and slurping.
Or: I like to spit, to drool, and to slurp.
Or: I like to spit, drool, and slurp.

Example 2:

You like spitting and drooling, but not to slurp.

Just because you don't like slurping does not mean that it shouldn't be parallel with spitting and drooling, which you do like.

Correct: You like spitting and drooling, but not slurping.

Example 3:

The juicer chops vegetables, squeezes oranges, and proctors can be liquefied with it.

Chopping vegetables, squeezing oranges, and liquefying proctors are all parallel actions. They should be expressed in the same way:

Correct: The juicer chops vegetables, squeezes oranges, and liquefies proctors.

Rule #8: Run-on Sentences and Sentence Fragments

A run-on sentence is usually two complete sentences that are incorrectly joined by a comma instead of separated by a period or a semicolon.

Example 1:

J.P. ate the mysterious object, it was a noodle.

This is a run-on sentence. It could be broken into two sentences:

1. J.P. ate the mysterious object.
2. It was a noodle.

It could also be combined into one sentence using a semicolon: J.P. ate the mysterious object; it was a noodle.

Sentence fragments are parts of sentences that are made up to look like real sentences. They are usually next to real sentences into which they should be incorporated.

Example 2:
All the kids had rashes on their bodies. Especially those with uranium lunchboxes.

In this example, the first sentence is complete, but the second is a fragment. The two could be combined like this: All the kids had rashes on their bodies, especially those with uranium lunchboxes.

Note: You only have to worry about run-ons or sentence fragments when you're working on the sentence correction or revision-in-context sections. Usage questions don't test for run-ons or fragments.

Rule #9: Totally Bogus Sight Questions

These are absolutely the most ridiculous questions on the test. They show how deeply and utterly absurd the Evil Testing Serpent is, to have included questions this ludicrous. They don't test anything that has to do with your ability to write. They don't even test your ability to identify correct grammar. They just test whether or not you'll fail to see a single wrong, or missing, letter. For example:

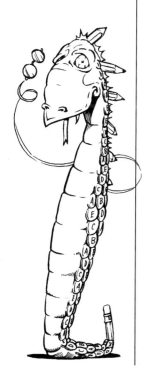

Late in the war, the Germans, <u>retreating</u> <u>in haste,</u> <u>left</u>
                            A   B

<u>many</u> of <u>their</u> prisoners go free. <u>No error.</u>
 C   D   E

If you didn't read the sentence carefully, you probably selected (E) (like Larry and Paul). Those of us who missed this question saw the word *let* where we should have seen *left*. With the word *let* the sentence is correct. With the word *left*, it is obviously wrong. In other words, we got this question wrong because we didn't see an *f*, not because we didn't know the grammar. In a sense, this question tests exactly the opposite of what it's supposed to test. People who are good writers know how the sentence is supposed to sound, so they imagine that the right word is there even when it's not. The moral of the story: *Read carefully*.

Rule #10: Dangling Modifiers

"Dangling modifier" is a fancy grammatical term for a simple concept. Here are some sentences with dangling modifiers.

Example 1:
Taking the test, his copy of *Up Your Score* was in his pocket.

This sentence does not mean what the person who wrote it wanted it to mean. This sentence implies that the copy of *Up Your Score* was taking the test. (This book can do many things, but it cannot take the test all by itself.) Whenever a sentence begins with a phrase like "Taking the test," which is supposed to modify (that is, describe) a word in the sentence, the word that it modifies must be in the sentence, and it must come right after the modifying phrase.

Correct: Taking the test, he had his copy of *Up Your Score* in his pocket.

The sentence can also be corrected another way.

Correct: While he was taking the test, his copy of *Up Your Score* was in his pocket.

Dangling modifiers will be on the sentence correction section of the test. Whenever you see a sentence with an "-ing" word in a phrase at the beginning, be on the lookout for a dangling modifier.

Example 2:
Conscientious about proper grammar, dangling modifiers were always on Bertha's mind.

Were the dangling modifiers conscientious about proper grammar? No, Bertha was. So she should come right after the comma.

Correct: Conscientious about proper grammar, Bertha always had dangling modifiers on her mind.

(Example 2 is an exception to the rule about dangling modifiers having an "-ing" word at the beginning.)

Example 3:
Parachuting over the Emerald City, the ant gasped in awe.

Was the ant parachuting? Hell, yes—so the sentence is correct.

Rule #11: Sentence Logic
On the sentence correction section of the test, there are often sentences that are grammatically correct but don't do a good job of saying what the writer wants them to say.

Example 1:
There are often sentences that are grammatically <u>correct, and do not say what</u> the writer wants them to say.
(A) correct, and do not say what
(B) correct and do not say that which
(C) correct but do not say what
(D) correct, with the exception that
(E) correct saying not what

The correct answer is (C). One would expect that if the sentences were grammatically correct, they would say what the author wanted them to say. *But* they don't. The word *but*

indicates that the part of the sentence after the comma contradicts what you would expect after reading the first part of the sentence.

> **Example 2:**
> It was dark in the closet, and they managed to find the exit.
> (A) It was dark in the closet, and they
> (B) It was dark in the closet, they
> (C) It is as dark in the closet, if they
> (D) Although it was dark in the closet, they
> (E) Until it were dark in the closet, they

The answer is (D). *Although* you would expect that in a dark closet, the exit would be hard to find, they did find the exit. The word *although* correctly conveys the author's intent that the part of the sentence after the comma should say something contrary to what one might expect after reading the first part of the sentence.

Rule #12: Commonly Messed-Up Expressions

Sometimes the ETS will deliberately mess up an expression to try to foil you. The only way to prepare for this type of question is by becoming familiar with standard, formal English and being able to hear or see which words or phrases just sound or look wrong. Like the Totally Bogus Sight Questions, these are pretty ridiculous. For example:

Example:
Since it's a beautiful day, I'd just assume walk.

The expression is "just as soon," but it sounds a lot like "just assume." You have to be able to see that it's wrong.

Correct: Since it's a beautiful day, I'd just as soon walk.

Rule #13: Logical Comparison

Remember when your math teacher said, "You can't compare apples and oranges"? That's basically what this rule is about. Make sure that when you make a comparison, you compare two like things.

Example 1:

My mother's salary is higher than Jane's mother.

Your mother's salary is higher than Jane's mother's salary, not higher than Jane's mother. How could a salary be higher than a person?

Correct: My mother's salary is higher than Jane's mother's.

Example 2:

Harry raised more cows than Jim's ranch.

Again, Jim raised the cows; his ranch did not raise anything.

Correct: Harry raised more cows than Jim did.

PRACTICE QUESTIONS

Okay—here are some pseudo-SAT II Writing Test usage and sentence correction questions. It's easier to practice the rules with these types of questions, although the revision-in-context section will also test the rules. There is one question for each rule, and two sentences that is correct. (You caught that mistake, didn't you? It should be "two sentences that *are* correct.")

Usage

1. After many <u>people</u> had been <u>strangely</u>
               A   B
    <u>painted</u> blue and yellow, the police <u>had</u>
     C   D
    <u>caught</u> the man with the spray can.

    <u>No error.</u>
      E

2. One <u>must listen</u> <u>carefully</u> to The Beastie Boys'
           A   B
    lyrics <u>otherwise</u> <u>you</u> might miss their
           C   D
    thematic significance. <u>No error.</u>
                        E

3. Confucius <u>says</u> that people <u>who</u> <u>stand</u> on
    　　　　　 A　　　　　　　 B　　 C
    the toilet <u>gets</u> high on pot. <u>No error.</u>
    　　　　　 D　　　　　　　　　 E

4. <u>Sagacious</u> <u>individuals</u> do not <u>construct</u>
    　 A　　　　 B　　　　　　　 C
    two-story <u>outhouses</u>. <u>No error.</u>
    　　　　 D　　　　 E

5. Every one of the <u>boys</u> in the class
    　　　　　　　 A
    <u>must</u> <u>have</u> <u>their</u> elbows <u>fumigated</u>.
    　 B　　 C　　　　　　 D
    <u>No error.</u>
    　 E

6. Brian and Matt <u>are</u> practicing <u>because</u>
    　　　　　　 A　　　　　 B
    <u>they</u> want to defeat Aliza and <u>she</u> in the
    　 C　　　　　　　　　　　 D
    wrestling match. <u>No error.</u>
    　　　　　　　 E

7. She <u>ran</u> away as <u>quick</u> as <u>she</u> could <u>from</u>
    　　 A　　　　 B　　 C　　　 D
    the ravenous poodle. <u>No error.</u>
    　　　　　　　　 E

8. Eggshell <u>was</u> <u>scattered</u> <u>around</u> the spot
    　　　 A　　 B
    <u>where</u> Humpty Dumpty <u>felt</u> to the ground.
    　 C　　　　　　 D
    <u>No error.</u>
    　 E

9. Last year, Jesse's <u>toes</u> <u>yielded</u> twice <u>as much</u>
    　　　　　　 A　　 B　　　 C
    toe cheese as <u>Jill</u>. <u>No error.</u>
    　　　　 D　　 E

10. What's <u>your</u> attitude <u>on</u> this <u>year's</u> Grammy
    　　 A　　　　 B　　 C
    nominees? <u>Do</u> any of them deserve to win?
    　　　 D
    <u>No error.</u>
    　 E

Sentence Correction

11. The most exciting thing about mushrooms is <u>their texture, a mushroom</u> is mushy and chewy.
    (A) their texture, a mushroom
    (B) their texture and mushrooms
    (C) their texture; a mushroom
    (D) their texture and that a mushroom
    (E) its texture; a mushroom

12. Betty enjoys putting itching powder in Chip's <u>jock strap, and Chip does not</u> enjoy it.
    (A) jock strap, and Chip does not
    (B) jock strap, but Chip does not
    (C) jock strap, being not as likely that Chip will
    (D) jock strap, being as Chip will not
    (E) jock strap, and Chip does not to

13. The fish on your <u>couch, although not as smelly</u> as might be expected, are making this date unpleasant.
    (A) couch, although not as smelly
    (B) couch, but not as smelly
    (C) couch, but quite that smelly
    (D) couch, and smells
    (E) footballed! It be greenly and whom that

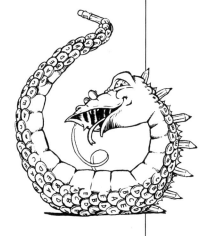

14. The rock star <u>enjoyed singing obscene lyrics, breaking guitars, and to make videos</u>.
    (A) enjoyed singing obscene lyrics, breaking guitars, and to make videos
    (B) enjoyed singing obscene lyrics, breaking guitars, and to try to make videos
    (C) enjoys singing obscene lyrics, breaking guitars, and to make videos
    (D) enjoyed singing obscene lyrics, breaking guitars, and making videos.
    (E) enjoyed singing obscene lyrics, breaking guitars, and arrested for starting a riot

15. Scaling the fortress <u>wall, the boiling oil</u>
    <u>scalded me</u>.
    (A) wall, the boiling oil scalded me
    (B) wall, I was scalded by the boiling oil
    (C) wall, the scalding oil boiled me
    (D) wall, oil boiled and I was scalded
    (E) wall, the boiling oil sure was hot

**The correct answers to questions 1–15, and the rules
that they test, are:**

1. D, rule 5
2. D, rule 4
3. D, rule 1
4. E (sentence is correct)
5. C, rule 2
6. D, rule 3
7. B, rule 6
8. D, rule 9
9. D, rule 13
10. B, rule 12
11. C, rule 8
12. B, rule 11
13. A (sentence is correct)
14. D, rule 7
15. B, rule 10

THE ESSAY

The essay on the SAT II Writing Test is your only opportunity in the entire SAT system to be creative—within limits. You see, the ETS graders are looking for certain qualities in each essay; if you deviate too much from those limits, the ETS will be frightened by your creativity and give you a low score. In this section, we will tell you how to write the kind of essay that the ETS wants to see.

As in another important aspect of life, length doesn't matter, skill does. Don't worry about how much you write, as long as it's good. The people who grade these look at thousands and thousands of essays. They spend about a minute on each essay.

*I thought we
were going to take
this part out.
— Lisa*

If your essay is short but solid they will be grateful.

Only you know how much time you have to set aside for planning the essay, writing it, and proofreading. But the time limit for the entire essay process is 20 minutes.

Here are some examples of recent essay topics:

"Describe a previously undiscovered cause of Napoleon's defeat at Waterloo."

"Interpret Shakespeare's *The Tempest* from a Freudian standpoint."

"If sulfur were to mix with lithium in a heated, pressurized container, what would be the result?"

"What is the meaning of life? Show work."

Just kidding. No essay will ever ask you for specific knowledge on a subject. The question will always ask you to write about a vague concept or to debate the validity of a statement. Here are some essay topics of the sort you might actually get on the SAT II:

1. "Progress always comes at a price." Use an example from literature, current affairs, history, or personal observation in which a difficult price had to be paid in order for progress to be made. Was the progress worth the price or was the price too high?

2. "The more difficult path can be the better path to take." Write an essay in which you explain why you agree or disagree with this statement. Support your argument with specific examples from history, current events, literature, or personal observation.

3. In a well organized essay describe a situation in which an individual or group at first resisted some form of change, then was convinced that change was necessary. Include in your essay:
   a. what the change was and why it was resisted at first
   b. how the person or group was convinced to change
   c. a discussion of the results of the change once it was made.

Be sure to include examples in your discussion. The examples may come from personal observation, or from your reading in history, literature, science, or current affairs.

You'll notice that in all three examples the subjects you can write about are extremely broad—"examples from history, contemporary affairs, literature, or personal observation"—basically anything except cartoons, video games, or group sex. So the first trick is to learn a lot about two or three subjects that interest you. Almost any will do. Read a few articles and books about these subjects and form some strong, well-thought-out opinions about them. Since the essay topics are so broad, you should be able to turn whatever you know into an essay that fits the topic.

For example, suppose you decide to become an expert on the civil rights movement in the U.S. You could answer the first question by talking about the great personal sacrifices that people like Rosa Parks, Martin Luther King, Jr., and Malcolm X made. Then you could talk about whether it was worth the high price they paid for progress in civil rights. You might give examples of the rights that these people won for our generation (desegregated schools, affirmative action). If you got question 2, you could basically write the same thing—about how people like Rosa Parks, Martin Luther King, Jr., and Malcolm X chose the difficult path of standing up for their civil rights.

If you got question 3, you could explain that racial intolerance and fear led many people to resist desegregation of schools, then you could outline how protests, court cases, and brave African-American students who had to attend school with armed guards helped change public opinion. Finally, you could talk about some ways in which America has become a more diverse, more tolerant place as a result of desegregation, while admitting that problems remain.

As you can see, the questions are broad enough for you to adapt them to whatever you feel like writing about. The most important thing is that you not waste even five seconds asking yourself, "Hmmm . . . what should I write about?" Know in advance the subjects you are prepared to write on; then all you have to do is figure out how to apply your knowledge to the question.

Write on One Subject

While the questions do not necessarily demand that you write about one specific subject, we think it is a good idea. If you take the first question and then say in your essay, "Everything has its price . . . when my gerbil died it cost a lot to freeze-dry it . . . and in the same way, Martin Luther King, Jr., paid a great price for social change . . . and it should also be noted that the price of renting a video has increased markedly," then you will get a low grade for failing to make any sense at all. You should use multiple examples to prove your points, but they should all relate back to a specific thesis statement. Don't write in general about how "everything has its cost" or your essay will wander. Your thesis statement should be quite specific: "The civil rights movement demonstrated that social change is accomplished at great cost."

"Personal Observation"

HELPFUL HINTS:
When making up stuff for your "personal observation" avoid the opening: "I learned a valuable lesson as admiral of the Spanish Armada."

If, as you read the remarks about the civil rights movement, you said to yourself, "Sure, that topic is interesting, but it isn't nearly as interesting as I am," then perhaps you should write an essay from "personal observation." Most of the questions will allow you to use examples from "personal observation." If you want to do this, then write about some issue in your own life or the life of someone close to you. Be sure to make it dramatic. Tell stories about the characters involved that illustrate the points you are making. Do not just blab your opinions without giving specific examples of why they are true. For example, if you are writing about how you have noticed that students do not show enough respect for the SAT, make sure to tell one story about how disrespectful the students are, and perhaps another story about how much joy and peace you have created by respecting the SAT. Our next point—that it's okay to make stuff up—is particularly applicable to personal observation essays.

Making Stuff Up

Suppose you are writing your essay and you are a little short of evidence. Our advice is to make stuff up. Because this test is not about how much you know, but about how well you can write, don't worry if you fudge some of your facts. Your essay will not be graded on factual accuracy. Remember, the readers spend about a minute on each essay—they aren't going to spend that minute running to the encyclopedia to make sure that you have your details right. They are just looking at the overall quality of your writing and organization.

This doesn't mean that you should say something that is obviously false. In the civil rights example, if you write, "The reason Malcolm X is still alive today is that . . ." they will know you don't know what you are talking about. But suppose you write, "80 percent of taxpayers in North Carolina opposed desegregation in 1961, but by 1971 only 20 percent opposed it." The graders will probably be impressed that you argue so convincingly (when actually, you made the numbers up). The reason the second example works is that it isn't completely a fantasy; it is based on an awareness of the shift in public opinion that did occur during the sixties.

If you're writing about personal observations, feel free to make up characters and events as long as they're within reason.

The ETS-Friendly Essay

On the essay section the ETS wants to see if you know the "rules" of good essay writing. The ETS does not care that the art of essay writing has been explored for centuries by great writers, each of whom discovered original ways of organizing and writing great essays. No, all the ETS graders care about is whether you know how to do the basic, no-frills high school essay. So, you should give them what they want and write an essay according to the formula they are expecting.

The formula they want is one that is organized just like an old-fashioned first date. Not a modern first date, which takes place in a mosh pit, but the kind you see in an old movie. An old-fashioned date has three parts: the introduction, the meal, and the goodnight.

Before you get down to your date, however, it's wise to spend a couple of minutes preparing. Organize your thoughts and jot down a few notes so that when you begin, you'll be smooth and polished and won't make a fool out of yourself trying to sound intelligent when you aren't sure what you want to say.

1. The Introduction

a. This begins with a "pickup line" in which you get the prospective date's (the reader's) attention.

b. Next there is a provocative sentence that explains the pickup line and gets you talking about something you know about.

c. Then you invite the prospective date (the reader) to join you for a meal. (This is the thesis sentence.)

THE Introduction

THE Meal

2. The Meal

We recommend that you divide the meal into three courses during which you continue talking about the stuff you started discussing in the opening, but now in greater depth, so that you can show your date how knowledgeable and interesting you are. Make sure that you move from one course to another by using smooth transitions.

3. The Goodnight

You conclude by talking about what a lovely discussion you have had, you make a hint about your future together, and then, if you get the right signals, there should be one goodnight kiss.

Now is your chance to do something you never get to do on a date. Review the experience a few times, correcting any part of it that didn't turn out exactly as you wanted it to. Add anything you wish you had said, and cross out anything you wish you hadn't said. As long as you do it neatly, no one will care that you didn't get it perfect the first time.

The Do-It-Yourself Essay Formula

To show just how easy it is to apply this formula to any essay topic, we have made a chart of the do-it-yourself essay. You'll see that no matter what the question is, you can write about whatever subject you planned to write about, and you can always make that subject fit the formula. We have written one essay about scientists, and one about the environment, but remember, you can write on almost any topic.

Note that Essay I agrees with the question, while Essay II disagrees. There isn't a "right" answer to any of the essay questions; remember, it isn't what you say that counts, but rather how well you say it.

This has been a perfect evening— a true 800!

THE Goodbye

Essay I: Question: "Progress always comes at a price," discuss . . . (same as question 1 discussed on page 230)

Essay II: Question: Depending heavily on others keeps us from realizing our own potential," agree or disagree. . . .

Part 1: The Introduction—Opening Paragraph

A. The attention-getting pickup line

There is an ancient Sudanese proverb that states, "To kill a tree is to kill oneself." (*We made this up. There's no such proverb, but how would the ETS know?*)

In tribute to the scientists who came before him, Isaac Newton said, "If I seem to see farther than others, it is because I stand upon the shoulders of giants."

B. Explain your pickup line; get the discussion going

In the search for better homes, transportation, and defenses, human beings have drained the earth's resources.

Newton was aware that his deep insights into science came from his mastery of the works of his predecessors.

C. Invitation to the meal (a good way to do this is to restate the essay question in relation to your topic and then say how you are going to organize your discussion)

Has the progress we have made in our standard of living been gained at too great a cost to the environment? We can begin to answer this question by exploring three areas of human progress and their environmental repercussions.

Depending heavily on the work of other scientists does not keep one from realizing one's own potential as a scientist. In fact three great scientists realized their potentials by depending heavily on others.

Part 2: The Meal—Paragraphs 2, 3, 4: Three examples that support your argument

1. The first example that supports your argument (1 paragraph)

One area in which human beings have made enormous technological progress is in transportation. Only two centuries ago, the only means of land transportation were on foot or on the backs of animals. Now we have high-speed

When Copernicus suggested that perhaps the planets revolved around the Sun instead of the planets and the Sun revolving around the Earth, this was a new way of looking at the world. However, most historians of science

trains, automobiles, airplanes, and spaceships. However, the environmental cost of all of this transportation has been vast. The burning of fossil fuels is ruining the ozone layer and causing global warming. Roads now scar the land that was once wilderness.

2. Another example that supports your argument (1 paragraph).

Humans have also paid a price for the improvements we've made in our dwellings. Once we lived in caves or in earthen huts. Now many of us live in manufactured homes in crowded cities. While this has brought us modern conveniences and greater safety from the elements, this lifestyle has ravaged the natural habitats of many animals. Scientists speculate that American cities are a prime cause of the extinction of at least three species of birds each year. (*We made this statistic up.*)

3. A third example that supports your argument (1 paragraph).

Finally, human beings have always sought defense from one another and from animals. In pursuit of this safety, we have advanced the science of weaponry to the point where our power to detsroy the environment is absolute. If nuclear war should occur, the environment would pay the ultimate price—the end of life as we know it.

agree that Copernicus's work depended heavily upon Ptolemy and on contemporary mathematicans. Thus, while he had conceived of an entirely new way of understanding the shape of the solar system, he did so with the help of other scientists.

Galileo also discovered new details of the universe— the moons of Jupiter, mountains on Earth's moon—which had never before been seen. Still, he was dependent upon the scientists who preceded him. He used Copernicus's model of the universe to track the planets. Also, the telescope that he used was made possible by the work of other scientists who had made progress in the field of optics.

Even though Newton's work on gravity seemed to depart radically from the scientists who preceded him, it too relied on his predecessors. As the quote above indicates, Newton was fully aware that his discoveries depended heavily upon Galileo and other scientists who had advanced the idea that the universe follows mathematical laws.

Part 3: The Goodnight—5th Paragraph Conclusion

A. Summarize your argument (explain what you proved in the previous three paragraphs)

B. Look to the future (this is optional, but they love it)

C. A goodnight kiss (one last cute point, perhaps referring back to your "pickup line")

We have made great progress in the fields of transportation, housing, and defense, but the environment has paid a tremendous price.

If our planet is to survive, we will have to realize that some forms of progress are not worth the environmental cost.

To invert the Sudanese proverb: To save a tree may be to save ourselves.

Copernicus, Galileo, and Newton fully realized their potential as scientists by depending heavily upon others.

Those who will make future contributions to science will likely also do so through careful study of other scientists.

By standing on the shoulders of those other scientists, they will be able to see further still.

If you find that the time allotted is not enough for you to write an essay according to the formula, then just put two paragraphs in "the meal" instead of three.

If you're saying to yourself, "I don't know enough facts about science to write an essay like the second one," don't worry. We didn't either. We just opened up our high school history book to the chapter about scientists and got our facts from there. Remember, because you are going to prepare your essays in advance, you can look up the facts you anticipate needing. And if you get to the test and forget some of those facts, you can just make them up. For example, you could have said, "After waking each morning, Isaac Newton allegedly spent four hours sitting in bed reading the works of scientists who preceded him." How would they know that wasn't true?

So, once again, the secret to the essay section is to write a couple of essays about two subjects that interest you before you even get to the test. Then, while everyone else is sweating about what to write about, you will just be making slight alterations in the essay you have already prepared. As practice, why not write two essays about your chosen subject in response to the two essay questions above?

CHAPTER

6

BUT WAIT! YOU ALSO GET...

A man walks down the street
Says, "Why am I short of attention?
Got a short little span of attention
But, oh, my nights are so long."—Paul Simon

CONCEN-
TRATION

Your *concentration span* is the length of time that you can direct your attention to a given task without spacing out. Every task also has what is called a *distraction potential*. The higher the distraction potential of a given task, the more difficult it is for you to apply your concentration span. We all know that the distraction potential of the SAT can be very high indeed. Not only is the test itself difficult and boring, but the test hall atmosphere, complete with creaking chairs, strange odors, ticking watches, squeaking pencils, sneezes, and shuffling papers can add to the distraction.

Imagine the following scenario. It's two hours into the test. You're on the second math section, and you get to this question:

If $a * b = 2ab$ and $a \dagger b = \dfrac{ab}{2}$ then what is the value of $a * (b \dagger c)$?
(A) $4ab$
(B) $4bc$
(C) $2abc$
(D) abc
(E) ac

This is not too hard a problem to do when you're fresh, but after two hours it can be tricky. If someone were to take a "brain transcript" of you trying to do this problem, here's what it might look like:

"Okay, it's one of those weird problems with the funny symbol thingies. Let's see, what's the deal? . . . Oh, I got it. You stick in the moochie for $b \dagger c$, which makes $ab/2$, then . . . no, no, no, crap, it's $bc/2$ that you plug in. Then that leaves $a * (bc/2)$. How much more time do I have left? Twelve minutes. That's ⅔ of the time for this section and I have more than ⅔ of the questions to do. Oh, no, I'm behind. Okay, okay, okay. Where was I? Oh yeah, you stick in $2a$, which makes

2abc/2 and then . . . I wish this idiot would stop tapping his foot. Tap. Tap. Tap. Tap. There he goes again. His hair is slimy. I wonder where he's applying to college. Tap. Tap. Why doesn't he wash his hair? Nasty! Okay, okay, okay. *2abc*/2 = *abc*, which is answer (D). Good. Fill in (D)."

Well, you got the question right, but only after much wasted thought. The worst mistake was checking the time. Never do this in the middle of a problem, only between problems. And never let the slightest distraction bother you—foot tapping, slimy hair, or whatever. Of course, this is much easier said than done. Simply deciding to concentrate can leave you with a brain transcript that looks like this:

"Concentrate. Concentrate, damn it. Okay. I'm just gonna focus my brain like you wouldn't believe. This is the most important three hours of my life and I am going to concentrate intensely for the whole time. Ooooh, I'm really concentrating now. His slimy hair isn't bothering me a bit. This is total concentration—no distractions. The tap tap tap noise that his foot is making right now, which I wish he would stop, isn't bothering me either. You could stick me with pins and I wouldn't feel it. Okay, what problem am I on? . . ."

You're concentrating so hard on concentrating that you're not concentrating on the test. The trick is to learn to concentrate without thinking about concentrating. Your mind should be effortlessly focused. To learn to do this you must practice. Training your brain is just like training any other part of your body—you have to exercise it.

Concentration exercises are usually pretty dopey. They're the kind of thing that you read about, say to yourself, "That's dopey," and move on without even trying them once. Typical concentration exercises are things like trying not to space out while running through the multiplication tables in your head. Any mental task that can be done for 20 consecutive minutes, but which is tedious enough that your brain would be tempted to space out, makes for a good concentration exercise.

We have discovered that drinking games make excellent concentration exercises. If you practice these games for 20 minutes a day for a month, you will find that your concentration span will improve dramatically. You will also be admired when you go to parties at college because you will be so good at these games.

Important Note: Usually these games are played in groups, and whenever someone screws up, that person has to take a drink. You, however, should play them alone and without doing the drinking. You will kill the whole value of the concentration game if you stop every few minutes to drink. You will also kill off so many brain cells after a month of these games that you will have no brain left with which to concentrate.

We've provided you with guidelines for two drinking games. We suggest that you play Game #1 for 10 minutes followed by Game #2 for 10 minutes. It is good practice to try to do these games with the television on to see if you can concentrate so intensely that you are not even aware the TV is on.

Game #1: Kerplunk!

This one starts off simply but gets difficult. Say to yourself, *in a steady rhythm,* the following sequence of sentences:

1. One frog—two eyes—four legs—in a pond—kerplunk!

Then multiply everything by two:

2. Two frogs—four eyes—eight legs—in a pond—kerplunk! kerplunk!

Then you do it with three frogs:

3. Three frogs—six eyes—12 legs—in a pond—kerplunk! kerplunk! kerplunk!

As you can see, the basic pattern is:

X. X frogs—two X eyes—four X legs—in a pond—repeat "kerplunk" X times

Keep doing the sequence. Whenever you say something wrong (i.e., 12 legs when you should have said 16 legs, or forgetting to say "in a pond," or not knowing how many times you have said "kerplunk," or forgetting which number is next) or whenever you lose the mental rhythm and have to pause to think of what to say next, you have to divide the number of frogs that you are on by two and then start again. For example, if you were on 10 frogs and you said that they had 40 eyes, you would have to go back to "five frogs—10 eyes—20 legs—in a pond . . ."

Game #2: Buzz

This is a counting game. Pick a number between 2 and 10, not counting 2 and 10. Then start counting *in a steady rhythm.* Whenever you come to a number that:

1. is a multiple of the number, or,
2. has the number as one of its digits

you don't say the number; instead you say, "Buzz." The best way to explain this is to give an example:

Suppose the number is 4, then you count:

1, 2, 3, buzz, 5, 6, 7, buzz, 9, 10, 11, buzz, 13, buzz, 15, buzz, 17, 18, 19 . . .

If you miss a "buzz" or lose the rhythm, you have to go back to the number that is half of the number that you screwed up on.

Game #3: SAT Practice Tests

This game has not gained widespread popularity in bars, but it is the most useful concentration game. If you take a lot of practice tests and really practice concentrating on each section for the entire half hour, you will concentrate better on the real test, too.

Moving On

Another concentration problem you might have is an inability to move right on to the next question if you have not been able to solve the previous one. This difficulty arises because your mind is unwilling to accept that it is unable to do the problem and wants to keep working on it. A brain transcript of this might look like:

Old Problem

New Problem

"Okay, screw this. Too diffi-cult. Can't figure it out."

NOT LOOKED AT YET

"This one looks easy. I can do this one. Choice (D) looks good but . . ."

"But wait! I can do this one. If I just knew what this part was. I've already spent two minutes on it. I might as well finish it. No. That's stu-pid. Move on to the next question."

"Where was I? Oh yeah. Choice (D) looks good."

"Hey, maybe choice (D) is also right on this problem. No, that can't be right. Move on to the next problem."

"Okay, it was (D). I'll fill that in on the answer sheet."

This sort of zigzagging really wastes time. When your brain tries to occupy itself with two problems at the same time, it doesn't work well on either of the problems. You have to trick your subconscious mind so that it will move on to the next problem without trying to go back. The three things that will help you do this are:

1. Guess—This is another good reason for guessing on all questions that you can't answer. When you guess, your subconscious is satisfied that it has found an answer and is more willing to move on.
2. You shall return—Tell your brain that you're going to come back to the problem after you've finished the test. Then your brain will be more willing to leave the

problem temporarily. (Put an X in the test book next to a problem you think you can't get, and a ? next to one you think you might be able to get with more time.)

3. Practice—The more timed practice tests you take, the more relaxed your brain will become with moving on.

PROCTORS: MINDLESS SLAVES OF THE ETS

SAT proctors tend to be selected haphazardly, and for the most part they do not give a flying poo about your life or your problems. They're paid only a pittance, not enough to make them care.

Sure we're being harsh, but we've interviewed students at many schools and we have heard some nasty horror stories about incompetent and ignorant proctors. On each test date, students across the nation go in to take the SAT in what they hope will be a fair environment. Instead, some of them must cope with bumbling idiots who forget to read instructions, eliminate break time, talk while you work, or give incorrect responses to student questions (responses like, "No, you shouldn't guess."). Many proctors simply haven't learned how to do their job. They are given a proctor's manual with specific instructions on what forms of ID are acceptable, how far apart to seat people, what to do if there's a fire alarm, etc. But since their wages are not incentive enough for them to read it and no one ever checks on them, they usually are left to say and do whatever they want. Here, once again, we discover the Evil Testing Serpent doing his foul work. He insidiously fails to insist on the quality of the proctors he selects.

Proctors come in three sizes. The first and most prestigious model is the Test Center Supervisor—a popular item, but available only in limited quantities. The TCS is, in short, The Big Cheese—she's in charge of the whole test center. She's supposed to find all of the underling proctors, procure rooms, and maintain contact with the ETS.

The next-sized proctor is the supervisor, who's the bigshot in each room. The supervisor is the dude who reads the directions in a clear and carefully modulated voice ("Please read

The Greek word proktos *means "anus." So does the English word* proctor.

the directions as I read them aloud to you . . ."). The supervisor is in charge of all the proctors in his room.

The actual proctors are the people who hand out the tests and answer sheets and make sure that you don't cheat. (Sometimes the proctor is the same as the supervisor.)

Proctors are selected by the test center. Often local teachers are chosen as proctors—people whose faces are familiar to students. Supervisors are paid in proportion to the number of students taking the test and proctors are paid a flat fee.

Because your proctor may not know all the facts, it is necessary for you to find out everything you need to know about the SAT before the test date. We hope this book has answered all of your questions. If it hasn't, read *Taking the SAT I*. If that doesn't help, call the ETS. If you still have an unanswered question, get a life.

If you happen to get good proctors, thank them, kiss them, and offer to nibble gently on their earlobes. (They'll love this.) However, you should be prepared for a bad one and know how to cope. This will save you from getting screwed.

To be on guard against a bad proctor, to misquote the Beastie Boys, "You've Got to Fight for Your Right to SAT." Your liberties, so generously granted to you by the ETS, include the following:

1. You have the right to 30 *silent* minutes to work on each section (except for the two 15-minute sections). The 30 minutes begin *after* the proctor has finished reading all instructions, not before!

2. You have the right to a five- to ten-minute break at the end of each hour.

3. You have the right to use the test booklet as scrap paper.

4. You have the right to have your seat changed if you give a legitimate reason. The proctor, of course, decides whether your reason is "legitimate" or not. Being placed

in a right-handed desk when you are left-handed, having the sun in your eyes, and sitting with water dripping on your head from a leak in the ceiling are all examples of legitimate reasons. Wanting to sit next to your girlfriend is not a legitimate reason.

5. You have the right to breathe.

If any of these rights are violated, *speak up*. If one of the proctors says something you think is questionable or even admits that he doesn't know something, go ask the supervisor, who we can only *hope* knows what she's doing. Never be afraid of "authorities" who actually know less than you do about their own jobs. Be polite, but insist. Remember, it's your future, and you don't want to spend it as an SAT proctor, do you?

RELAXATION

Welcome to our section about relaxation. Please sit back, close your eyes, and imagine that you are on a beach next to the bluest of oceans. The sun is warm on your skin and your toes are wriggling in the soothing sand. The smell of coconut suntan lotion washes over you in a delicate sea breeze. As you take deep breaths of this beautiful air, you feel more and more at peace.

That sure would be relaxing. But the SAT isn't anything like that. The SAT is when you get up from the beach and stroll into the blue ocean and a black cloud of stingrays surrounds you and stabs you until ravenous sharks smell your blood mixing with the salt water and begin a feeding frenzy on your flesh.

Nevertheless, there are ways to become a little bit more relaxed while taking the SAT. Although the SAT will never be a day at the beach, it doesn't have to be a gruesome drowning either. If you learn how not to panic it can be sort of a lukewarm, slightly grimy, but not uncomfortable bath. Scientists

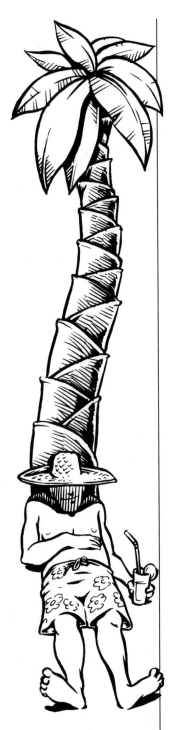

have made considerable progress in recent years in the field of "stress management." In consultation with some experts in the field, we have developed the *Up Your Score* Lower Your Stress Plan™.

Because people are frightened of the unknown, the best thing you can do to lower your stress is to prepare yourself. If you've memorized the test directions, know how to approach all of the question types, and have practiced on numerous old SATs, then there won't be any "unknowns" to stress you out. On top of that it may be soothing to have a routine that you follow when you take the test. For example, some people like to pause every five questions, close their eyes for five seconds, take a deep breath, and then go on. One relaxation expert suggested that the most relaxing way to do deep breathing is to spend four seconds breathing in and six seconds breathing out. Try it. It works.

Another way to reduce your anxiety is to do what is called "positive visualization." In the weeks before the test, each night before you go to bed, make a movie in your mind about exactly what it will be like to arrive at the test center, show them your admission ticket and ID, sit down, get your answer sheet, listen to the incomprehensible proctor read the directions, hear the smelly kid in front of you crack his knuckles. Then visualize yourself being completely relaxed throughout the whole ordeal. No, you are beyond relaxed— you are totally focused with intense energy on the test. Yet your body is not showing any signs of stress. You are breathing deeply, your palms aren't sweaty, your pulse is slow. If you visualize this scenario numerous times before the real test, you'll be amazed at how similar to your visualizations the real test will be. Of course, you'll be more nervous than you were in your imagination, but you won't feel any need to panic, and that extra bit of nervous energy might help keep you alert.

Another relaxing thing to remember is that you are *not supposed* to know all of the answers. Sure, an occasional whiz gets a 1600, but the SAT is not like a classroom test on which your teacher will be disappointed in you for each question that you get wrong. In fact, you can get tons of questions wrong and still do okay. For example, you can skip 30 questions and still score around 1300. You can skip about half of the questions and still get a score that is around the national average. So, don't worry about whether or not you can solve a particular problem. Work on it for a reasonable amount of time, then say, "It just doesn't matter. I'm not supposed to know all of the answers," mark it in the test book so you can come back to it if you have time, use one of our guessing techniques to make an educated guess for the time being, and then go on with the test.

Finally, we checked with the heads of the world's major religions and they all agree that while a poor performance on the SAT might make it less likely that you will get into the college of your choice, it will not have any effect upon your chances of getting into the heaven of your choice.

So enjoy your bath.

YOGA AND THE SAT

A Body-Oriented Experience

In order to succeed on the SAT, it is most important to use your *mind*. If you arrive at the testing area without your *mind*, you are sure to do poorly on the test. (There have been reports of test-takers in California who scored above 600 without their minds; these rumors have been investigated and have been found to be vicious hoaxes.) Most of this book is devoted to training the mind to meet the intellectual challenge that the SAT presents. However, a certain amount of physical conditioning is necessary as well. Each year thousands of students all across the nation suffer from muscle fatigue, leg cramps, and spinal curvature as a direct result of the SAT. Yes, the SAT can be a grueling, bone-breaking, lung-collapsing experience for the ill-prepared. How can this be? How can taking a test be so physically draining? Simply stated, all the misery is caused by this little beastie:

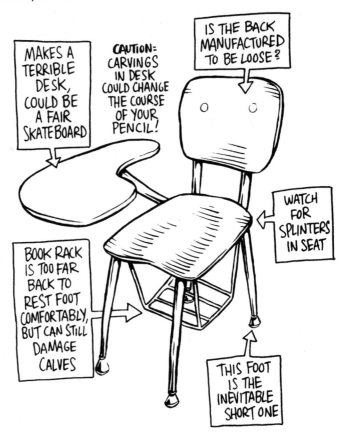

And well you should gasp! This demented version of a chair, or one much like it, will be your home during the three most important hours of your high school career. Equipped with hardly ample desk space of about one square foot, this chair undoubtedly will have you making a fool of yourself as you attempt to keep your test booklet and answer sheet together on the desk and not let them fall all over the floor. They will fall on the floor anyway, making a rustling sound, and you will wind up annoying everyone in the testing hall. If you are left-handed, the situation will be even worse—you will wind up with the book on your lap and the answer sheet on the desk—leaving your left arm wrapped across your body to mark the circles. This is misery. Demand from the proctor a more appropriate place to take the test. He will probably just laugh wickedly and enjoy watching you suffer.

To make matters worse, the legs of the chair are usually too short and the edges too sharp. If you're not careful, you'll cut yourself and there'll be blood everywhere. And if you don't keep your posture (practically impossible to maintain), you'll wind up in traction with a slipped disc. Only the strong survive.

But there is hope. For help, we suggest you turn to knowledge that has existed for centuries in the eastern regions of the world. The ancient art of yoga, we have found, offers the most relevant conditioning for the serious-minded. If you practice the following exercise, starting at least a month before the test, you will suffer minimal discomfort from your immediate surroundings during the test.

CHEATING

Cheating is rampant at many test centers. Among the cheating methods we have encountered are: sharing answers during the breaks between sections, peeking at other people's answer sheets, communicating answers through sophisticated body language codes, leaving a dictionary in the bathroom and looking up words during the breaks, and even having one student take the test for another student.

Two kids with whom we went to high school cheated by using the following method. Since their last names were Basset and Bates (the names have been changed to protect the guilty) they knew that they would be sitting next to each other during the test. Basset was a math whiz and Bates was a vocabulary guru. So Basset did both of his own math sections while Bates did both of his own verbal sections. When the proctor turned around, they traded tests. Basset did Bates's math sections and Bates did Basset's verbal sections. They both did very well and—what a surprise—they both got exactly the same score.

Another way of cheating that we heard of involved using M&M's. Throughout the test, one kid would eat different-colored M&M's, each one standing for a letter—yellow for A, green for B, etc. The other kid would watch him and know what the right answer was.

A few years back, the ETS lost a lawsuit to a high school student it suspected of cheating. Brian Dalton's score rose from 620 in May 1991 to 1030 in November 1991, and the large increase caused ETS to withhold his score from colleges until it had "investigated" further. Dalton explained that he had been sick the first time he took the test, and that he had subsequently completed a prep course. But the ETS still refused to release his scores because a handwriting expert suggested that another person might have filled out his answer sheet. Dalton took the ETS to court, and the judge ruled in his favor because the ETS hadn't thoroughly investigated information that Dalton had submitted, including testimony by proctors and another handwriting expert. However, it was too

Cheating by glancing at a neighbor's answer sheet is likely a losing proposition; not all tests have the sections in the same order.

late for Brian: St. John's University had already rejected him due to his initially low SAT score.

Should you cheat? *No. You should not cheat.* You see, there's nothing wrong with beating the system by learning what you've learned in this book because, although we do teach you a lot of tricks, we don't break any rules. But if you beat the system by breaking the rules, you are doing something that's wrong. You will feel guilty and wish you hadn't done it. When your friends who didn't cheat don't get into their first-choice colleges and you do, you will feel awful. Just ask Basset and Bates.

So why did we write this section? To make you aware that cheating is a reality and that you shouldn't let people cheat off you. In fact, you should screw them over when they try. Suppose that during the break someone asks you what you got for number 22. Even though you know that the answer is (B), tell them that you got (C) and you're totally sure that you got it right. Then after the test say to that person, "Did I tell you (C)? I meant to say (B). Golly, I'm really sorry."

Note: If you were planning to cheat by looking at the answer sheet of the person next to you (which you shouldn't have even thought of doing!), you should know that while all the tests on a given test date have the same sections, they are in different orders. While your first section may be a math section, the first section of the person next to you may be a verbal section. The ETS devised this plan to thwart cheaters.

A Gray Area

Cheating by getting answers from other people is clearly wrong. The most common form of cheating, however, does not involve getting answers from others. The most common method of cheating is working on sections of the test after the 30 minutes allotted for that section are over. At the bottom of every section the Evil Testing Serpent warns you in big, bold, letters:

STOP

IF YOU FINISH BEFORE TIME IS CALLED, YOU MAY CHECK YOUR WORK TO THIS SECTION ONLY. DO NOT TURN TO ANY OTHER SECTION IN THE TEST.

Bet you guys were real popular in high school
—Lisa

At many test centers, no one checks what section you are on. We would estimate that about half the kids at our test center cheated by using this method. The five of us were good boys and girl and didn't. But after the test when we realized how many of our friends had done this, we felt like we were at an unfair disadvantage for not having done it.

Clearly, this kind of cheating is not as bad as getting answers from other people. It could be argued that when your future is in the balance, why not borrow a minute from the math section to work on the verbal section that you didn't quite finish, especially if half your classmates are doing it? On the other hand, it's still cheating.

LITTLE CIRCLES

Robert Southey, the author of *The Three Bears* and arguably the worst poet ever, once said, "The desert circle spreads like the round ocean." He was referring, of course, to the metaphorical relationship between circles and the SAT.

Circles are quite significant in that there are many of them that you will have to fill in during the course of the test. This is about how to fill in those little circles. (Actually, they're not really circles, they're ovals.)

Undoubtedly, you've had to fill in lots of little circles in your life. You probably never gave much thought to technique or speed. In fact, as far as we know, no one in modern science has ever researched the science of filling in circles. We are the first ones. We'll probably win the Nobel prize.

In the course of our research, we have discovered that some students spend as much as 2.3 seconds per circle. At that rate, they will spend 7 minutes and 4 seconds of their total testing time filling in circles. On the other hand, those students who master this chapter will spend only 0.4 seconds per circle and will therefore spend only 1 minute and 12 seconds filling them all in. That's almost 6 extra minutes that can be spent working on the test.

We consulted with Dr. Elizabeth Mandell to develop an

anatomically correct description of the technique that we believe to be most efficient:

> Grasp your number 2 pencil between the distal closed space of terminal phalanx II and the palmar surface of the corresponding area of the distal phalanx of the pollicis. Additional support is derived from the radial border of the distal interphalangeal joint of the third phalange of the upper extremity. The flexor pollicis brevis, which is innervated by the median and deep ulnar nerves and is in close proximity to the princeps pollicis artery, assists in this action as do the tendons of the flexor, the digiti superficialis, and those of the flexor digiti profundis. (Certainly, the ulnar surface of the upper extremity distal to the olecranon process may rest upon the writing surface *provided that* the flexor carpi ulnaris, flexor carpi radialis, and the palmaris longus maintain a tonic contraction.)

> The abductor pollicis brevis, which originates from the flexor retinaculum, the tuberosity of the scaphoid and the trapezium, and the extensor pollicis longus engage in antagonistic movements with the flexor pollicis brevis and the abductor pollicis obliquus, assisted by the first and second lumbricales, which insert upon the tendon of the extensor digiti communis.

Got that? In other words, use a circular motion that works from the inside to the outside. Time trials and super-slo-mo analysis have proven that the most efficient method is:

The In-to-Out Circle Method

Common mistakes made by high school students who are not familiar with our ground-breaking research include:

The Vertical Lines Method

The Horizontal Lines Method

The Out-to-In Circle Method

The Artist Cross-Hatching Method

The Unfocused Method

Unclear on the Concept

Uh, What Was the Question?

The Suicide Doodle Method

The Moron Dot Method

To perfect your technique follow the rules below:

1. Don't be compulsive about filling in every nook and cranny. Just make sure that in one swift movement, at least 90 percent of the circle is filled in. Make it black, but don't waste time going over it twice to make it black again.

   If you don't fill in each circle perfectly, you can fill them in more thoroughly during one of the breaks between tests. Just take care not to waste time during the test.

2. Leave the point of one of your pencils *dull*. Although you don't want to use a dull pencil on the math section (you want a good pencil for scratch work) it will save you time on the verbal section because the more surface area the point of your pencil has, the fewer strokes you need to make to fill in the circle.

3. Although you don't want your arm to be too stiff, you should press hard on the answer sheet. The darker the mark, the more likely the scanner is to see it. This is

an important factor if you're not filling in your circles all the way.

4. On the math grid-in questions, there is space above the grid to write in the answer. But the computer only registers the circles, so you don't have to waste time writing in the answer.

5. Practice, practice, practice. Try to get your time below 0.5 seconds per circle. The following pages are filled with 800 (our favorite number) circles for you to practice on. If you get your time below 0.3 seconds, you may be able to qualify for the O-lympics.

Ⓐ	Ⓑ	Ⓒ	Ⓓ	Ⓔ		Ⓐ	Ⓑ	Ⓒ	Ⓓ	Ⓔ		Ⓐ	Ⓑ	Ⓒ	Ⓓ	Ⓔ

Ⓐ Ⓑ Ⓒ Ⓓ Ⓔ   Ⓐ Ⓑ Ⓒ Ⓓ Ⓔ   Ⓐ Ⓑ Ⓒ Ⓓ Ⓔ
Ⓐ Ⓑ Ⓒ Ⓓ Ⓔ   Ⓐ Ⓑ Ⓒ Ⓓ Ⓔ   Ⓐ Ⓑ Ⓒ Ⓓ Ⓔ
Ⓐ Ⓑ Ⓒ Ⓓ Ⓔ   Ⓐ Ⓑ Ⓒ Ⓓ Ⓔ   Ⓐ Ⓑ Ⓒ Ⓓ Ⓔ
Ⓐ Ⓑ Ⓒ Ⓓ Ⓔ   Ⓐ Ⓑ Ⓒ Ⓓ Ⓔ   Ⓐ Ⓑ Ⓒ Ⓓ Ⓔ
Ⓐ Ⓑ Ⓒ Ⓓ Ⓔ   Ⓐ Ⓑ Ⓒ Ⓓ Ⓔ   Ⓐ Ⓑ Ⓒ Ⓓ Ⓔ
Ⓐ Ⓑ Ⓒ Ⓓ Ⓔ   Ⓐ Ⓑ Ⓒ Ⓓ Ⓔ   Ⓐ Ⓑ Ⓒ Ⓓ Ⓔ
Ⓐ Ⓑ Ⓒ Ⓓ Ⓔ   Ⓐ Ⓑ Ⓒ Ⓓ Ⓔ   Ⓐ Ⓑ Ⓒ Ⓓ Ⓔ
Ⓐ Ⓑ Ⓒ Ⓓ Ⓔ   Ⓐ Ⓑ Ⓒ Ⓓ Ⓔ   Ⓐ Ⓑ Ⓒ Ⓓ Ⓔ
Ⓐ Ⓑ Ⓒ Ⓓ Ⓔ   Ⓐ Ⓑ Ⓒ Ⓓ Ⓔ   Ⓐ Ⓑ Ⓒ Ⓓ Ⓔ
Ⓐ Ⓑ Ⓒ Ⓓ Ⓔ   Ⓐ Ⓑ Ⓒ Ⓓ Ⓔ   Ⓐ Ⓑ Ⓒ Ⓓ Ⓔ
Ⓐ Ⓑ Ⓒ Ⓓ Ⓔ   Ⓐ Ⓑ Ⓒ Ⓓ Ⓔ   Ⓐ Ⓑ Ⓒ Ⓓ Ⓔ
Ⓐ Ⓑ Ⓒ Ⓓ Ⓔ   Ⓐ Ⓑ Ⓒ Ⓓ Ⓔ   Ⓐ Ⓑ Ⓒ Ⓓ Ⓔ
Ⓐ Ⓑ Ⓒ Ⓓ Ⓔ   Ⓐ Ⓑ Ⓒ Ⓓ Ⓔ   Ⓐ Ⓑ Ⓒ Ⓓ Ⓔ
Ⓐ Ⓑ Ⓒ Ⓓ Ⓔ   Ⓐ Ⓑ Ⓒ Ⓓ Ⓔ   Ⓐ Ⓑ Ⓒ Ⓓ Ⓔ
Ⓐ Ⓑ Ⓒ Ⓓ Ⓔ   Ⓐ Ⓑ Ⓒ Ⓓ Ⓔ   Ⓐ Ⓑ Ⓒ Ⓓ Ⓔ
Ⓐ Ⓑ Ⓒ Ⓓ Ⓔ   Ⓐ Ⓑ Ⓒ Ⓓ Ⓔ   Ⓐ Ⓑ Ⓒ Ⓓ Ⓔ
Ⓐ Ⓑ Ⓒ Ⓓ Ⓔ   Ⓐ Ⓑ Ⓒ Ⓓ Ⓔ   Ⓐ Ⓑ Ⓒ Ⓓ Ⓔ
Ⓐ Ⓑ Ⓒ Ⓓ Ⓔ

IS THE SAT BIASED?

In recent years, the SAT has been called unfair. Why? Because of its alleged bias against women, minorities, and the poor, all of whom consistently do worse than rich white males on the tests. (If you're rich, white, and male, shame on you!)

In previous editions of *Up Your Score*, we gave you statistics on specific questions that were proven to be biased by gender, race, or income. But because so many people recognized the obvious biases in these questions, the ETS has stopped publishing statistics for specific questions. It has also tried to eliminate openly biased questions, and in fairness, we could not bring ourselves to lambaste them for questions they used years ago.

Because of the nature of the SAT, however, many still considered it biased. Basically the test is a fast-paced game which stresses speed and strategic guessing. (Unfortunately, it's used to predict success in college, which does not necessarily depend on speed or strategic guessing.) This type of test favors the way American boys behave. Female students and students from cultures that don't place an emphasis on speed and guessing are therefore at a disadvantage when taking the SAT.

Sex bias: In 1995, the average SAT score for boys was 43 points higher than the average score for girls. Since the SAT is supposed to be an indicator of how well students will do in college, one might deduce that women must do worse in college than men. However, women, on the average, get better grades in high school and college than men get. If the SAT is supposed to predict freshmen grades, women should be out-scoring men on the SAT.

Boys scored 40 points higher on math than girls. Most people believe boys generally are better math students than girls, but a study conducted at ETS itself indicated that while men were somewhat more likely to take advanced math courses at college, on the average women received higher grades.

Race bias: On the 1995 SATs, the following were the average scores for various racial and ethnic groups (note that these scores were issued before recentering; see page 7):

Asian Americans	956
Whites	946
Native Americans	850
Hispanics	827
Mexican Americans	802
Puerto Ricans	783
African-Americans	744

Minorities may also do worse on the SAT because of income bias since in general minorities have lower incomes than whites do. (See below.)

The ETS tried to bridge the racial gap in 1970 by the lame gesture of adding one reading passage per test concerning minorities. However, the benefit of the passage is questionable, except for *Up Your Score* readers who use it to their advantage (see page 44).

Income bias: The scores on the 1995 SAT were shown to be directly proportional to income level, with an average score of 1004 for students with family incomes over $70,000, and 769 for under $10,000.

In addition to diminished educational opportunities, another important reason poorer students may do worse on the SAT is a lack of access to coaching, which can raise scores but costs as much as $600. Poorer students often cannot afford the luxury of an expensive prep course or even the advantage of the informative score reports described in Chapter 1. However, you, the informed consumer, paid only $8.95 for this book and will have your score, and your consciousness, raised immensely.

Most of the information for this section came from FairTest (The National Center for Fair and Open Testing), which leads the fight against the ETS. If you have any questions or would like to subscribe to their newsletter, call (617) 864-4810 or write to FairTest, 342 Broadway, Cambridge, MA 02139. Tell them *Up Your Score* sent you.

SATING FOR DOLLARS

After you ace the SAT, you will decide that, because you are such a good, involved student with a kick-butt SAT score, you could get into a prestigious college that costs more than you were planning to spend on your first house. You will develop a passion for this particular college, but your dreams of attending will be crushed you learn that it costs about three times as much as you can possibly afford.

At this point you have several options. You could turn your back on the material world and join a socialist commune where money is not an issue. You could create a charity called Educating Our Future Leaders and solicit everyone in the phone book. Then take their donations and spend them on your college education. (This is probably illegal, by the way.) You could sell your little brother, but you probably wouldn't make enough money.

Or you could try to win some scholarship money. Ask your guidance counselor about scholarship opportunities and research them in the library in the most recent college scholarship books you can find. Many of these books are huge and daunting, but you will soon realize that you don't qualify for many of the scholarships in them unless you live in Santa Fe, your birthday is February 29, and you're a direct descendant of an original signer of the Declaration of Independence. Many of the scholarships that you do qualify for will require transcripts, essays, and lists of extracurricular activities, so be prepared to submit these materials. Although scholarship applications are less fun to fill out than tax forms, they can be much more rewarding.

SATitis

What do you do if you wake up on the day of the test and you don't feel well? Panic, scream, beat your fists against the wall, and scream, "Why me?"

Then sit back and assess how you feel. If you really feel vile, consider postponing the test and asking the ETS for a refund. If, however, you just have a cold, slight nausea, and a mild headache, you should still take the SAT. First of all, your "illness" could just be nerves, in which case it might go away after you take a shower. Even if it doesn't, adrenaline might well carry you through the test (you can come home and allow yourself to wallow in your symptoms afterward), and you won't have the SAT looming in front of you for another few months. Take some cold or headache or tummy medicine as long as you're certain it won't make you drowsy. (It's very difficult to succeed on the SAT if you take it while you are sleeping.) Try to relax and breathe deeply and focus on the test, not on your scratchy throat, runny nose, watery eyes, throbbing head, clogged sinuses, or aching stomach. And remember, the SAT makes everyone nauseous. Finally, if you know you didn't do well, just cancel your scores. . . .

CANCELING COUNSELING

If, after the test, you feel like you might have screwed up, it's only natural and you shouldn't worry about it. However, if you *know* that you screwed up, you should cancel your scores. If you made some grievous error like choosing (E) for all the Quantitative Comparisons, or falling asleep during a section, then it is probably wise to cancel. But don't cancel just because you made a few stupid mistakes.

The simplest way to cancel is to fill out a Test Cancellation Form before you leave the test center. However, if you decide to cancel after you've left the test, you must notify the ETS by the Wednesday after the Saturday that you took the test. (For details, refer to your *SAT Student Bulletin*.)

If you're set on getting an amazing score, memorize all the problems that you weren't sure about and then go home and see if you guessed correctly. If you did guess correctly, keep your score. Otherwise, cancel. (We only recommend this if you want to take the test over and over again until you get 1600.)

If you cancel, your score report will read "Absent or Scores Delayed."

THE SSS AND THE SDQ

With his spare time, the Evil Testing Serpent likes to play matchmaker. This is why he invented the Student Search Service (SSS). The SSS (sounds like something the Serpent would say) is like a computer-dating service, except that instead of matching sexually frustrated singles, it matches colleges with potential students. It's free, and it's a good way to get lots of mail, so you might as well do it. However, if you're eco-conscious, you may not want to waste all that paper. One way to save trees is to share college brochures with your friends. Just make sure you have your own application when the time comes.

In order to enroll in the program, you have to fill out the **Student Descriptive Questionnaire (SDQ)** in the Student Bulletin for either the SAT or PSAT (both of which are available in your high school guidance office; or you can enroll when you sign up for an Advanced Placement test). By the way, doing this questionnaire is a great opportunity to practice filling in little circles.

Unless you're a compulsively ethical person, there is no reason why you have to tell the truth when answering the questionnaire. If you have no artistic ability, but you still want to see the pretty pictures in the brochures that the art schools send out, then fill out question 6 to say that you got an "A or Excellent in Art and Music." Also, do not be modest when answering the questionnaire. If you're good at something, say that you're great at it. That way you'll be sure to get mail from the colleges that are interested in that skill. The way it works is, the colleges send the ETS a list of characteristics that they are looking for in their students, and the ETS sends them the name, address, sex, date of birth, social security number, high school, and intended major of students who match those characteristics. The college doesn't know your answers to individual questions; it only knows that the matchmaking Serpent thought you might be compatible.

Another similarity between the SSS and a dating service is that they both make mistakes, matching you up with some real losers. The Registration Bulletin claims that you will get mail only from schools with "the academic programs and other features you find important." This is false. If you put on the questionnaire that you are an Alaskan native who wants to study philosophy and has no mechanical ability, you will still get mail from the Mormon School of Interplanetary Auto Mechanics.

THE SAT AND THE INTERNET

Many of you already know all the fun stuff you can do on the Internet. You can get the words to any Alanis or Oasis song you want, you can play Doom with someone in South Dakota, you can even flirt with 40-year-old men. Now, for your extreme convenience and pleasure, you can also prepare for the SAT on the Internet. Most of the following SAT sites are still under construction, but already there are some useful things out there.

The College Board has a site on the World Wide Web that is surprisingly peppy for such a stuffy organization. They have a "Question of the Week" that is a good place to see SAT practice questions. They also have a site on America Online which is mostly just no-frills Q and A about the test and promotions for their books. We asked a few tough questions such as "Why do you still have last year's test dates posted instead of this year's?" and they were very courteous and apolegetic. You won't get better at the test by visiting this site, but if you have any practical questions, might be helpful.

Several SAT schools now have on-line versions of their courses that are less expensive than their classroom offerings, and have the excellent advantage that when you get bored (and you will get bored if you expect the other guys to be as witty and charming as we are), you can always log off.

America Online has a huge "Kaplan University," which is identical to a real university except that it lacks the campus, the beer, the professors, the football team, the parties, the sex, the dorms, the freedom, and the education. But it does have one graphic of a building with ivy on it. The SAT course itself seems solid enough. They even have some little SAT verbal and math games. Their WWW site is mostly the same stuff—but where's the virtual university?

The *Princeton Review* site on the WWW isn't bad. It has a lot of career and internship information in addition to its test prep stuff. It has one highly promising feature— on-line dissection of recent tests—but unfortunately the dissections are pretty superficial. They tend to say things like "The verbal section had no particular surprises," but don't get down to detail about specific questions.

Princeton Review also has a huge site on AOL that spends a lot of time promoting its own products, a little bit of time teaching its approach to the SAT, and a lot of time discussing everything from "lima beans" to "writing jobs for college students." They also have free "downloadable practice testlets."

One of the better sites we found was the home page of Stanford Testing Systems on the Web. Although they too hawk their book, they've also put their complete test preparation guide, including dozens of math and verbal lessons, online. Although their lessons aren't as entertaining or interesting as *Up Your Score*'s, they're reasonably well thought out.

The best site on the Internet, according to our international review panel, will be the "*Up Your Score* On-Line SAT House Party" site. As this book went to press, we had just started developing it; we promise that it will feature the best, most up-to-date test information, cool graphics, and lots of chances to meet and discuss things the grownups never tell you about high school and college. There's even a top-secret plan to publicly expose some of the Serpent's insidious flaws. To find us, check out www.workmanweb.com/upyourscore. Sites on the WWW are constantly growing and changing. Our advice is to point an Internet search engine at "Scholastic Assessment Test" or "SAT" and see what comes up. We will of course have pointers to the best stuff on our website. Happy Surfing!

FOOD SMUGGLING

The ETS says that food is strictly prohibited in the test center. Forget that. If you're going to be hungry, or you want an extra bit of energy, bring some food with you.

You shouldn't eat the food during the test because that would waste valuable time. Instead, snack between sections. Choosing your SAT menu can be lots of fun. Here are a few guidelines and suggestions:

1. Nothing noisy: no potato chips, carrots, rice cakes, or tuna casseroles (at least not the kind with cornflakes on top)
2. Nothing sticky: no cookie batter, maple syrup, toffee, or Superglue
3. Nothing big: no turkeys, cotton candy, melons, or shish kebabs

As long as you stay within the above guidelines, we leave the specific choices up to you. However, we do recommend the following recipe:

Sweet And Tasty 800 Bars

Ingredients:

½ pound butter
1 box dark brown sugar
3 eggs
3 cups flour
1 teaspoon vanilla extract
2½ teaspoons baking powder
2 jumbo Hershey bars (the kind with the little squares)

Melt the butter and let it cool until you can put your nose in it for three seconds and feel no pain. Stir in the brown sugar. Then add the flour slowly. Beat the eggs and add them one at a time. Add the vanilla and baking powder. Break the chocolate bars into _____ squares with your _____ and add them to the batter.

(A) Hollywood . . . remote
(B) little . . . fingers
(C) liquid . . . fly swatter
(D) gaseous . . . squirt gun
(E) coconut . . . willpower

Answer: (B)

Pour everything into a buttered baking dish with a volume of 216 cubic inches. If it's 2 inches deep and 12 inches long, how many inches wide is it?

(A) 8   (B) 9   (C) 10   (D) 25   (E) $8x - 5$

Answer: (B)

Take a big handful of the batter and eat it. (Don't you wish all recipes said that?) Preheat oven to the average of 100 and 600. It takes 35 minutes for them to turn golden brown in a standard oven. If an oven is slow, it takes 40 minutes.

Quantitative Comparison (Remember them? If not, see p. 188.)

Column A

Column B

The length of time it takes to turn golden brown in a slow oven.

The length of time given for an SAT math section.

Answer: (A)

When they are golden brown, remove them from the oven. Now you can cut them into whatever shape you choose.

Sneaking Food into the Test Center

If you're taking the test during the winter, it's no problem to get the food in. Just hide it in your coat. Smuggling food to the May and June dates can be trickier. Your best bet is one of those hooded sweatshirts with the pockets in the front. These can hold a lot of food, and the food is easily accessible because it's in your front pocket. Pocketbooks are also useful. Do not do what Larry did. He cleverly concealed a chocolate bar in his back pocket. Before he had a chance to eat it, two of the Musketeers had melted.

FASHION AND BEAUTY TIPS

Just as it's important not to be hungry during the SAT, it's important to be comfortable. You don't want to waste time wishing you'd worn looser jeans or that your shirt wasn't itching you. Make sure you dress in layers no matter when your test date is. The test room could be heated, air-conditioned, both, or neither. Be prepared for any climate. Bear in mind that cardigans and sweatshirts that zip up the front are easier to wriggle out of quickly than garments you have to pull over your head. Avoid loose floppy sleeves; as fashionable as they may be, you don't want to have to keep swishing them out of the way to fill in your answer sheet. The same goes for bangle bracelets (which also have a tendency to jangle annoyingly). Finally, a lucky pair of socks or the underwear you wore when you won the basketball tournament couldn't hurt.

Hand care is crucial to the SAT. Your hands will grip your pencil, they will punch numbers on your calculator, they will strangle the proctor if he or she is absolutely incompetent and unreasonable. Cut your fingernails so you don't waste time biting them; the same goes for your cuticles. If you like, paint your nails a soothing color like green. Begin treating your hands with natural minerals and creams at least one week before the test and do isometric hand exercises in order to increase the ease with which you grasp your pencil.

Hair care is also very important. Even if you're otherwise attired in your oldest floppiest sweats, go to the test with squeaky clean hair—it'll make you feel pulled together and competent. Plus, its brilliant shine might distract other students and therefore increase your percentile score. Also bear in mind that the weeks before the SAT are no time to start growing your hair out. The last thing you want is to be constantly pushing your hair out of your eyes and cursing yourself for ever cutting it in the first place.

Finally, choose the watch you wear carefully. Because you will constantly be checking how much time is left, you want to feel comfortable with your watch. Digital ones are preferable because in the heat of the moment you could forget how to tell time. Also, make sure your watch doesn't beep, or if it does, that you know how to turn off the alarm. Otherwise you risk being the object of intense hatred of the other test-takers.

STICK IT IN YOUR EAR

At this point in the book, we would like to recommend that you find two cylindrical objects, rub them back and forth between your fingers, and then insert them into two of your body's orifices simultaneously.

The orifices are your ears and the cylindrical objects are foam ear plugs. These little squishy thingies are great. They

SAT-WEAR THAT SCORES BIG!

SWELLE

PANTS: MULTIPLE CHOICE

Hide Those Dark Circles

Dating Out of Your Percentile

Pamper Yourself **800 HERBAL 800 BATH!**

Test Day Nightmare: "But I Wore It To The PSATs!"

HAIR:CONCENTRATION::NAILS:?

cost about 50 cents a pair at your local pharmacy—a small price to pay for cutting out most of the distracting noises at the test center. They are comfortable once you get used to them. In fact, some people we know at college have become addicted to them and can't study without them.

When you put in the earplugs, you suddenly hear your own breathing more intensely and sometimes even your own heart-beat. These are precisely the things that you are supposed to listen for when trying to meditate. So once you get used to them, you'll find yourself concentrating and relaxing with a meditative intensity.

They are also helpful for blocking out those annoying teacher-noises in high school classes you'd prefer to sleep through.

SOME OTHER THOUGHTS ON GETTING INTO COLLEGE

Remember, the SAT is only one aspect of your college application. If your score isn't that strong, make sure the rest of your application is.

Your grades and courses: These should always be your first priority. Colleges will usually insist on a minimum standard of grades and courses before they will look at the rest of your application.

Essays: College admissions officers read hundreds of essays—your goal is to write one that will stick in their minds. You might want to reveal something about yourself in your essay that didn't come out in the rest of your application. You can write about your summer job as a camp counselor, but remember that many others will probably write similar essays about their summer experiences. Make yours stand out. Humor can be effective, but if the admissions committee doesn't find your humor funny, it's worse than not using any humor at all. So make sure you get feedback on your essays before you send them in. (This goes for all essays, not just humorous ones.) Show them to your family, your friends, your teachers, your plumber. However, don't let them write the essay for you—it should always reflect you.

Extracurriculars: Remember, these are always secondary to grades. But one extracurricular that is irresistible to colleges is organizing and leading something socially responsible. Ask yourself what your school or community needs and then get your friends to work with you on a project, such as organizing a recycling program. This is not only a good deed, it may get you into college. Admissions officers also love self-propelled activities—one kid we know organized his own summer trip to work at a Moscow newspaper, and he got into Harvard. Conversely, bear in mind that dinky extracurriculars aren't that impressive. Being a leader (editor of the school paper, captain of the basketball team) looks a lot better than just being a member of a club that meets once a week.

Note: "If at first you don't succeed, try, try again." If for some reason you have your heart set on one school (although there is usually no good reason for that) and you don't get in, think about taking a year off to make yourself fascinating and smart, and apply again.

Parting Words of Advice

(To Be Read the Night Before the Test)

Congratulations! You've made it through (or else you're peeking at the end of the book). You know what the word *cerebration* means, and you're all set to be cerebral. You have your ID, your admission ticket, three sharp pencils and one dull pencil, a calculator with charged batteries, and some good food to smuggle into the test all waiting by the door. Maybe you've studied everything in a day; maybe you started with verbal flash cards four and a half years ago. Who cares? It's over now; no amount of studying the night before the test is going to help you significantly. If you need a boost of confidence, just remember that there are people out there who will be taking the test tomorrow without having read this book first. (Unthinkable, isn't it?) If you botch the test, you'll just take it again on the next test date. If you don't get into the college of your choice, you can choose another one that probably doesn't cost as much and has a better football team.

We hope that you enjoyed our book and that you learned a lot. Our objective was to teach you how to take the SAT, but we hope that along the way you learned some stuff that will help you for the rest of your life. You now know a lot of vocabulary words that you didn't know before, you are a more clever test-taker, and you're a better thinker than you used to be.

The five of us went through the same thing that you are going through right now. We know how you feel. There is a lot of pressure. It feels as if someone is scratching her finger-nails on your mental chalkboard.

So, go outside and look at the stars. There are lots of them and they're trillions of miles away. In the Grand Scheme of the Universe, how big a deal can the SAT be? Be chill. You're going to cruise tomorrow. Sit back. You only live once . . . and then they send you your score report.

Good luck,

Larry, Manek, Paul, Michael, Lisa

Larry, Manek, Paul, Michael, Lisa

P.S. You do know what the word *lamia* means, don't you?

We'll look this one up for you. According to the *American Heritage Dictionary*, it's "a monster represented as a serpent with the head and breasts of a woman; reputed to prey upon humans and suck the blood of children." Sweet dreams!

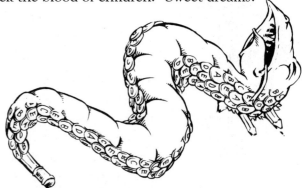

Larry Berger

Larry Berger is finishing his dissertation for a doctoral degree in English so as to enhance his performance on the SAT verbal section. He has written two other books: *Tray Gourmet: Be Your Own Chef In The College Cafeteria* and *I Will Sing Life: Voices From the Hole In The Wall Gang Camp*, which is about seven children at Paul Newman's camp for children with life-threatening illnesses, where Larry was a creative writing counselor for three years.

He graduated Summa Cum Laude from Yale and went on to be a Rhodes Scholar at Oxford. At Yale he received the Herson Prize for an outstanding student of English, the Wallace prize for the best student short story, and the Connecticut Student Poetry prize. He also co-directed the Children in Crisis Big Sibling Program and the Booksgiving Book Drive. He expands to three times his normal size when placed in water.

Michael Colton

Michael Colton is known for his superior achievements and for his modesty. Currently a senior at Harvard majoring in English, he grew up in Newton, MA, where he edited the school newspaper, became a National Merit Scholar, and lusted after the captain of the women's soccer team. Since then he has written for the *Boston Globe*, the *Los Angeles Times*, and *Might* magazine. He also edits and writes a gossip column for *Fifteen Minutes*, the weekly magazine of the *Harvard Crimson*. When he grows up he would like to be taller.

Lisa Fran Exler

Lisa Fran Exler, currently a freshman at Brandeis University, is hoping to study pet detection with Ace Ventura. In high school at Beth Tfiloh Community School in Baltimore, MD, she edited *Insight*, her high school newspaper, co-chaired the Judaic Action Committee, and participated in the cultural enrichment club, community service activities, and the volleyball team. She is also a Bronfman Youth Fellow, a National Merit Scholar, a Justice Brandeis Scholar, and a lefty. In her rare moments of leisure, she enjoys reading, sleeping, listening to music, hanging out with friends, and rooting for her home team, the Orioles. Her favorite M&Ms are the green ones.

Manek Mistry

Manek Mistry grew up in Ithaca, NY. He graduated from Cornell University in 1990, with a degree in biology. He then switched course and spent the next three years at Cornell Law School, receiving a JD in 1993. Now that he's out in the real world (after 20 long years of schooling heading in many different directions), he's realized that the only thing he really wants to do is write. Of course, he knew that in first grade, too. He's had short stories published in a number of literary journals, and (like everyone else in the world) is working on his first novel. No, really, he's going to finish it someday. He lives in the Pacific Northwest.

Paul Rossi

Since graduating (with distinction) from Cornell University, Paul Rossi has traveled to several cities, searching for permanent employment. In the process, he has discovered that the street value of his education in French Literature and Nineteenth Century European History is not easily convertible into U.S. currency. Currently he is living in San Francisco, writing experimental fiction and (yes) poetry, while trying to keep his houseplants from dying on him. His friends consider him to be a fine and peace-loving citizen.